W9-CUD-009

schools.

DIVERSITY
IN SCHOOLS

DEBATING ISSUES
in American Education

EDITORIAL BOARD

DIVERSITY
IN SCHOOLS

VOLUME EDITORS

FRANK BROWN
UNIVERSITY OF NORTH CAROLINA AT CHAPEL HILL

RICHARD C. HUNTER
UNIVERSITY OF ILLINOIS AT URBANA-CHAMPAIGN AND
BAHRAIN TEACHERS COLLEGE, UNIVERSITY OF BAHRAIN,
KINGDOM OF BAHRAIN

SARAN DONAHOO
SOUTHERN ILLINOIS UNIVERSITY CARBONDALE

3

VOLUME

DEBATING ISSUES
in American Education

SERIES
EDITORS

CHARLES J. RUSSO
ALLAN G. OSBORNE, JR.

⑤SAGE reference

Los Angeles | London | New Delhi
Singapore | Washington DC

Los Angeles | London | New Delhi
Singapore | Washington DC

FOR INFORMATION:

SAGE Publications, Inc.

2455 Teller Road

Thousand Oaks, California 91320

E-mail: order@sagepub.com

SAGE Publications Ltd.

1 Oliver's Yard

55 City Road

London EC1Y 1SP

United Kingdom

SAGE Publications India Pvt. Ltd.

B 1/I 1 Mohan Cooperative Industrial Area

Mathura Road, New Delhi 110 044

India

SAGE Publications Asia-Pacific Pte. Ltd.

3 Church Street

#10-04 Samsung Hub

Singapore 049483

Publisher: Rolf A. Janke

Acquisitions Editor: Jim Brace-Thompson

Assistant to the Publisher: Michele Thompson

Developmental Editor: Carole Maurer

Production Editor: Tracy Buyan

Reference Systems Manager: Leticia Gutierrez

Reference Systems Coordinator: Laura Notton

Copy Editor: Matthew Sullivan

Typesetter: C&M Digitals (P) Ltd.

Proofreader: Ellen Howard

Indexer: Mary Mortensen

Cover Designer: Janet Kiesel

Marketing Manager: Carmel Schrire

Copyright © 2012 by SAGE Publications, Inc.

Printed in the United States of America.

Library of Congress Cataloging-in-Publication Data

Diversity in schools/volume editors, Frank Brown, Richard C. Hunter, Saran Donahoo.

p. cm.—(Debating issues in American education ; v. 3)

Includes bibliographical references and index.

ISBN 978-1-4129-8764-6 (cloth)

1. Multicultural education—United States. 2. Minorities—Education—United States. 3. Marginality, Social—United States. I. Hunter, Richard C., Dr. II. Brown, Frank, 1935- III. Donahoo, Saran.

LC1099.3.D59 2012

370.1170973—dc23   2011048280

SUSTAINABLE FORESTRY INITIATIVE Certified Sourcing
Label applies to the text stock www.sfiprogram.org SFI-00341

12 13 14 15 16 10 9 8 7 6 5 4 3 2 1

CONTENTS

ABOUT THE
EDITORS-IN-CHIEF

Charles J. Russo, JD, EdD, is the Joseph Panzer Chair in Education in the School of Education and Allied Professions and adjunct professor in the School of Law at the University of Dayton. He was the 1998–1999 president of the Education Law Association and 2002 recipient of its Mcghehey (Achievement) Award. He has authored or coauthored more than 200 articles in peer-reviewed journals; has authored, coauthored, edited, or coedited 40 books; and has in excess of 800 publications. Russo also speaks extensively on issues in education law in the United States and abroad.

Along with having spoken in 33 states and 25 nations on 6 continents, Russo has taught summer courses in England, Spain, and Thailand; he also has served as a visiting professor at Queensland University of Technology in Brisbane and the University of Newcastle, Australia; the University of Sarajevo, Bosnia and Herzegovina; South East European University, Macedonia; the Potchefstroom Campus of North-West University in Potchefstroom, South Africa; the University of Malaya in Kuala Lumpur, Malaysia; and the University of São Paulo, Brazil. He regularly serves as a visiting professor at the Potchefstroom Campus of North-West University.

Before joining the faculty at the University of Dayton as professor and chair of the Department of Educational Administration in July 1996, Russo taught at the University of Kentucky in Lexington from August 1992 to July 1996 and at Fordham University in his native New York City from September 1989 to July 1992. He taught high school for 8½ years before and after graduation from law school. He received a BA (classical civilization) in 1972, a JD in 1983, and an EdD (educational administration and supervision) in 1989 from St. John's University in New York City. He also received a master of divinity degree from the Seminary of the Immaculate Conception in Huntington, New York, in 1978, as well as a PhD Honoris Causa from the Potchefstroom Campus of North-West University, South Africa, in May 2004 for his contributions to the field of education law.

Russo and his wife, a preschool teacher who provides invaluable assistance proofreading and editing, travel regularly both nationally and internationally to Russo's many speaking and teaching engagements.

Allan G. Osborne, Jr. is the retired principal of the Snug Harbor Community School in Quincy, Massachusetts, a nationally recognized Blue Ribbon School of Excellence. During his 34 years in public education, he served as a special education teacher, a director of special education, an assistant principal, and a principal. He has also served as an adjunct professor of special education and education law at several colleges, including Bridgewater State University and American International University.

Osborne earned an EdD in educational leadership from Boston College and an MEd in special education from Fitchburg State College (now Fitchburg State University) in Massachusetts. He received a BA in psychology from the University of Massachusetts.

Osborne has authored or coauthored numerous peer-reviewed journal articles, book chapters, monographs, and textbooks on legal issues in education, along with textbooks on other aspects of education. Although he writes and presents in several areas of educational law, he specializes in legal and policy issues in special education. He is the coauthor, with Charles J. Russo, of five texts published by Corwin, a SAGE company.

A past president of the Education Law Association (ELA), Osborne has been an attendee and presenter at most ELA conferences since 1991. He has also written a chapter now titled "Students With Disabilities" for the *Yearbook of Education Law*, published by ELA, since 1990. He is on the editorial advisory committee of *West's Education Law Reporter* and is coeditor of the "Education Law Into Practice" section of that journal, which is sponsored by ELA. He is also on the editorial boards of several other education journals.

In recognition of his contributions to the field of education law, Osborne was presented with the McGhehey Award by ELA in 2008, the highest award given by the organization. He is also the recipient of the City of Quincy Human Rights Award, the Financial Executives Institute of Massachusetts Principals Award, the Junior Achievement of Massachusetts Principals Award, and several community service awards.

Osborne spends his time in retirement writing, editing, and working on his hobbies, genealogy and photography. He and his wife Debbie, a retired elementary school teacher, enjoy gardening, traveling, attending theater and musical performances, and volunteering at the Dana Farber Cancer Institute in Boston.

ABOUT THE
VOLUME EDITORS

Frank Brown is the Cary C. Boshamer Distinguished Professor of Educational Leadership and Dean Emeritus, School of Education, University of North Carolina at Chapel Hill. Brown holds a PhD from the University of California at Berkeley and has held several academic and administrative positions: lecturer in education and acting director of mathematics and science education, University of California at Berkeley; associate director, New York State Commission on the Quality, Cost and Financing of Elementary and Secondary Education; assistant professor and director of University's Urban Institute, City College of New York; professor of educational administration and PhD program in public policy and director of the Cora P. Maloney College, State University of New York at Buffalo; and visiting scholar, Graduate School of Education, University of California at Berkeley. He has authored more than 300 publications and is listed in *Who's Who in America* and *Who's Who in Black America.*

Richard C. Hunter is a professor of educational administration and former head of the Educational Organization and Leadership Department at the University of Illinois at Urbana-Champaign. He holds an EdD in policy, planning, and administration from the University of California at Berkeley and was professor and chair of the Educational Leadership Program at the University of North Carolina at Chapel Hill. He has worked as a teacher, a principal, and an assistant and associate superintendent in the public schools of Berkeley, California; U.S. Air Force Schools in Tokyo, Japan; Richmond, California; and Seattle, Washington. He also was the district superintendent of the public schools of Richmond, Virginia; Dayton, Ohio; and Baltimore, Maryland. He was an associate director for education for the U.S. Department of Defense Education Activity in Arlington, Virginia. He was given a Fulbright Scholar Program Award from the U.S. Department of State and is currently serving as a lecturer at the Bahrain Teachers College of the University of Bahrain.

Saran Donahoo is an associate professor in the Department of Educational Administration and Higher Education and the director of the College Student Personnel Program at Southern Illinois University Carbondale. She earned both her PhD and her MA at the University of Illinois at Urbana-Champaign. She completed her BA in secondary education at the University of Arizona. Her published works include coediting *Teaching Leaders to Lead Teachers: Educational Administration in the Era of Constant Crisis* and articles in *Teachers College Record, Equity & Excellence in Education, Christian Higher Education, Urban Education,* and *Education and Urban Society,* as well as an array of book chapters. She also serves as associate editor for Media Reviews for the *Journal of Student Affairs Research & Practice.* In 2009, she received both the Joyce Cain Award for Distinguished Research on African Descendants from the Comparative and International Education Society (CIES) and the American Educational Research Association (AERA) Division J Outstanding Publication Award.

ABOUT THE CONTRIBUTORS

Nimo Abdi is a doctoral student in K–12 educational administration at Michigan State University. Her research interests include issues relating to school experiences of Somali refugees/immigrant students in public schools. More specifically, she is interested in student identity and self-perceptions in both school and community contexts.

Katrina A. R. Akande is a PhD candidate in the Department of Family Science at the University of Kentucky. Her research interests are family diversity, fatherhood, and racial socialization.

Wendy W. Amato is a doctoral student at the University of Virginia in the department of Curriculum and Instruction. Her research focuses on culturally congruent pedagogy for English language learners.

Clare Beckett-McInroy is a coactive coach/psychometrist, senior consultant, and president of Bizladies, Bahrain Chapter, at Bahrain Teachers College, University of Bahrain, and lecturer/tutor with University of Strathclyde (United Kingdom). Clare has worked in a variety of leading positions including university dean. She has presented at numerous international universities and conferences, including Harvard University and the University of Manchester (United Kingdom), and has many publications.

Lynda Brown Wright is a professor of in the Department of Educational, School and Counseling Psychology at the University of Kentucky. She has 24 years of experience as a trainer and instructor of multiculturalism. A primary research interest includes the examination of factors related to the cognitive development and schooling experiences of children and youth of color.

Mona Bryant-Shanklin is associate professor with the Department of Early Childhood, Elementary Education, and Special Education at Norfolk State University (Virginia). Her background with "at risk" populations is the basis for her current research and publication interests, which among other topics include social justice issues for traditionally underrepresented groups.

Jennifer L. Burris is a PhD student in the Department of Educational, School, and Counseling Psychology at the University of Kentucky. Her research interest is academic motivation and achievement among African American children.

Sonja M. Feist-Price is a professor in the Department of Special Education and Rehabilitation Counseling at the University of Kentucky where she has been on faculty since 1992. In addition to her doctoral degree in rehabilitation research from Southern Illinois University Carbondale, in 2006, Feist-Price completed a PhD in counseling psychology from the University of Kentucky.

Brandon Fox is a PhD student in curriculum and instruction with an emphasis in multicultural education at Texas A&M University. His research interests include culture and mathematics, equity and access, and multicultural teacher education.

Jesulon S. R. Gibbs is an assistant professor of educational leadership at the University of South Carolina in Columbia. Her research and teaching foci are public school law and educational policy analysis. She is also a contract attorney for Boykin & Davis, LLC, a school law firm. Dr. Gibbs's recent book is titled Student Speech on the Internet: The Role of First Amendment Protections.

Cosette M. Grant is a senior instructor and also serves as an adjunct professor at Pennsylvania State University Greater Allegheny. Her research focuses on the challenges and opportunities offered by increasing diversity in education. Her work includes published research on gender, diversity, and mentoring in peer-reviewed publications

Paul Green is on the faculty in the Ethnic Studies Department at the University of California, Riverside. His research and teaching focus on policies, practices, and laws that impede or advance educational and social opportunity for children and youth of color.

Dana Griffin is an assistant professor at the University of North Carolina at Chapel Hill. Being a former school counselor, she researches school-family-community collaboration and parental involvement in African American and Latino populations. Further, she explores culturally appropriate strategies for working with parents from these populations.

Miguel A. Guajardo is an associate professor in the Education and Community Leadership Program at Texas State University–San Marcos. His research interests include community building, community youth development, leadership development, race and ethnicity, university and community partnerships, and Latino youth and families.

Deborah A. Harmon is a professor of curriculum and instruction at Eastern Michigan University and the director of the Office of Urban Education and Educational Equity in the College of Education. Dr. Harmon's research is in multicultural education, urban education, and gifted education.

Valerie Hill-Jackson is a national award–winning educator, AERA/Spencer and Geraldine R. Dodge fellow, and clinical associate professor in the

Department of Teaching, Learning and Culture at Texas A&M University. Her interests are passionately located in critical teacher education, community studies, and STEM education for underserved learners.

Rachel Jackson is an undergraduate senior with a major in human resource development, a minor in creative studies, while seeking a teaching certificate from Texas A&M University. On completion of her bachelor's degree, Jackson plans to continue research in giftedness for the underserved and using organization development in revamping the public education system.

E. Lincoln James is professor of communication and managing editor of *The Western Journal of Black Studies* at Washington State University.

Marlon C. James is an assistant professor in the School of Education at Loyola University Chicago. His teaching and research focuses on developing social justice educators and fostering transformative schooling environments for African American males.

Enid Beverley Jones, professor emeritus, earned an EdD in educational administration from University of Florida, Gainesville, and held several positions as faculty, department chair, and director of doctoral universities. She has made presentations on educational administration and education finance at local, state, national, and international conferences. Her publications include a textbook on education finance and several journal articles.

Carl Byron Keys, II is an educator specializing in program development and in the doctoral program at University of Virginia. His research interests lie in understanding how educational leaders can build agency for members of their schools and use the affective nature of the schooling process to improve achievement. Keys is currently engaging in praxis in San Diego, California.

Muhammad Khalifa is a faculty member in K–12 educational administration at Michigan State University. He was previously an urban school teacher and administrator. His research addresses culturally appropriate school leadership practice. He has looked at successful urban school leadership, as well as principals in alternative schools and in Middle Eastern and African countries. His current research examines disparities in school suspension, urban school closures, and educational experiences of refugee children.

Robert C. Knoeppel is an associate professor and chair of the Faculty of Leadership, Counselor Education, and Human & Organizational Development at Clemson University. His research interests include school finance, leadership, and accountability policy.

Wayne D. Lewis is an assistant professor in the Department of Educational Leadership Studies at the University of Kentucky. His teaching and research are in the areas of education politics and policy, school reform, school-family-community collaboration, and diversity in education.

James E. Lyons is professor of educational leadership in the Department of Educational Leadership at the University of North Carolina at Charlotte. He joined the UNC–Charlotte faculty in 1979 and served as Department Chairperson for 15 years. During the last 25 years, he has published more than 40 articles and book chapters.

William J. Miller is assistant professor of political science at Southeast Missouri State University where he specializes in public opinion and American public policy.

John A. Oliver is an assistant professor of educational and community leadership at Texas State University–San Marcos. His research explores intersections of effective partnerships between communities, schools, and institutions of higher education for community change. Oliver was a public school teacher and assistant principal in Michigan for over 8 years.

Paul E. Pitre is an associate professor of educational leadership at Washington State University. His research focuses on underrepresented students' experiences in the college choice process and factors that predict college attendance. His research interests include P–16 education policy and higher education governance.

Patrice Preston-Grimes is an assistant professor at the University of Virginia's Curry School of Education. Her research interests include civic education, African American educational history, the sociocultural contexts of teaching and learning, and, more recently, the use of technology in social studies instruction.

Linwood J. Randolph, Jr. earned an EdD in curriculum and instruction from the University of North Carolina at Chapel Hill in 2011. He is a National Board–certified teacher and currently is assistant professor of Spanish and coordinator of foreign language teacher education at the University of North Carolina at Wilmington. His research interests include heritage language maintenance and multiculturalism in world language education.

Latish Reed is an assistant professor of educational leadership at the University of Wisconsin–Milwaukee. Her previous experiences as an urban school teacher and administrator influence her current research agenda, which centers on school leadership with focus on serving the needs of traditionally marginalized students.

Xue Lan Rong is professor at the University of North Carolina at Chapel Hill. Her research focuses on culture, race/ethnicity, and education, and the effects of immigrant generation on young adolescents' schooling. Rong's publications include 5 books, 3 edited journal volumes, and more than 40 journal articles and book chapters.

Martin Scanlan is on the faculty in the College of Education at Marquette University. His scholarship focuses on how schools work to create educational opportunities for traditionally marginalized students. His current research is on schools meeting students' special needs and dual immersion schools, as well as on collaboration among institutes of higher education, K–12 schools, and community organizations.

Christopher N. Thomas is an assistant professor and department chair of the leadership studies program at the University of San Francisco and was recently named 2010 Professor of the Year by the Association of California School Administrators. His primary responsibility is training and preparing educators to become instructional and social justice leaders.

Deneia M. Thomas is an associate professor in counseling and educational psychology at Eastern Kentucky University in Richmond, Kentucky. She has vast experience promoting equity and accountability within K–12 settings and postsecondary institutions. Thomas maintains a record of scholarship relating to the examination of factors that promote success among diverse populations.

Natalie A. Tran is an assistant professor in the Department of Secondary Education at California State University, Fullerton. Her research focuses on instructional practices and social contexts affecting student achievement in science. Her methodological interests include hierarchical linear modeling, experimental design, quasi-experimental design, and survey studies.

Tiffany R. Wheeler is an assistant professor of education at Transylvania University in Lexington, Kentucky. Her teaching and research interests include culturally responsive pedagogy, sociocultural perspectives of literacy instruction, race and ethnicity issues in education, and immigrant children. She received the Bingham Award for Excellence in Teaching in 2011.

Miguel Zavala is assistant professor in the Department of Secondary Education at California State University, Fullerton. His research focuses on the role teacher-led community organizing spaces play in fostering social justice teaching and action-research projects. Zavala has extensive experience working with urban and migrant Latino youth.

INTRODUCTION

This volume covers several salient diversity indicators, including race, ethnicity, language, and socioeconomic status, that must be considered in order to ensure quality education in public schools for all students. These indicators are discussed in the context of efforts to achieve educational equity through multicultural education and broader social policies addressing issues such as school funding, segregation, and teacher training.

Efforts to provide educational equity for all students can be traced to the women's rights movement of the 19th century and the civil rights movement of the 1950s. These efforts accelerated after the landmark 1954 Supreme Court decision in *Brown v. Board of Education* supporting school desegregation. In the 1960s, we witnessed the racial and ethnic pride movements. These activities were followed by demands for changes in school curricula, more minority teachers and administrators, and later, gender equity.

However, resistance to demands related to diversity has been strong and persistent (Brown, 2004a; Brown, 2004b). There was resistance at all levels of the federal government, state governments, and local school boards. Individuals in these units of government expressed opposition to school desegregation, changes in the curriculum, affirmative action plans to employ more minority personnel, ethnic studies, and bilingual education. Several states banned the use of state funds for racial desegregation, teaching of English as a second language, and the establishment of ethnic studies programs. Some school districts and their supporters pressured book publishers to remove or reduce the multicultural content in their books and school libraries to ban books popular among minority students.

Recently, policymakers have attempted to replace the nation's commitment to public education with an emphasis on school choice and to define educational excellence in terms of student achievement on standardized tests. There are many other controversies related to how best to meet the needs of diverse students, but we have chosen the topics for this volume because of their relevance to diversity and excellence as keys to the nation's ability to meet the challenges of the 21st century, especially with respect to effectiveness in the global economy. An underlying assumption is that effective implementation of goals related to diversity will lead to quality education for all students. The debates in this volume focus on a number of broad issues relating to diversity and quality education, ranging from desegregation and multicultural instruction, to educational and funding equity. These topics introduce the readers to the nature and complexity of diversity in public education.

DIVERSITY AND QUALITY EDUCATION

Quality public education has been deemed important at all levels of government, and imperative for the country's survival in the global economy (Byrd, 2004; Spring, 2008; Wilson, 2009). Diversity in education is influenced by the racial, ethnic, and linguistic diversity of the U.S. population. The United States has one of the most financially unequal systems of education with respect to educational funding per student enrolled in public K–12 schools. Most countries have a single national funding system for public education, with equal expenditures per student nationwide. The United States has 50 separate state systems, with expenditures per student that differ between the states, and between school districts within each state, with one exception: The state of Hawaii has only one school district with equal funding per pupil across the entire state. Education achievement in the United States lags behind other rich countries (Darling-Hammond, 2010, pp. 26–64). In addition, achievement gaps exist between minority and nonminority students and between low-income students and their more affluent counterparts.

There are several reasons for our approach to diversity in this volume. First, we are concerned about equity in the funding of schools that promotes a better chance for an equal educational opportunity for all children within each school district within each state. Students' test scores serve as a gatekeeping function for success in school. In today's economy, high academic skills are important, and in an era of high-stakes testing, the penalty for having lower academic skills is greater (Magnuson & Waldfogel, 2008, p. 2; Winerip, 2011, p. A17). Thus, an achievement gap in education means unequal opportunities in the larger society. An example of such a gap is that between test scores of Black and White students. The test score gap between Black and White students narrowed until 1988, but then it began to widen. This narrowing of the gap was evident for both Black boys and girls until 1988, but after 1988, Black girls began to outscore Black boys (Magnuson & Waldfogel, 2008, pp. 6, 13). This achievement gap also exists for other racial and ethnic minorities. Second, this country needs more and better educated citizens to compete successfully in the global economy. Finally, academically, there is a lack of quality education for most minority students, who live in poorer school districts with less educational funding per pupil. The lower levels of education funding result in these children having less qualified teachers, which usually results in an inferior education compared to most White students who reside in wealthier school districts (Darling-Hammond, 2010; Magunson & Waldfogel, 2008).

This volume debates several significant issues that are central to achieving this goal of providing students in each public school an equal educational opportunity between the states and within individual states.

DESEGREGATION

After 1865, slavery ended, but 31 years later in *Plessy v. Ferguson* (1896), the Supreme Court held that states could meet the equal protection requirements under the Constitution by providing "separate but equal" opportunities for Blacks and Whites. It wasn't until 1954 that the Supreme Court in *Brown v. Board of Education* ruled that racially segregated schooling was unconstitutional. Even after that decision, major progress in implementing desegregation did not occur until 1970 (Brown, 2004a; Brown, 2007), and after 1980, school integration declined (Brown, 2004a; Cashin, 2004). More recently, in its 2007 ruling in *Parents Involved in Community Schools v. Seattle School District No. 1*, the Supreme Court struck down voluntary assignment plans in Seattle, Washington, and Louisville, Kentucky. The Court held that that a public school student assignment plan that gave preference to racial minority students was unconstitutional where there was no preponderant proof that such a plan was necessary to achieve racial diversity. The case arose when parents in two school districts challenged voluntarily implemented assignment plans that gave preference to minority students. The Court found that the two districts did not have a compelling interest in adopting the assignment plans since they were not being used to remedy the effects of past intentional discrimination. Further, the Court indicated that the objective of creating racial balance, while laudable, was not compelling. This decision represented a setback for the diversity movement, in that it limited a neighborhood school's racial and ethnic population to that of the immediate geographic area (Brown, 2007).

In this volume, the first chapter specifically examines the question of whether litigation should be the primary focus in efforts to desegregate the schools, while several other chapters look at other means of providing equal educational opportunities to diverse student populations. In this respect, Chapters 1, 2, and 3 debate various diversity strategies, such as racial and ethnic school desegregation, multicultural counseling, and school personnel preparation programs that should educate such personnel to deal effectively with such a diverse student population.

INSTRUCTION
Curriculum

Establishing a school's instruction and curriculum has traditionally been a function of state and local governments. State boards of education set curricula standards and approve textbooks. However, special interest groups often request funding for additional instructional activities and curricula offerings to supplement the district's standard curriculum. The movement toward curriculum diversity has stimulated an ongoing political and legal debate that often becomes highly charged. Many curricula disagreements end in court and become issues in political elections to statewide offices and local school boards. Indicative of the ongoing struggle, some educators have suggested that elements of popular youth culture, such as hip-hop, should be incorporated into the curriculum, a proposal that is debated in Chapter 8. As this debate clearly shows, there are both pros and cons to using pop culture to teach a diverse student population, and some argue that the decision of whether to adopt such a strategy should depend on the overall culture of the school and community.

Personnel

Academic achievement among African American, Latino, and some other ethnic minority students continues to lag behind that of White students and some groups of Asian Americans. One cause of this gap is that many teachers have a low expectation of minority students and assign a disproportionate number of minority students to lower level academic courses or tracks (Darling-Hammond, 2010; Oakes, 2005). A second cause of this achievement gap may be that minority schools have less experienced teachers and higher rates of teacher turnover. Another issue is the lack of male teachers of all races. Chapter 15 debates the merits of gender-based student loan forgiveness programs to increase the percentage of male teachers and administrators.

America is a capitalist society, and attracting better teachers to work effectively with all racial and ethnic groups will require better financial benefits. When the talent pool for teachers declined in the 1960s, the National Science Foundation and the Ford Foundation spent hundreds of millions of dollars to help elite colleges prepare teachers. Both programs recruited the best and brightest into education by paying the total cost of their education and providing spending money. After the U.S. Congress enacted the Civil Rights Act of 1964 that opened better opportunities for racial and ethnic minorities and females of all races to enroll in greater numbers in academic professions such as medicine, law, and business, many of these individuals no longer sought careers in public school teaching. This resulted in fewer academically talented individuals entering the teaching profession. In addition, most elite colleges and universities beginning in the late 1960s eliminated their teacher preparation programs. These events caused a decline in the quality of teachers, which contributed to a decline in students' test scores by 1980 (Magunson & Waldfogel, 2008). The earlier National Science Program had provided fellowships to practicing teachers to enroll in programs in science and mathematics with all expenses paid by the government. The current STEM program that began under President George W. Bush has a much smaller budget and aims primarily to encourage more college students to seek majors in the sciences, technology, engineering, and mathematics (STEM)—not teaching careers. Despite current programs designed to attract a talented pool of candidates into teaching, such as Teach for America, a large number of young teachers leave the profession within 5 years (Darling-Hammond, 2010; Klein, 2011; Ravitch, 2011, p. A25). This suggest that states may need to pay teachers higher salaries (a) to attract more of the most academically talented college students into the teaching profession to accomplish this goal and (b) to encourage more elite colleges and universities to enter the field of preparing public school teachers and administrators. Further, there is a need for greater diversity among our teaching force. Several essays in this volume examine ways of bringing more diverse and talented candidates to education. Chapter 15 looks at ways to attract more males to the teaching profession, a profession that is currently dominated by female teachers.

Title I and Race to the Top Programs

The primary purpose of public education is to provide instruction/teaching for students. Thus, several chapters in this volume review efforts to improve instruction for all students. The first national effort dealing with the country's diverse student population began with the Elementary and Secondary Education Act (ESEA) of 1965. This program recognized the lack of quality instruction for poor minority children. This statute has been reauthorized several times, most recently as the No Child Left Behind Act (NCLB) of 2001. The ESEA was originally approved to bridge the academic gap between economically disadvantaged and advantaged students. Specifically, Title I of the statute provides compensatory education for students and supports the education of students with disabilities and bilingual education. It also allows students to transfer from low-performing schools to better schools.

Recently, President Barack Obama's Race to the Top (RTT) program, designed to improve underperforming schools, has supplemented the NCLB. RTT supports such programs as charter schools, magnet schools, private management of public schools, vouchers, and alternative teacher preparation programs. Authors in several of the chapters in this volume debate the merits of Title I and RTT. With regard to Title I, Chapter 6 takes up the issue of whether aid to schools under Title I of ESEA is an appropriate strategy for closing the achievement gap that exists between White and minority students. Chapter 5 discusses whether Title I is effective in closing the achievement gap between those who are economically disadvantaged and their more affluent peers. Chapter 4 addresses RTT and whether this and related programs can be successful in meeting the goals of improving underperforming schools.

Support Services

Counselors and administrators are a valuable resource for teachers as well as for students and their families. Disadvantaged minority students and their parents may need special assistance from school personnel, and there may be a greater need for more face-to-face interaction between parents and school personnel. For example, parents of special education students may not fully understand their rights or why their child is not progressing academically. As children progress through school, parents should be informed personally as to what is required of their children. Given the high dropout rate among disadvantaged minority students, it is also important for counselors and administrators to assist students and their parents in managing the demands of school so that students are better able to succeed academically. Several chapters in this volume deal specifically with issues that touch on the support services that can be provided to a diverse student population. Chapter 2 in this volume deals specifically with the question of whether multicultural counseling programs are needed to improve the academic achievement of students. Another chapter, Chapter 11, examines support services for students from limited English speaking families and different cultures. This chapter also asks whether English-only is the best method for teaching English language learners. Chapter 9 examines the many issues surrounding the use of ability grouping and tracking in schools. Chapter 13 examines ways to provide additional support services to minority students and their parents, specifically utilizing full-service community counseling models to assist students enrolled in majority-minority schools to improve the students' chances of being more successful in school.

EDUCATIONAL EQUITY

Research has shown that in the United States, family wealth is related to children's academic achievement (Cashin, 2004; Darling-Hammond, 2010; Wilson, 2009). Yet, being poor and minority is not the same as being poor and White in the United States (Stricker, 2007; Wilson, 2009). There are more opportunities to escape poverty for Whites than for racial minorities (Stricker, 2007; Wilson, 2009). As stated earlier, there is an academic achievement gap between minority students and White students, as well as between low-income students and higher income students. One proposal for providing equitable educational opportunities is the full-service community school model, in which public health, social, and/or community services are provided along with education services. Chapter 13 of this volume debates whether such full-service models are useful for achieving educational equity.

Educational Funding

State Funding

Public education is a state function, but the financial ability to support education varies from state to state and district to district within a state. Also, there are funding disparities between neighborhood schools within each school district. Wealthier school districts are better able to attract the best school personnel to meet the high standards that all school districts desire. However, more minority students tend to live in low-income neighborhoods with less funding for their schools.

As is apparent from the essays in the Finance volume in this series, public school funding is complex, and because public education is a state responsibility, funding is highly political. District level funding is based on support from state and local funds, and the source of local and state funds varies widely by state. For example, some states support up to 75% of the cost with 25% coming from local funds, with other combinations in between, and the amount of local funding also varies widely. Some states generate funds from sales or income taxes, and some generate funds from a combination of sales and income taxes. Basically, local funds are drawn mainly from property taxes, and local sales taxes if permitted by the state.

There are state formulas for providing funds for schools. First, states may provide local school districts' funds based on their enrollment, property wealth, property assessment ratio, and tax rate. Second, most states provide each school district a basic support level regardless of its wealth or property tax rate. But several states provide each local school district a single funding rate per teacher per class without regard for property value or tax rate.

Federal Funds

The federal government provides about 7% of local school budgets to support such programs as special education, meals for poor children, compensatory education (Title I programs), bilingual education, dropout prevention, and Native American education. These programs address special needs but do not address the unequal funding among the states or among schools within a single district.

The Future of Educational Funding

In 1973, the Supreme Court in *San Antonio v. Rodriguez* held that unequal state funding across school districts did not violate the Constitution. After 1973, school funding equity cases were processed through state courts with not much success (Odden & Picus, 2008), and some scholars believe this situation is unlikely to change (Guthrie, Springer, Rolle, & Houck, 2007). These legal challenges have not to date resulted in increased revenues for poor schools servicing largely disadvantaged minority children.

Given such funding disparities and the high correlation between federal education programs and the overrepresentation of minority students, Chapter 10 debates whether current funding structures marginalize ethnic and racial minority students.

CONCLUSION

It has been more than 50 years since the Supreme Court outlawed racial segregation in schools with *Brown v. Board of Education* (1954), and 40 years since *Swann v. Charlotte-Mecklenburg Board of Education* (1971), when the Court authorized the use of race to desegregate schools. It has now reversed that 1971 decision by its ruling in *Parents Involved* against the use of racial criteria to desegregate schools, thereby returning schools back to the neighborhood concept. Equal funding through the courts also has not been successful for plaintiffs. Using the federal courts to equalize state funding across school districts in 1973 was not successful (*San Antonio v. Rodriguez*). Also, subsequent challenges in state courts for equal school funding have not been very successful.

The ability to racially desegregate schools beyond one's neighborhood or the ability to equalize funding of schools across all neighborhoods within each school district could have a positive impact on the ability of schools to address the needs of their diverse student populations. Unfortunately, school districts may have difficulty desegregating public schools or receiving equal funding for all schools within a school district.

Attracting more diverse and talented college students into teaching as a career will incur additional costs. Top schools, academically, are able to recruit and retain top college graduates, and schools that cannot afford to attract top teachers should not expect to be highly ranked (Klein, 2011, p. 76). Although there are many reasons why schools have difficulty in diversifying their staff, financial shortcomings may restrict their ability to diversify the teaching faculty and administration by race, ethnicity, and gender. Financial restrictions may also impede efforts to diversify the curriculum, including extracurricular activities.

The challenge for education policymakers is how best to provide schools with the tools and conditions needed for programs that meet the needs of diverse populations of students, teachers, administrators, and parents necessary to secure a quality education for all students.

Frank Brown
University of North Carolina at Chapel Hill

Richard C. Hunter
University of Illinois at Urbana-Champaign and
Bahrain Teachers College, University of Bahrain, Kingdom of Bahrain

Saran Donahoo
Southern Illinois University

FURTHER READINGS AND RESOURCES

Brown, F. (2004a). The first serious implementation of *Brown*: The 1964 Civil Rights Act and beyond. *Journal of Negro Education, 73*(3), 182–190.

Brown, F. (2004b). Nixon's "Southern Strategy" and forces against *Brown*. *Journal of Negro Education, 73*(3), 191–208.

Brown, F. (2007). Ending the *Brown* era: What is the future for equal educational opportunity? *School Business Affairs, 73*(9), 8–10.

Byrd, R. (2004). *Losing America*. New York: W. W. Norton.

Cashin, S. (2004). *The Failure of Integration: How race and class are undermining the American dream*. New York: PublicAffairs.

Darling-Hammond, L. (2010). *The flat world and education: How America's commitment to equity will determine our future*. New York: Teachers College Press.

Guthrie, J. W., Springer, M. G., Rolle, R. A., & Houck, E. A. (2007). *Modern education finance and policy*. Boston: Pearson/Allyn & Bacon.

Klein, J. (2011). The failure of American schools. *The Atlantic, 307*(5), 66–77.

Magnuson, K., & Waldfogel, J. (2008). *Steady gains and stalled progress*. New York: Russell Sage Foundation.

Oakes, J. (2005). *Keeping track: How schools structure inequality* (2nd ed.). New Haven, CT: Yale University Press.

Odden, A. R., & Picus, L. O. (2008). *School finance: A policy perspective* (4th ed.). Boston: McGraw-Hill.

Ravitch, D. (2011, May 31). Waiting for a school miracle. *The New York Times*, p. A25.

Spring, J. (2008). Research on globalization and education. *Review of Educational Research, 78*(2), 330–363.

Stricker, F. (2007). *Why America lost the war on poverty—and how to win it*. Chapel Hill: University of North Carolina Press.

Wilson, J. W. (2009). *Why the poor stay poor: Being Black and poor in the inner city*. New York: W. W. Norton.

Winerip, M. (2011, February 13). Closing the achievement gap without widening a racial one. *The New York Times,* pp. A15, A17.

COURT CASES AND STATUTES

Brown v. Board of Education, 347 U.S. 483 (1954).
Elementary and Secondary Education Act of 1965, 20 U.S.C. § 6301 *et seq.* (1965).
No Child Left Behind Act of 2001, 20 U.S.C. §§ 6301–7941 (2006).
Parents Involved in Community Schools v. Seattle School District No. 1, 127 S. Ct. 2738 (2007).
Plessy v. Ferguson, 163 U.S. 537 (1896).
San Antonio Independent School District v. Rodriguez, 411 U.S. 1 (1973).
Swann v. Charlotte-Mecklenburg Board of Education, 402 U.S. 1 (1971).

Should the courts be the primary focus in efforts to achieve desegregation?

POINT: Richard C. Hunter, *University of Illinois at Urbana-Champaign and Bahrain Teachers College, University of Bahrain, Kingdom of Bahrain*

COUNTERPOINT: E. Lincoln James and Paul E. Pitre, *Washington State University*

OVERVIEW

The debate in this chapter focuses on the issue of whether court-ordered mandates, as opposed to legislated school desegregation policies, should be the primary focus in addressing unequal educational opportunities for students of color. Studies have shown that since de facto segregation continues, unequal educational opportunities for students of color continue to exist nationwide even though state-mandated racial segregation no longer exists. Thus, children of color do not always have equal educational opportunities (Cashin, 2004). The question is whether current legislation can adequately address this problem.

Legal racially segregated public schools existed in southern and most border states until the 1954 U.S. Supreme Court's landmark decision in *Brown v. Board of Education* (1954). In *Brown,* the Court ruled that racially segre-gated public education was unconstitutional and, in doing so, reversed its 1896 decision in *Plessy v. Ferguson. Plessy* held that racial segregation was constitutional if the state provided "separate but equal" facilities for both Whites and non-Whites.

Brown combined five school cases from the lower federal courts to review challenges to racially segregated public schools. The cases came from four states and the District of Columbia. The Court held a second hearing in 1955 to discuss implementation of *Brown* and ordered the lower courts to proceed "with all due deliberate speed." In 1968, in a Virginia school desegregation case, *Green v. County School Board,* the U.S. Supreme Court ordered the lower courts to act affirmatively in enforcing *Brown.* The *Green* opinion listed six factors needed to achieve unitary desegregation status: student assignments, faculty assignments, staff assignments, facilities, transportation, and extracurricular activities.

The school desegregation process was slow. First, school districts refused to voluntarily integrate their schools. Second, seeking a legal remedy against school districts required lawsuits on behalf of Black plaintiffs with children enrolled in each of approximately 5,000 school districts that required racially segregated schools. This process was dangerous and costly for Black plaintiffs. Civil rights organizations were able to finance a limited number of cases through the courts. Finally, it took 4 to 6 years for such cases to reach the Supreme Court, and if the plaintiffs were successful, the cases were remanded to the lower federal district courts for implementation. These were the same judges who often had ruled against plaintiffs when their cases initially had come before the trial courts. Lower courts approved limited remedies that failed to adequately desegregate schools. In many cases, the courts supervised integration efforts for decades that never achieved unitary desegregation status.

The Civil Rights Act of 1964 aided in this process by bringing legal action against offending school districts by the U.S. Attorney's Office that covered legal expenses. By 1990, the Supreme Court began to retreat from its positive views on school desegregation by allowing school districts to be removed from lower courts' supervision without meeting all of the six *Green* factors required by the Court in its 1968 decision.

In 2007, the Court in *Parents Involved in Community Schools v. Seattle School District No. 1* held that the use of race in busing to achieve integration was no longer constitutional by overturning its 1972 Court decision that allowed such use of busing to desegregate schools. *Parents Involved* ended the 50-year practice of using race in assigning students to schools to promote racial desegregation. This case involved voluntary racial diversity. In 2001, prior to *Parents Involved,* a Fourth Circuit federal court decision allowed North Carolina's Charlotte-Mecklenburg Public schools' opposition to busing of students by race to stand (*Belk v. Charlotte-Mecklenburg Board of Education,* 2001). As was expected, racially isolated schools returned to Charlotte-Mecklenburg. In 2001, the 140,000-pupil Wake County Schools of North Carolina enacted another standard to help achieve racial diversity: the use of socioeconomic measures in assigning students to schools. This policy of using socioeconomic measures to achieve more racial diversity is currently under attack by opponents of busing.

Richard C. Hunter in the point essay in this chapter concludes that overall research suggests that court-ordered school desegregation had a positive impact on the academic and mental health of racial and ethnic minority students. He feels that public school desegregation is still the best option for addressing the unequal educational opportunities for students of color in this country. E. Lincoln James and Paul E. Pitre argue, on the other hand, that court-ordered school desegregation did not achieve its goal, even though a few good things happened to Black children after *Brown*. In their counterpoint essay, James and Pitre contend that legislated school desegregation policies by themselves have been insufficient in bringing about equal educational opportunities for students of color for a number of reasons.

In reading this chapter, you may want to think about how resources between schools in poor neighborhoods can be equalized with resources available to schools in wealthier neighborhoods. Resistance to school desegregation is still strong among many White Americans (Brown, 2004a, 2004b; Cashin, 2004). Therefore, in this new environment of racially segregated neighborhood schools where required attendance at neighborhood schools is the norm, how do we bring about equal funding between wealthy and poor neighborhood schools? Are courts more likely to support plans to bring about equality between children in different neighborhoods? Since it is unlikely that the U.S. Supreme Court will reverse its 2007 decision in *Parents Involved* and allow the use of race to achieve racial diversity in public schools (Brown, 2007), what other options exist?

Frank Brown
University of North Carolina at Chapel Hill

POINT: Richard C. Hunter
University of Illinois at Urbana-Champaign and Bahrain Teachers College, University of Bahrain, Kingdom of Bahrain

According to David J. Armor (1995), there is more than one source of public school desegregation policy—the roots of this policy lie in both school desegregation law and social science theory. The U.S. Supreme Court, in its landmark decision in *Brown v. Board of Education*, enacted a sweeping school desegregation policy. In evaluating the need for a school desegregation policy, it is important to discuss the history of public education in the United States, which was racially segregated by law throughout the Southern region of the United States and by housing patterns in most of the rest of the country. This condition for public education was the pattern for several generations and was supported by the 1896 decision of the U.S. Supreme Court in *Plessy v. Ferguson*. This case held that Homer Plessy, an African American man who was traveling on a public railroad, could not sit in the White section because of his race. The Court's decision continued the prevailing policy of racial segregation for African Americans, as long as they were provided "separate but equal" treatment. Although this legal decision related to public transportation, it was extended to all sectors of American life, including public education. Practically speaking, this meant that racial segregation of African American students in public education could continue, as long as they received a free public education. Because of *Plessy* and the overt racism in the South, African American public school students continued to receive a substandard education for an additional 50 years. They attended racially segregated schools with African American teachers, who were paid less than White teachers; their schools were built with less money and did not have the same libraries and science laboratories; and they received textbooks that had been discarded by White schools. Education for African American students was separate, but not equal, in comparison to their White counterparts.

The cumulative effects of the "separate but equal" doctrine, coupled with the policy of racial segregation that preceded it, had produced a demonstratively inferior education for students of color. Because of this, a number of lawsuits were brought on behalf of African American plaintiffs, who alleged that their rights were being violated under *Plessy*. Most of the early public education desegregation cases were brought on behalf of graduate students in higher education because some states did not provide an opportunity for

African American students to obtain a legal education. These early school desegregation cases forced states to create new degree programs for African American university students, who heretofore had gone to Northern universities to receive their graduate education (Hunter, 2004).

THE BROWN DECISIONS

The first Supreme Court decision in *Brown v. Board of Education* (*Brown I*) was handed down in 1954. This case was the result of consolidating four separate public school desegregation cases, the most famous of which involved the public schools of Topeka, Kansas. In this case, Thurgood Marshall, using the Equal Protection Clause of the Fourteenth Amendment of the U.S. Constitution, convinced the High Court that these public school districts had violated the civil rights of students of color. *Brown II* was issued by the Supreme Court in 1955 to address the responsibilities of the federal district courts in establishing remedies for the plaintiffs in *Brown I*.

Derrick Bell, a distinguished academic who has done extensive research on race and law, maintains that even though the *Brown* decisions were important and furthered race relations, the Supreme Court made an error in approving *Brown* and should have continued support for the "separate but equal" doctrine espoused in *Plessy* by the Court. He suggests that *Plessy* could have been used to require school districts to provide truly equal education instead of the unequal education provided for African American public school students after *Brown*. Bell also maintains that *Brown* was not successful because of a bad calculation and misunderstanding of the effects of White racism on public education (Bell, 2004).

John C. Boger and Gary Orfield (2005) maintain that the courts and political leaders who are of the opinion that *Plessy* should have been maintained are misguided. They believe these persons do not adequately consider that under *Plessy*, equal education for students of color was denied in the South from 1896 through 1954. These authors cite data regarding the funding of public education in the South, which indicates that White students received 33% more financial resources for their education than African American students did in 1940, and 43% more in 1954.

OTHER IMPORTANT SCHOOL DESEGREGATION CASES

Early federal court decisions in school desegregation did not place much emphasis on educational improvements. The primary focus of these decisions was the requirement that African American and White students attend the same schools and that faculties be integrated. The public school desegregation case in Virginia, *Green v. County School Board* (1968), was responsible for the now famous six *Green* factors, which are student assignment, faculty assignment, staff assignment, facilities, transportation, and extracurricular activities. Even though school facilities were one of the six *Green* factors, it was not given as much attention as student assignment and transportation. The six *Green* factors have been used by federal district courts to determine whether the vestiges of deliberate and unlawful segregation in public schools have been eliminated. In some cases, school districts are not given unitary status until they have satisfied the court that all of the *Green* factors have been met.

Swann v. Charlotte-Mecklenburg Board of Education* (1971), which involved the public schools of Charlotte and Mecklenburg County, North Carolina, is another of the landmark public school desegregation cases. *Swann* decided the issues of whether racial quotas and busing students could constitute a remedy to achieve school desegregation. Another famous school district case involving the attempt to consolidate or create a metropolitan school district to enhance the racial balance of students was *Milliken v. Bradley* (*Milliken II,* 1977), which was struck down by the Supreme Court. *Milliken II* would have permitted the Detroit public schools to be combined with several neighboring school districts in Wayne County. What makes this case additionally famous is that, unlike other cases, the Court supported other remedies for the racial segregation of Detroit schools. The state of Michigan was required to fund compensatory education programs designed to improve public education for Detroit's students. This decision included funding instructional improvements such as reduced class sizes, which heretofore had not been ordered in *Milliken I* (1974) or in other school desegregation cases. After *Milliken II,* public school desegregation litigants began taking a more comprehensive view of public school desegregation and asked federal district courts to fashion broader remedies (Hunter, 2004). The *Jenkins v. Missouri* 1995 case is viewed by some as the most far-reaching school desegregation case in the United States. In this case, the state of Missouri was required to fund many remedial education programs—including full-day kindergarten, expanded summer school, before- and after-school tutoring, an early childhood program, and a comprehensive magnet school program—and to make salary payments for underpaid school district personnel. The Court also ordered the community to pass a tax increase, which had not been increased for over 30 years. Additionally, the state of Missouri was required to fund extensive capital improvements. The capital improvements required by *Jenkins* included funding the initial phase of the capital improvements plan at a cost of $37 million and the school district's long-range capital improvement plan of $187 million. Overall, the district's capital plan called for the renovation of approximately 55 schools, closure of 18 facilities, and construction of 17 new schools (Alexander & Alexander, 2009; Hunter, 2004).

RETREATING FROM BROWN

There have been several decisions by the Supreme Court that indicate its retreat from public school desegregation. One such case was the decision in *Board of Education of Oklahoma v. Dowell* (1991), which allowed this school district to end its desegregation plan and supervision by the Court. The *Dowell* case led to what is now referred to as "unitary status," which is the process of releasing a school district from federal district court supervision (Clotfelter, 2004). Other decisions of the Supreme Court discontinued the policy of making race-conscious student assignments to remedy past discrimination against African American students in public schools. These decisions include *Parents Involved in Community Schools v. Seattle School District No. 1* and *Meredith v. Jefferson County Public Schools (Louisville)*, 2007. In these decisions, the Court struck down race-conscious student assignment plans even if such reassignment reduced student racial isolation and increased diversity. Against the backdrop of other Supreme Court cases, these decisions dealt a fatal blow to public school desegregation and are leading the country to racial resegregation (Wells & Frankenberg, 2007). Christina Asquith (2006) indicates that legal experts predicted the Supreme Court would strike down the use of race-conscious admission policies in their decisions on these cases. This change, experts maintain, resulted from the appointments of Justices John Roberts and Samuel Alito—conservatives who tipped the balance of the Court to a more conservative ideology, opposed to using race as a criterion for assigning public school pupils, even if it improves student diversity. Some view the decision of the Court in these cases as shortsighted in that they had the potential to decrease student diversity, while public school districts like Seattle and Louisville were going against popular beliefs by maintaining student diversity. The approach of using race as a factor in student assignment policy has never been popular in the United States, even after the landmark *Brown* decision. The efforts in Seattle and Louisville to achieve student diversity were designed to permit minority students to attend schools outside their racially segregated neighborhoods, thus improving diversity.

PROSPECTS FOR THE FUTURE

In his opinion in the Seattle and Louisville cases, Justice Kennedy presented options for school districts to achieve student racial integration:

- Locate schools between racially distinct neighborhoods.
- Redraw school attendance zones.
- Target recruitment of students from particular schools.

However, social scientists and educational practitioners do not favor measures such as those suggested by Justice Kennedy. The use of race-conscious criteria in student assignment decisions has demonstrated success in creating more diversity in public schools. This assertion is supported by the recent experience of the Charlotte-Mecklenburg Schools in North Carolina, which changed policy from a comprehensive race-based system of student assignment to a race-neutral one. This change increased student racial segregation and resulted in less student diversity. Wake County (Raleigh) Public School System, also in North Carolina, chose to assign all district pupils on the basis of socioeconomic status and achieved great success. Because of this, Wake County was recognized by the U.S. Department of Education for its success in maintaining racially diversity. However, recently, Wake County rescinded its policy to assign students using socioeconomic data. This change was brought about by a change in the composition of the board of education and its decision to return to neighborhood schools. Additionally, the decision has created considerable tension in the community (Schrader, 2009). Other approaches to student assignment that school districts could use to create diversity among their student bodies, in light of the Seattle and Louisville decisions, include the following (Wells & Frankenberg, 2007):

- The use of managed school choice approaches, where parents can send their children to schools other than the neighborhood schools, such as magnet schools that are based on themes and use nonracial criterion for student assignment
- Use of criteria that coincide with race, such as using neighborhoods or native languages to assign students to schools

THE AUTHOR'S POSITION

Public school desegregation is still the best option to address the unequal educational opportunities for students of color in the United States. This view is based on the following: First, state and local governments, including many public educational systems, have not uniformly and consistently demonstrated throughout history a desire to address discrimination against students of color. This failure caused plaintiffs of color to take legal action in federal courts. If we were forced to rely on the vagaries of local and state government to address the educational problems of students of color, we would not be as far along in terms of educational quality as we are today. Consider the unequal funding of public education that has forced plaintiffs in just about every state in the union to sue for equalized and equitable funding in support of the nation's students of color. Race has been a major issue in public education, and it remains so even after *Brown*, even though *Brown* has improved public education for many students.

Second, federal court judges have great authority to fashion remedies to address constitutional violations found on the part of students of color. The remedies ordered for students of color in *Milliken II* and in *Missouri v. Jenkins* are examples of the latitude judges have in such cases. Admittedly, the Supreme Court has become more conservative. It has also taken a negative view of race in public school student assignments as a remedy for civil rights violations. However, federal courts could order the use of socioeconomic status to assign public school students or use one of the other criteria presented in this essay to ensure schools are desegregated. We should take into consideration that the Supreme Court approved broad remedies and that new cases could be filed using such remedies.

Third, there are a number of public school districts that have achieved unitary status and probably cannot be sued again for civil rights violations against African American students. This is true, but there are other students of color on behalf of whom legal actions could be brought, especially Hispanic students. Moreover, the minority population is shifting from the large cities to the suburbs, which have not been declared unitary and might be practicing de facto segregation in their public schools. Perhaps litigation could be brought on the behalf of these students.

Fourth, some have suggested we should not rely on *Brown* because *Plessy* offers greater promise in addressing the educational conditions of students of color than *Brown* did. As mentioned above, *Plessy* did not work so well for public school students of color while it was in force. Nor does this position acknowledge the impact that race has on public educational decisions. Again, it is suggested that the school finance litigation movement in this country offers concrete evidence that judicial intervention for children of color is necessary.

CONCLUSION

Presently, the Supreme Court is controlled by conservative jurists who do not appear to favor diversity in public education. This condition is very troublesome, but the ideological leaning of the Court could change over time. The struggle for equal education for students of color has not been a short journey, nor is it over because conservative jurists and others believe it is.

Consider an interpretation from one of the legal framers of *Brown*, who indicated in a conversation on school desegregation policy with the author of this article that the civil rights attorneys in *Brown* elected to attack *Plessy* not because they wanted African American children to be educated with White children, or because they believed that African American children could not receive a high quality public education unless they were in classrooms with White students. After all, the attorneys who represented the plaintiffs in *Brown* had attended segregated schools. Most of them received their graduate education at universities in the North, because they were not permitted to receive a graduate legal education in their Southern home states. We should not lose sight of the fact that the legal framers of *Brown* attended segregated schools and experienced firsthand the effects of *Plessy* in their public educations. They believed that a "separate but equal" education for students of color delivered in racially segregated schools would not be truly equal education. They maintained the view that Whites would not allocate equal economic resources to students of color who attended racially segregated schools. Again, the school finance litigation movement in this country recognizes the predilection of many Whites who by their actions appear to favor unequal education for public school students of color. Further, the development and implementation of new legal theory takes time and requires imaginative attorneys like Thurgood Marshall, who are dedicated to the cause of equal educational opportunity for students of color. Also, the legal obstacles that conservatives and others will create to deny educational opportunity for students of color must not easily deter these persons. Rather, they must be steadfast and willing to develop new legal theories and strategies that will find favor with the courts, using *Brown* as the primary vehicle to deliver school desegregation policies that address the unequal educational opportunities for all students.

REBUTTAL STATEMENT

What the counterpoint authors, James and Pitre, do not adequately consider is that public school desegregation, when it was being enforced, allowed more Black students to attend public schools that were racially integrated. In fact, the number of Black public school students increased dramatically after the first few years of desegregation. Moreover, Black student achievement increased, and the achievement gap between Whites and Blacks was less than it has been at any other time in our history (Boger & Orfield, 2005; Clotfelter, 2004; Schrader, 2009). Also, they fail to consider the growing body of research that indicates that Black or poor students do better when they attend racially and socioeconomically integrated schools (Coleman, 1966; Rothstein, 2004). Moreover, there are very effective public school districts that maintain that racial and socioeconomic diversity are necessary for Black students to have the same educational opportunity as their White counterparts and have gone to great lengths to maintain diversity in their schools (Schrader, 2009).

COUNTERPOINT: E. Lincoln James and Paul E. Pitre
Washington State University

T he popular sentiment during the 1950s and 1960s was that Black children would benefit enormously from attending integrated schools. Further, it was believed that these students would experience adverse educational effects by attending schools with a high concentration of students from low socioeconomic status backgrounds. The civil rights movement and judicial and legislative actions of the era gave impetus to fairly successful desegregation of public education in the United States. However, as the court retreated from its strong stance on school desegregation in the 1980s, resistance by states and school districts resulted in an increasing trend toward resegregation. It has resulted in a widening achievement gap between White and minority students as measured by standardized test scores, mainly in the areas of math, reading, and science. This gap is reflected in poorly funded schools—especially in urban areas—low attendance and graduation rates, and high dropout rates for Blacks and Latinos (Orfield, 2004).

Ever since the *Brown v. Board of Education* (*Brown I*) ruling in 1954, there have been questions about the effectiveness of desegregation laws and policies in creating equal opportunity for Blacks and other minorities. These questions have revolved around particular desegregation strategies, some mandated by *Brown*, and others by programmatic specifications emanating from legislative acts such as the Civil Rights Act of 1964 and the Elementary and Secondary

Education Act (ESEA) of 1965. We are of the view that legislated school desegregation policies by themselves have been insufficient in bringing about equal educational opportunities for students of color because of the following:

1. Political, economic, and social resistance at state and local levels reflecting innate subscription to and protection of White privilege

2. Lack of enforcement and the systematic dissolution of policy by the courts

3. Malaise and disinterest in desegregation by the federal government and the U.S. Congress beginning in the 1980s

4. Inadequate funding

5. Loopholes in legislation and court rulings that have been exploited by those who still harbor segregationist sentiments.

In this debate, we approach the fact of low education achievement for students of color as a function of desegregation's failure.

We begin by first presenting a general background to the problem, followed by our identification and analysis of three strategies used historically in the education desegregation effort. Five factors that have impacted the quest for equality are embedded in these three strategic actions. In our conclusion, we address some remedies that have been suggested as keys to improving the life chances of students of color at the K–12 level.

GENERAL BACKGROUND: THE FIGHT FOR EQUALITY AND SCHOOL DESEGREGATION

The fight for equality began in the 19th century with *Plessy v. Ferguson,* which codified the already universal de facto segregation practiced in the South. The law mandated a dual society where Blacks and Whites were "separate but equal." In terms of public education, this meant that Black and White students did not have the same rights and were not allowed to share the same facilities, including attending the same school. This segregationist doctrine persisted for the next 50 years or so during the Jim Crow era as Black schools remained undersupported, underfunded, and of extremely poor quality when compared to their White counterparts. Indeed, Stephen J. Caldas and Carla L. Bankston (2007) have observed that Jim Crow legislation in states and localities across the South both disenfranchised Blacks politically and slowly separated Blacks from Whites in many social spheres, including restaurants, public transportation, and housing.

However, in the 1950s, the stage was set for a new era in desegregation law and educational opportunity through the U.S. Supreme Court's decision in *Brown v. Board of Education* (1954). The issue before the court in *Brown*, according to Chief Justice Warren, was whether or not the "segregation of children in public schools solely on the basis of race, even though the physical facilities and other 'tangible' factors may be equal, deprive the children of the minority group of equal educational opportunities?" In a unanimous decision, the court ruled that segregation of public schools on the basis of race violated the Equal Protection Clause of the Fourteenth Amendment. The intent of *Brown I* was to have schools that formerly practiced de jure (by law) as well as de facto (by fact) segregation eliminate all vestiges of prior segregation, to the extent practicable, and to actively pursue integration bearing in mind that "the mere cessation of discriminatory activities was insufficient" (*Brown v. Board of Education*, 1954). Thus, the *Brown* decision mandated the desegregation of public education, provided equal protection to Blacks under the Fourteenth Amendment, and mandated a unitary system where Blacks and Whites living in the same neighborhoods had to attend the same school. When it became clear to the courts that hostility and resistance would delay or entirely stymie implementation of the desegregation law, a further ruling, in *Brown II* (1955), dictated that school districts had to comply with *Brown I* by desegregating with "all deliberate speed," and that district courts had the authority to implement the rulings.

THE COURTS, CIVIL RIGHTS, AND THE ESEA

Three landmark events that occurred within 11 years of each other have shaped the landscape of American public education. The first was the *Brown* ruling, the second was the Civil Rights Act of 1964, and the third was the ESEA of 1965. The civil rights movement in the 1960s raised public consciousness surrounding the issue of poverty and played a critical role in affecting equal education opportunity in public schools. No doubt the plight of the poor helped guide the intent of the Civil Rights Act and reaffirmed the sentiment expressed in *Brown*. Most importantly, Title IV of the Civil Rights Act demanded that schools desegregate forthwith, and empowered the U.S. Attorney General to prosecute noncompliance. Title VI allowed the federal government to provide or withhold funding from any government agency that engaged in discrimination.

Through the ESEA, the federal government provided billions of dollars to fund state education. This funding allowed the government to exert a greater amount of influence at the state level than was possible before. ESEA comprises four titles, each addressing critical aspects of nationwide education change.

The act provided funding for primary and secondary education and authorized resources for professional development and instructional resources. The expectations were that these compensatory education provisos would help overcome poverty by the 1970s, as well as help the United States stay competitive with other education systems through the combined effect of funding for disadvantaged children noted in Title I and new programs such as Head Start.

The reauthorization requirement of ESEA has allowed various administrations to influence the direction of public education. For example, President Johnson's democratic leadership amended ESEA in 1967 to include funding for bilingual education; in 1994, the Clinton administration's modification allowed the creation of charter and magnet schools. The Bush administration's No Child Left Behind Act of 2001 mandated high-stakes testing for elementary and secondary schools as well as punitive measures for school districts that failed to meet adequate yearly progress criteria. Since assessment became a priority of education policy in 1994, it has been a feature in all reauthorizations of ESEA, including the Obama administration's Race to the Top.

THREE DIFFERENT KINDS OF DECISIONS IN THE HISTORY OF EDUCATION DESEGREGATION

Legislation and judicial decisions from *Brown I* until the early 1970s, most often addressing equal opportunity for Black students, established the foundation for many current rules and regulations governing the rights of racial and ethnic minorities in public education. Many of these rules were hotly contested, appealed, and modified, through the judicial and legislative systems as well as in the court of public opinion. The years following *Brown* are characterized by three strategies affecting the success of desegregation in public schools: legislative and judicial actions aimed at dismantling segregation, expansion of judicial authority, and the use of funding to affect the behavior of states and school districts. The resegregation of American schools is closely linked to changes to these strategic approaches.

The judicial and legislative dismantling of segregation began in 1954 with provisos for equal protection under the Fourteenth Amendment and a direct ban on segregation. These efforts extended into specification of direct actions that states and school districts needed to undertake to ensure desegregation. Requirements by the courts included orders not only to end school segregation but also to "undo the harm" that segregation had caused by racially balancing their schools under federal guidelines. The courts fully understood the various tactics used to avoid desegregation and, during these early years, treated them with short shrift. But many of the gains made under the above rulings were lost by 2000; by then, the courts, in a series of reversals, had begun to facilitate the resegregation of public schools.

A second strategy in the desegregation struggle could be seen in the expanding scope of judicial authority. As early as *Brown II* (1955), district courts were granted the authority to implement and supervise desegregation plans, which were to proceed with "all deliberate speed" (p. 301). Opposition to *Brown* expressed itself in Arkansas just 3 years later. The Little Rock school district had developed a plan to integrate all public schools within a year and a half. However, the Arkansas legislature passed its own law declaring desegregation illegal. Tension and violence erupted when nine African American students attempted to enroll in public school and the governor sent in the National Guard to block their entry. President Eisenhower sent in federal troops to quell mob violence and enforce desegregation orders. In subsequent action, the Eighth Circuit reasserted the federal courts' authority to enforce desegregation orders by firmly reiterating the supremacy of the federal constitution over state law. In *Cooper v. Aaron* (1958), the Supreme Court affirmed this ruling, clearly stating that a state governor and legislature could not refuse to implement its orders.

Yet a third approach to overcoming resistance to *Brown* was financial control. This was first exercised in the Court in 1964 when Virginia amended its constitution, outlawed integration, closed the public schools in Prince Edward County to bar Black children from attending, and issued vouchers and grants for Whites to attend private schools (*Griffin v. County School Board*, 1964). Financial leverage was used by courts in prohibiting the use of public funds to support private segregated education. Financial leverage for compliance was especially useful in enforcing various aspects of the Civil Rights Act and ESEA. Through its enforcement of the ESEA, the federal government became deeply involved for the first time with education on a state level. It offered billions of dollars to state and district boards to help them develop curriculum, acquire resources, and improve teacher training. But states received federal funds only if the state and its institutions followed strict accountability policies. The government also exerted influence on states by making money available to them through the provisos of the Civil Rights Act. Title VI allowed the federal government to withhold funding from any government agency that engaged in discrimination.

Because public education was funded in several states by a combination of property taxes and state funding, poorer school districts—which tended to be mainly minority and largely segregated—were, and in some cases still are, unable to maintain education quality. As a consequence, activists have often brought lawsuits on the basis of the Fourteenth Amendment in an effort to use financial reform as a substitute for desegregation. The battle for school finance reform today is based exclusively on provisos in state constitutions, and the battle to desegregate schools has yet to be won.

CONCLUSION

The thrust for desegregation was met with strong resistance from Whites, who fled en masse to the suburbs, where they campaigned vigorously for the right to choose which schools their children could attend. They battled against incursions by Blacks through busing and fought bitterly against increased property taxes that could help support poorer urban districts—which in time have become increasingly complex with large influxes of immigrant populations. The main impediments during the first 20 years following *Brown* took the form of political, economic, and social resistance at state and local levels reflecting White racism and a determination to protect White privilege and segregation in housing, one legacy of Jim Crow.

As the federal government became more involved in public education, courts became less enthusiastic about desegregation. By the mid- to the late 1970s, weak enforcement and systematic dissolution of policy by the courts was accompanied by the malaise and disinterest shown by the federal government. During the 1980s, the Department of Justice actively sought to dismantle and dissolve voluntary and mandatory school desegregation plans; meanwhile, the courts allowed school districts to end court-ordered busing and return to neighborhood school choice. The federal courts had come to believe, like the federal government, that the pervasive racial isolation was due to residential segregation and not actions of the school district.

The Reagan administration ushered in a new era of segregation in which decisions were made with a greater focus on socioeconomic status than race. A 1983 commissioned report, *A Nation at Risk*, assessed the nation's education system and provided evidence to show that (a) American students were being outperformed on 19 different international academic tests; (b) some 23 million adults and 13% of 17-year-olds were functionally illiterate; and (c) high school student scores on all standardized tests, including those demonstrating superior achievement on the SAT, had declined. The recommendation was that state and school boards take responsibility for governing, with the federal government providing and managing funding for projects that would preserve the equal rights and protection of students. It was also recommended that a new curriculum with five foundation courses be required for high school graduation, that more rigorous measureable performance standards be implemented, and that a "nationwide (but not federal) system of state and local" standardized testing be administered at key points in the education process. The purposes of these tests were to provide remediation, credentials and certification, and advanced or accelerated work.

Legislation such as the No Child Left Behind Act (2001) has not delivered on the success first touted when it was formulated. The failure of legislated policies to address unequal opportunity in education is a direct result of failure to understand the importance of desegregation. The segregated history of the United States has given rise to the concept of "Whiteness as property"—property that comes with certain rights and privileges. White schools have historically been better funded, with better facilities and better teachers. Undoubtedly, some see school integration as a threat to White privilege and the concomitant rights associated with Whiteness. Granted, there is more to closing the achievement gap than desegregating public education. There are other variables that matter—variables that cannot be legislated or controlled, such as family values, fair housing, poverty, and so on. A majority of students of color are not being helped by legislated policies because they have been overwhelmed by stronger forces, such as family circumstances and the changing racial composition of inner cities.

Further Readings and Resources

Alexander, K., & Alexander, M. D. (2009). *American public school law* (7th ed.). Belmont, CA: Wadsworth, Cengage Learning.

Armor, D. J. (1995). *Forced justice: School desegregation and the law.* Oxford, UK: Oxford University Press.

Asquith, C. (2006). Legal experts await Supreme Court's ruling on race-conscious admissions in public schools. *Diverse Issues in Higher Education, 23*(13), 13.

Au, W. (2004, Spring). No child left untested: *Brown v. Bush. Rethinking Schools.* Retrieved from http://www.rethinkingschools.org/archive/18_03/nclu183.shtml

Bell, D. (2004). *Brown v. Board of Education and the unfilled hopes for racial reform.* New York: Oxford University Press.

Boger, J. C., & Orfield, G. (2005). *School segregation: Must the South turn back?* Chapel Hill: University of North Carolina Press.

Brown, F. (2004a). The first serious implementation of *Brown*: The 1964 Civil Rights Act and beyond. *Journal of Negro Education, 73*(3), 182–190.

Brown, F. (2004b). Nixon's "Southern strategy" and forces against *Brown. Journal of Negro Education, 73*(3), 191–208.

Brown, F. (2007). Ending the *Brown* era: What is the future for equal educational opportunity? *School Business Affairs, 73*(9), 8–10.

Caldas S. J., & Bankston, C. L., III. (2007). A re-analysis of the legal, political and social landscape of desegregation from *Plessy v. Ferguson* to *Parents Involved in Community Schools v. Seattle School District. B.Y.U. Education and Law Journal, 2,* 217–256.

Cashin, S. (2004). *The failure of integration: How race and class are undermining the American dream.* New York: Public Affairs.

Clotfelter, C. T. (2004). *After Brown: The rise and retreat of school desegregation.* Princeton, NJ: Princeton University Press.

Coleman, J. (1966). *Equality in educational opportunity.* Baltimore: Johns Hopkins University.

Hunter, R. C. (2004). The administration of court-ordered school desegregation in urban school districts: The law and experience. *The Journal of Negro Education, 73*(3), 218–228.

Orfield, G. (2004). *Dropouts in America: Confronting the graduation rate crisis.* Cambridge, MA: Harvard Education Press.

Rothstein, R. (2004). *Class and schools using social, economic, and educational reform to close the Black–White achievement gap.* New York: Teachers College, Columbia University.

Schrader, J. (2009, November 1). More districts use income, not race, as basis for busing. *USA Today.* Retrieved from http://www.usatoday.com/news/education/2009-11-02-busing02_ST_N.htm

Wells, A. S., & Frankenberg, E. (2007). The public school and the challenge of the Supreme Court's integration decision. *Phi Delta Kappan, 89*(3), 178–188.

COURT CASES AND STATUTES

Belk v. Charlotte-Mecklenburg Board of Education, 269 F.3d 305 (4th Cir. 2001).

Board of Education of Oklahoma v. Dowell, 498 U.S. 237 (1991).

Brown v. Board of Education (Brown I), 347 U.S. 483 (1954).

Brown v. Board of Education (Brown II), 349 U.S. 294 (1955).

Civil Rights Act of 1964, 42 U.S.C. § 2000 *et seq.* (2006).

Cooper v. Aaron, 358 U.S. 1 (1958).

Elementary and Secondary Education Act of 1965, 20 U.S.C. § 6301 *et seq.* (1965).

Green v. County School Board, 391 U.S. 430 (1968).

Griffin v. County School Board, 377 U.S. 218 (1964).

Jenkins v. Missouri, 515 U.S. 70 (1995).

Meredith v. Jefferson County Public Schools, 127 S. Ct. 2738 (2007).

Milliken v. Bradley (Milliken I), 418 U.S. 717 (1974).

Milliken v. Bradley (Milliken II), 433 U.S. 267 (1977).

Missouri v. Jenkins, 495 U.S. 33, 110 S. Ct. 1651 (1990) (Jenkins I).

Missouri v. Jenkins, 515 U.S. 70, 115 S. Ct. 2038 (1995) (Jenkins II).

No Child Left Behind Act, 20 U.S.C. §§ 6301-7941 (2006).

Parents Involved in Community Schools v. Seattle School District No. 1, 127 S. Ct. 2738 (2007).

Plessy v. Ferguson, 163 U.S. 537 (1896).

Swann v. Charlotte-Mecklenburg Board of Education, 402 U.S. 1 (1971).

2

Are multicultural counseling programs in schools needed to improve the academic performance of students?

POINT: Deneia M. Thomas, *Eastern Kentucky University*
Lynda Brown Wright, *University of Kentucky*

COUNTERPOINT: Jennifer L. Burris, Katrina A. R. Akande, and
Sonja M. Feist-Price, *University of Kentucky*

OVERVIEW

According to the American School Counselor Association (ASCA, 2010), the role of the school counselor is to work with children, teachers, and parents to ensure that each student receives the appropriate advice and support needed to foster academic achievement, career preparation and development, and personal growth. Acting as educators who fulfill their primary functions outside of the classroom, school counselors can trace the origin of their roles back to ancient Greece when teaching philosophers worked to help individuals identify the purpose of their lives. More recently, beginning in the Middle Ages, Catholic priests also took on many of these duties with the added emphasis on confidentiality, especially within the context of religious confession. In the United States, modern school counseling began at the outset of the 20th century as psychology, sociology, and social disciplines started to professionalize and craft spaces in which to study human development, identify theoretical perspectives, and practice their skills (ASCA, 2010).

Despite the long-established presence of school counselors within American education, it is not always clear how best to use these educators within schools. At the high school level, parents and students want information on academic preparation for college and careers. Counseling professionals in secondary schools spend much of their time gathering and distributing information about entrance exams such as the ACT and SAT, helping students learn about federal financial aid and other available funds, preparing students to complete various elements of the college application process, and generally encouraging students to think about and work toward a positive future. However, school counselors working in middle and elementary schools do not always have such clear foci. Rather, these educators spend more of their time working with students and families on addressing present needs such as academic performance as measured both in class and on standardized exams, maintaining environments that support positive social interactions by addressing bullying and peer conflicts, and helping to connect students with resources that assist with their needs outside of school, thus creating conditions that allow them to focus consistently on their education. In all settings, school counselors help with the development and implementation of individualized education plans, assessments related to Response to Intervention, addressing and preventing school violence, and otherwise sustaining healthy educational environments.

Based on the changing context of public education, the duties of the school counselor expand each year as more children enter school with unmet needs. As a result of high-stakes testing and rising economic pressure on education, schools also face increased accountability for nonacademic factors that influence academic performance. Recognizing this wide range of responsibilities, programs for preparing candidates to be school counselors include curricula that emphasize many professional skills, such as helping students achieve competencies for various grade levels; developing individual plans for students, especially those who require direct, personal counseling services and responsive services related to preventing problems in public education; and intervening when students face crises both at home and at school. Since school counseling programs generally focus on providing master's degrees and postbaccalaureate training, many states also require individuals interested in becoming school counselors to obtain classroom teaching experience first, which helps to prepare them to identify the issues present in public school and assists students, teachers, and administrators in addressing these concerns (ASCA, 2010).

While school counseling programs focus on providing these future professionals with general preparation for working in various school settings, some
speculate that this is not enough for the current climate affecting and surrounding public education. As the debates in this section consider, do we need to
make more of an effort to prepare school counselors to address multicultural
issues?

The debate over multicultural preparation for school counselors springs
from the ongoing debate over the place and value of multicultural education in
general for students and all other education professionals. Proponents of multicultural education believe that such curricula provide the content and context
needed to address racial, ethnic, religious, and other cultural misinformation
and misunderstandings that continue to complicate social arrangements in a
multicultural society. Instead of hiding or avoiding negative elements of history,
multicultural educators believe that discussing negative aspects of the past
honestly and openly provides the foundation that will allow people to reconcile
their feelings about these events and move ahead in positive ways. Supporters
of these efforts suggest that openly teaching and talking about these differences will help children and educators to develop both understanding and
appreciation for various perspectives.

Conversely, those who oppose multicultural education maintain that emphasizing social and cultural differences helps to widen existing gaps that already
impair and inhibit the development of a cohesive and cooperative society.
Rather than increasing cultural understanding, opponents of multicultural education contend that highlighting existing cultural differences hinders the ability
of the United States to establish and maintain a common national identity by
constantly dwelling on past racial and cultural structures, thus preventing the
nation from moving forward. In their view, students from cultures presented
negatively are forced to carry the stigma of events and policies in which they
have no direct involvement. On the other hand, students from cultures presented as oppressed may equally feel shame or sorrow over depressing conditions from days gone by.

Building on the foundation of the general debate within multicultural education, the two essays in this chapter consider these issues as they specifically
relate to the preparation and professional practice of school counselors. Similar
to the larger debate on this topic, in the point essay, Deneia M. Thomas and
Lynda Brown Wright support the use of multicultural education in counseling
programs because this curricular emphasis will better prepare these educators
to meet the needs of the various students that they will encounter while working
in public schools. Thomas and Wright contend that counseling services must
accommodate the changing population and demographic shifts evident in our

society. On the opposing side, Jennifer L. Burris, Katrina A. R. Akande, and Sonja M. Feist-Price, in the counterpoint essay, advocate that these programs would do better to prepare future counselors to meet a variety of student needs regardless of their cultural backgrounds. They conclude that what is needed is solid implementation of school counseling interventions rooted in best practices for all youth.

Saran Donahoo
Southern Illinois University Carbondale

POINT: Deneia M. Thomas
Eastern Kentucky University

Lynda Brown Wright
University of Kentucky

The premier psychological and counseling organizations, including the American Psychological Association (APA) and the American Counseling Association (ACA), have identified ethical principles that specify the critical importance of infusing diversity into practice. Moreover, multiculturalism is a strand that permeates the entire *ACA Code of Ethics*. Specifically, the ACA preamble states, "ACA members are dedicated to diversity and embrace a cross-cultural approach in support of the worth, dignity, potential and uniqueness of people within their social and cultural contexts" (ACA, 2005, p. 3). Finally, to ensure that students receive the optimal services, the American School Counseling Association National Model (ASCA, 2005) has an established philosophy and emphasizes that to meet the academic and social/emotional needs of all students, cultural competence in congruence with the implementation of multicultural counseling is a critical process that is essential for all counselors to be effective in meeting the needs of students. The inclusion of these ethical principles serves as a baseline supporting the need for multicultural counseling programs in schools to improve the academic performance of students.

The United States is a nation composed of immigrants and those who have ancestry from other countries who reside temporarily or permanently in America. As population shifts occur, there must be continued efforts to offer services that are more consistent with and sensitive to various dimensions of ethnic minority worldviews (Sue, Arredondo, & McDavis, 1992). Counseling services must accommodate the changing population and demographic shifts evident in our society. For example, the 2010 U.S. Census Bureau reports that racial and ethnic minority groups make up 33% of the U.S. population. By 2030, an estimated 26% of older Americans will be a member of a visible racial/ethnic group. Moreover, the increasing diversity among the PK–12 populations affirms the need that multicultural counseling programs integrated systemically within schools can improve the achievement outcomes for all students.

THE RATIONALE FOR MULTICULTURAL COUNSELING PROGRAMS

Although the literature is limited regarding empirical findings specifically linking multicultural counseling services directly to improved academic achievement, research clearly supports a link between the infusion of multicultural counseling services and both a decrease in attitudinal racism and an increase in racial identity and social advocacy (Sue et al., 1992). The *ACA Code of Ethics* (2005) address nondiscrimination, stating that

> counselors do not condone or engage in discrimination based on age, culture, disability, ethnicity, race, religion/spirituality, gender, gender identity, sexual orientation, marital status/status, language preference, socioeconomic status, or any basis proscribed by law. Counselors do not discriminate against clients, students, employees, supervisees, or research participants in a manner that has a negative impact on these persons. (standard C.5)

Moreover, the literature indicates that multicultural counseling programs improve student self-perception and shape identity development among African American students, which directly influences school engagement and school belonging, which in turn directly impacts academic outcomes (Oyserman, Harrison, & Bybee, 2001). Several studies found that in comparison to their same-age peers, high-achieving Black students seem to define themselves positively in terms of race (e.g., cultural pride). One study found that gifted achievers maintained the most positive racial orientation. This is significant because those highly gifted achievers also maintained positive racial identities, which significantly influenced their academic outcomes (Ford & Harris, 1997). In another study, Carla O'Connor (1997) observed that a collective Black identity may promote academic aspirations and achievement rather than limit them. The overall findings suggest a positive relationship between a pro-Black identity and proschool attitudes and behaviors.

Daphna Oyserman, Kathy Harrison, and Deborah Bybee (2001) found that minority youth in middle and high school get better grades if they connect their racial ethnic identity (REI) with academics. In another study, researchers interviewed a diverse population of adolescents (e.g., African American, Hispanic, Native American, and Israeli youths) focusing on REI to learn how racial identities affected their grades, school attendance, or persistence on mathematics tasks. The research findings suggested that some forms of identity can reduce the risk that a student will feel disengaged from school. However, the risk increased when the student did not have a positive REI, or had one that only focused on his or her group and not its place in society. The researchers also found that African American students who felt good about being Black and American did well in school. In fact, they excelled when they reflected positively on the Black community, even if they viewed society as racist toward them.

The same study, which included eighth-grade multicultural youths, asked students open-ended questions about their racial ethnic identity. Those identifying with peers of the same race and their entire society had better grades than students who did not develop their own REI or who identified only with other races. These findings suggest that a strong REI could add to students' abilities to achieve academically (Oyserman et al., 2001).

Given the understanding that REI development is significantly correlated with high academic achievement among diverse students, it is essential that multicultural counseling services be integrated in PK–12 programs to increase student personal development, which in turn translates into school belonging and affects overall academic outcomes. This is a critical aspect of professional school counseling that must be examined, given the increasing student diversity of U.S. schools and the movement to restructure school counseling programs for higher achievement among marginalized student populations. If professional school counselors do not perceive that they are capable of performing tasks related to equity and diversity, then they will likely avoid those tasks or downplay the importance of such tasks. This is an important consideration to improve the academic performance and school efficacy among multicultural student populations. The literature widely documents the influence of these programs and achievement. Therefore, the most significant factor connecting multicultural counseling and academic achievement is the type of service implementation. It is incumbent on counselors to obtain and retain the skills needed to develop practices that support student social/emotional needs of diverse populations. It is important to examine counseling programs and clinical experiences that ensure such competencies are achieved and maintained. Such competencies and their execution are mandated to ensure that skills are current and effective. According to the *ACA Code of Ethics* (2005), "Counselor educators actively infuse multicultural/diversity competency in their training and supervision practices. They actively train students to gain awareness, knowledge, and skills in the competencies of multicultural practice" (standard F.11.c).

To ensure that counselors are competent and effective in changing potentially prejudiced attitudes, it is important to combat prejudice within the counseling profession itself. One study found that although mental health organizations have developed specific multicultural competencies necessary for practitioners and guidelines to support practice, they acknowledge discriminatory practices at the social and community level that may be affecting the mental health and well-being of the population served (Chae, Foley, & Chae, 2006). APA emphasizes the importance of infusing multiculturalism in all areas of clinical training and practice. For example, they implore counselors and counselor trainers to employ a culture-centered approach, acknowledging that all individuals are influenced by sociocultural, ecological, and other contextual factors.

Multicultural counseling is defined by ACA (2005) "as a capacity whereby counselors possess cultural and diversity awareness and knowledge about self and others, and how this awareness and knowledge is applied effectively in practice with clients and client groups." (p. 20). Thus, it is vital to develop and enhance training programs to ensure that multiculturalism/diversity is taught, and that awareness is integrated and explored, as a part of the training to eliminate prejudice within the counseling profession.

MULTICULTURAL TRAINING MODELS

To help counselors increase their multicultural competencies and embrace these practices, three different multicultural training models have emerged in the psychological literature: (1) separate course, (2) integration or infusion, and (3) area of concentration (Constantine, Hage, Kindaichi, & Bryant, 2007).

The Separate Course Model

In the separate course model, two different approaches are frequently included, both didactic and experiential (Lee, 1997). Although these courses offer important information about different ethnic groups, one limitation is that students can develop stereotypes about clients from certain groups. Moreover, according to Mark Chae, Pamela Foley, and Sung Chae (2006), focusing on the cultural characteristics of clients, the therapist runs the risk of potentially losing the clients as people, because they could lose focus on their humanness by centering in on racial and cultural characteristics. The study recommends that counselors use this knowledge to help conceptualize clients' presenting problems in therapy from a cultural context. Therefore, we can view multicultural knowledge as a guide or model for developing hypotheses that may or may not be confirmed by the client's experiences. Although a knowledge-based curriculum is an important component to multicultural training, scholars contend that there is a need for programs to emphasize experiential learning. The authors suggest that an effective approach to multicultural training is for therapists to engage in tasks and skills that facilitate the development of awareness and understanding of one's own racial and ethnic identity (Chae et al., 2006).

The Integration or Infusion Model

The integration or infusion model emphasizes the importance of infusing multicultural issues into all coursework. The advantage of this approach is that students are able to learn multicultural applications in all areas of training (e.g., career development and abnormal psychology) (Chae et al., 2006). A benefit of this approach is that students recognize that multiculturalism is not merely a "subfield" but that it is a relevant component affecting all aspects of clinical training. However, the Chae et al. article mentions that for the first competency to be effective, it is dependent on the availability of opportunities for experiential self-evaluation within this curriculum. The research contends that unless there are opportunities for practical application of this knowledge in fieldwork with racial and ethnic minorities, the infusion of information may have limited impact in the competence of trainees to develop a full understanding of minority cultures and culturally sensitive therapeutic interventions.

The Area of Concentration Model

A third type of multicultural training is an "area of concentration." This training experience allows the student to enroll in various didactic and experiential courses, as well as take part in specially designated practicum sites, which place particular emphasis on multicultural training (Chae et al., 2006). The research suggests that this is the question all counseling programs must answer and evaluate each year to ensure that students are getting a balance of didactic and experiential learning in diversity training. This kind of training will allow students to have exposure to professionals experienced in the application of culturally appropriate interventions (Chae et al., 2006). Thus, providing students with opportunities to develop competence should lead to confidence in working with clients from cultures different from their own.

Combining Approaches

Lastly, several studies contend that each of the programmatic typologies has advantages and disadvantages, and it is even suggested that a combination of all three approaches would be the most effective in training therapists to become culturally competent. However, Chae et al. (2006) contend that this approach may not be practical due to the limited resources available to many counseling programs across the nation.

Considering the current state of affairs, studies overwhelmingly find that clinical and counseling programs are required to provide the minimum of a separate course with both didactic and experiential components. A didactic course may help to develop the second competency of knowledge of ethnic minorities, but without an experiential component, it would be difficult to provide adequate training in the other competencies. Even if many clinical and counseling programs do not have access to fieldwork experiences that specialize in working with clients from diverse backgrounds, all programs can be required to develop curricula that increase the self-awareness of trainees regarding their own racial and ethnic identities (Chae et al., 2006).

ADDRESSING RACIAL PREJUDICE

It is the ethical responsibility of counselors not to discriminate against anyone from a different ethnic or cultural background. One study suggests that Caucasian therapists provide the majority of services in schools; therefore, it is imperative for counselor educators to understand the various factors that contribute to racial prejudice from a historical-dominance point of view. Such knowledge may help counselor educators in designing interventions to promote the professional development (Castillo et al., 2006). Most interesting is that this study examines racial prejudice by combining previously identified predictors to determine their relative importance in contributing to racial prejudice. The findings suggest that White racial identity significantly predicted racial prejudice when demographic variables were controlled. The authors of the study concluded that understanding these variables is important for counseling programs in the quest to train culturally competent counselors, as well as to combat racial prejudice within the counseling profession. Such counseling strategies will influence multicultural counseling programs in PK–12 settings to increase REI and affect the overall academic performance of students from multicultural populations.

RESPONSE TO COUNTERPOINT

Interestingly, the counterpoint essay focuses on research conducted on university campuses rather than with P–12 populations, which is the focus of our point essay. We contend that multicultural counseling programs are needed to improve academic performance in P–12. We further argue that such programs are not as effective if they begin at the postsecondary level—they must begin early in the school experience.

One of the most salient points from the counterpoint essay addresses the fact that fundamental training programs have "responded to the moral and social responsibility to remedy past inequities," specifically "within helping professional preparation programs within the fields of education, psychology, counseling, and social work" (Platt, 2002). While the authors contend that there is an inherent limitation within the methodological approaches to teaching multicultural pedagogy and within professional organizations' agenda to advocate for such teaching, it cannot be denied that such practices are *necessary* to "remedy past inequities." Additionally, the authors contend that the literature is "replete" with studies that indicate positive diversity outcomes, yet void of evidence of their effectiveness. Our point clearly identifies positive outcomes for all students when multiculturalism is infused within the curriculum; it can have a direct influence on academic efficacy and personal development. Such efforts, however limiting, are a first step to ensure that accountability is included in professional practices that directly influence student development.

COUNTERPOINT: Jennifer L. Burris, Katrina A. R. Akande, and Sonja M. Feist-Price
University of Kentucky

P roponents of multicultural counseling programs assert that students, most notably those from diverse ethnic, racial, and cultural backgrounds, benefit substantially from culturally competent service provision. In addition, the American School Counseling Association (ASCA) espouses within its National Model a philosophy stating that counselor cultural competence is critical to counselor effectiveness in meeting the needs of students (ASCA, 2005). This counterpoint essay discusses opinions expressed by scholars in the fields of education, counseling, and psychology that offer a contrasting perspective regarding multiculturalism. First, the efficacy of guidance programming in schools is examined. Then, the essay explores broader issues related to the efficacy of multiculturalism and its influence on professional practice, including (a) scholarly critiques related to the conceptualization of multiculturalism, (b) impediments to logical inquiry involved in multicultural research due to a cultural relativist philosophical stance, and (c) limitations of research methodology seeking to unearth the efficacy of multicultural interventions. While there are data supporting the view that counseling programs in schools provide benefits to students, it is not yet evident that a focus on multicultural guidance programming is necessary to effectively support student achievement.

EFFECTIVENESS OF SCHOOL COUNSELING PROGRAMS

In a review of school counseling literature, Susan C. Whiston and Robert F. Quinby (2009) focused on the effectiveness of school counseling interventions based on current outcome research. Using the four components of the ASCA National Model as a framework (guidance curriculum, individual planning, response services, and program management), the authors found that, overall, students who took part in school counseling interventions performed one third of a standard deviation better than their nonparticipant counterparts on a variety of outcome measures. However, they noted that more empirical investigations were needed to validate the effectiveness of all school counseling interventions, as many are being used without having been empirically vetted.

This also applies to the efficacy of multiculturally based interventions and supports for students. As noted by Markeda L. Newell et al. (2010), scholars are still being challenged to find ways to develop multicultural competence in professionals that will translate into effective service provision and positive outcomes for students and their families. While there is much support for multiculturally based interventions from both philosophical and theoretical stances, a gap remains in the empirical literature base that illustrates how employing these competencies translates into better academic outcomes for students.

BROADER ISSUES IMPACTING THE EFFICACY OF MULTICULTURALLY BASED PROGRAMS

Over the past 3 decades, a notable shift toward multiculturalism has occurred on university campuses. In an effort to acknowledge the changing population demographics in our society, university administrators have responded to the moral and social responsibility to remedy past inequities and prepare competent graduates by teaching diversity as a standard part of university programs. This shift has been most noticeable within *helping* professional preparation programs within the fields of education, psychology, counseling, and social work (Platt, 2002). Yet, some scholars question whether it is necessary to engage in efforts to teach multiculturalism, in particular since empirical evidence directly linking improved outcomes to multicultural practices and interventions is sparse.

Tony Platt (2002) highlights the ineffectiveness of infusing multiculturalism into graduate (preprofessional) education curricula. This claim has drawn criticism regarding the impact that multicultural training has on competent professional practice. More research is needed to determine whether professionals who are taught from a multicultural perspective achieve better outcomes compared to professionals who were not taught from a multicultural perspective.

The debate over the endorsement of multicultural competencies in the field of mental health counseling exemplifies further the complexity surrounding the concept of multicultural practice. Weinrach and Thomas (2004) suggest that multicultural education and training for counselors, while hypothetically appropriate, does not transition well into the reality of professional practice. Education objectives set on elucidating the cultural milieus of individuals and groups found within U.S. society focus on preparing professionals to provide services to diverse people, but at best, they leave them with a cumbersome knowledge base and unwieldy sets of methods and techniques that do not prove realistic and helpful in practice (Patterson, 2004).

C. H. Patterson (2004) highlights the following faulty assumptions of teaching multicultural practice:

a. Human differences are more important than human similarities.

b. Cultural groups in our social reality exist as discrete and separate groups.

c. Developing different theories/methods/techniques for diverse groups will improve competency in practice.

d. Teaching professionals to be prepared to uniquely attend to all difference is plausible and practical.

Patterson goes on to explain that no counselor is equipped to handle the cultural characteristics of all individuals. Therefore, multicultural competency training cannot provide counselors with specific techniques to develop interventions designed to meet the needs of all people from various cultural groups. Given this limitation, it is difficult to conceive how multicultural counseling programs can be an effective means of improving the academic achievement of students in K–12 schools.

Individuals with culture-related issues are better served when counselors create empathetic relationships by building a guidance environment based on mutual trust and respect for a person's culture (Vontress & Jackson, 2004).

The Danger of Overlooking Issues Not Related to Race/Ethnicity?

Weinrach and Thomas (2004) contend that counselors who focus on race as a central component of intervention protocol are actually doing individuals a disservice. To assume that race is salient imposes unethical intervention protocols onto individuals whose issues are not necessarily related to race, ethnicity, or culture—for example, a student may need help in applying effective learning strategies in the classroom or improving his or her test-taking skills. Racial saliency assumptions can further perpetuate stereotypes. Student behavior or life circumstances do not reflect monolithic dimensions of race or ethnicity. A "cultural cookbook" approach for understanding individual behavior or developing appropriate treatment protocols does not exist. In the applied sense, counselors must understand that while culture affects individual student functioning at some level, it is not the sole determinant impacting educational and social development.

Political Agendas

On the other hand, mandating cultural competencies at the national level of any profession promotes a universal standard of practice where individual's needs are based on their membership within a specific cultural group (Weinrach & Thomas, 2004). This view of multiculturalism has a hint of propaganda rooted in the movement to promote social equality rather than developing professional guidelines based on relevant data that has proven to be effective for people (Sasso, 2001). Even so, some scholars argue that helping professionals should not be about the business of promoting political agendas related to mandating multiculturalism (Platt, 2002; Sasso, 2001; Weinrach & Thomas, 2004).

Weinrach and Thomas (2004) point out that the Association of Multicultural Counseling and Development's Multicultural Counseling Competencies has its own political undertone related to eradicating social injustice. A political agenda based on multiculturalism should not negate the empirical inquiry of appropriate intervention modalities that foster guidance relationships aimed at helping students resolve issues that are critical in their academic achievement. Gary M. Sasso (2001) illustrates that such value-laden inquiry disrupts the process of logical inquiry. Justification for multicultural facets of counseling should be grounded in empirical inquiry rather than the value standards of the community.

Suzette L. Speight, Linda J. Myers, Chikako I. Cox, and Pamela S. Highlen (1991) raise concerns regarding the conceptualization of multiculturalism and its implication on the education and training of counseling professionals. Current conceptualizations of multiculturalism tend to promote one of two perspectives. Proponents of multiculturalism emphasize the need for professionals to understand "regular" individuals who represent the "standard" and "multicultural" individuals who represent "difference." Other scholars emphasize the importance of having professional cultural competencies that are grounded in understanding ethnic groups within the context of their cultural norms without the use of comparison groups. Classification based on race promotes segmentation and an external focus that categorizes individuals according to cultural affiliation. This may lead counselors to overemphasize the influence of cultural difference with their students and obscure the complex nature of human individuality. What is more beneficial than developing culturally specific knowledge bases is to take a more holistic worldview that emphasizes an understanding of common strands across the human experience that will be applicable to all students regardless of their cultural group affiliation. The goal of "multicultural work" with helping professionals should be to help counselors gain an understanding of human universalities and individual uniqueness, along with cultural influences for a balanced and respectful view of human difference and interrelatedness.

Postmodernism and Cultural Relativism

Postmodernism refers to a philosophy that many apparent realities are only social constructs subject to inherent change. Postmodernism rejects classifications such as those related to gender, race, ethnic origin, and sexuality. Cultural relativism, on the other hand, is the principle that individuals should be understood in terms of their own culture. Thus, postmodernists would reject many of the well-founded empirical claims about cultural practices that can be helpful in counseling practice.

Scholars have also offered arguments about the logic of the postmodernist and cultural relativist philosophical underpinnings with which proponents of multiculturalism have developed their cultural competencies agenda. While no one will dispute the importance of understanding the role of injustice, oppression, and discrimination within our society, Sasso (2001) asserts that our pursuit to generate knowledge and apply this knowledge within our respective fields should not lead us to engage in pseudo-inquiry. The process of pseudo-inquiry negates the role of objectivity, the process of logical inquiry, and the quality of empirical evidence. Instead, multiculturalists and others who adhere to a postmodernist stance seek evidence for their beliefs rather than structure their beliefs around empirically based reasoning. Postmodernist truth claims are based on the assertion that "there are other 'ways of knowing' or truth that can be determined through means other than logical, rational inquiry" (Sasso, 2001, p. 180).

Sasso (2001) described how this misguided logic renders postmodernistic knowledge claims vulnerable and indefensible:

> A number of basic misunderstandings lead postmodernists to a corruption by beliefs. These misunderstandings include the notions that logical inquiry is just a matter of social practice; truth claims can only be considered good relative to the standards of the community; [and] science as a social enterprise means that scientific knowledge is "socially constructed...." (p. 182)

Therefore, argumentation based solely on social values and moral reasoning creates a segue to the development of cultural competencies that lacks empirical evidence. Proponents of multicultural counseling must be careful not to compromise the rigor of the inquiry process in the hopes of finding evidence supportive of their beliefs.

CRITIQUES OF RESEARCH METHODOLOGY

Our final discussion highlights critiques of multicultural interventions in research. For example, Mark E. Engberg (2004) examined the influence of cultural interventions on students' racial bias in higher education. This synthesis of empirical studies related to racial sensitivity efforts such as multicultural courses, workshops, and peer-based interventions yields mixed results. Threats to internal validity have compromised findings of many multicultural research endeavors. Engberg found that many studies designed to test the effects of multicultural interventions on students were inadequately designed. Study limitations reported by Engberg included (a) reliance on quasi-experimental designs that do not control for group differences; (b) reliance on convenience or purposive sampling that limits generalizability; (c) lack of longitudinal studies that can explain changes in students' racial bias attitudes over time; (d) lack of measures that control for confounding variables; (e) lack of research plans that test for long-term intervention effects; and (f) the lack of randomized samples across race, gender, and academic disciplines. Engberg stressed that future studies need more explanatory power. Although this example is taken from multicultural research in higher education, it illustrates the need that multicultural scholars must endeavor to be clearer about which components of multicultural interventions are most effective to substantiate claims that these interventions are necessary.

CONCLUSION

The need for multicultural mandates within schools warrants more scholarly discussion. We are confident that most professionals in various helping fields strive to promote self-efficacy and self-sufficiancy among individuals they serve. However, the axis of multicultural debate centers on what is the best approach to assist students from cultural groups that are marginalized and disenfranchised. Some scholars believe that professional standards related to multicultualism help eradicate racist or biased aspects of guidance programming used by counselors. Conversely, opponents of multicultural mandates argue that rigid standards equate to a "one size fits all" approach for students from minority groups. Scholars who oppose multicultural mandates also argue that the present multicultural logic is situated within an obscured political agenda to promote social justice—not the primary role counselors are to fulfill. These scholars emphasize the need for guidance programming that is evidence based rather than value laden. Political agendas corrupt the process of the empirical pursuit of truth. As research efforts improve, we may yet find a definitive answer about the benefits of multicultural-based guidance programming to students. What is effective for students is solid implementation of school counseling interventions rooted in best practices for all youth. The need for multicultural counseling programs has yet to be firmly established.

FURTHER READINGS AND RESOURCES

American Counseling Association (ACA). (2005). *ACA code of ethics*. Retrieved June 14, 2010, from http://www.counseling.org/Files/FD.ashx?guid=ab7c1272-71c4-46cf-848c-f98489937dda

American School Counselor Association (ASCA). (2005). *The ASCA national model: A framework for school counseling programs*. Alexandria, VA: Author.

American School Counselor Association (ASCA). (2010). *Careers/roles*. Alexandria, VA: Author.

Castillo, L. G., Conoley, C. W., King, J., Rollins, D., Riveria, S., & Veve, M. (2006). Predictors of racial prejudice in White American counseling students. *Journal of Multicultural Counseling and Development, 34*, 14–35.

Chae, M. H., Foley, P. F., & Chae, S. Y. (2006). Multicultural competence and training: An ethical responsibility. *Counseling and Clinical Psychology Journal, 3*(2), 71–77.

Constantine, M. G., Hage, S. M., Kindaichi, M. M., & Bryant, R. M. (2007). Social justice and multicultural issues: Implications for the practice and training of counselors and counseling psychologists. *Journal of Counseling & Development, 84*, 24–25.

Engberg, M. E. (2004). Improving intergroup relations in higher education: A critical examinaiton of the influence of educational interventions on racial bias. *Review of Educational Research, 74*(4), 473–524.

Ford, D. Y., & Harris, J. J. (1997). A study of the racial identity and achievement of Black males and females. *Roeper Review, 20,* 105–110.

Lee, C. C. (1997). Cultural dynamics: Their importance in culturally responsive counseling. In C. C. Lee (Ed.), *Multicultural issues in counseling: New approaches in diversity* (2nd ed., pp. 15–30). Alexandria, VA: American Counseling Association.

Newell, M. L., Hatzichristou, C., Shanding, G. T., Nastasi, B. K., Jones, J. M., & Yetter, G. (2010). Evidence on multicultural training in school psychology: Recommendation for future directions. *School Psychology Quarterly, 25*(4), 249–278.

O'Connor, C. (1997). Dispositions toward (collective) struggle and educational resilience in the inner city: A case analysis of six African American high school students. *American Educational Research Journal, 34,* 593–629.

Oyserman, D., Harrison, K., & Bybee, D. (2001). Can racial identity be promotive of academic efficacy? *International Journal of Behavioral Development, 25*(4), 379–385.

Patterson, C. H. (2004). Do we need multicultural counseling competencies? *Journal of Mental Health Counseling, 26*(1), 67–73.

Platt, T. (2002). Desegregating multiculturalism: Problems in the theory and pedagogy of diversity education. *Social Justice, 29*(4), 41–46.

Sasso, G. M. (2001). The retreat from inquiry and knowledge in special education. *The Journal of Special Education, 34*(4), 178–193.

Speight, S. L., Myers, L. J., Cox, C. I., & Highlen, P. S. (1991). A redefinition of multicultural counseling. *Journal of Counseling and Development, 70,* 29–36.

Sue, D. W., Arredondo, P., & McDavis, R. J. (1992). Multicultural counseling competencies and standards: A call to the profession. *Journal of Multicultural Counseling and Development, 20,* 64–89.

Vontress, C., & Jackson, M. (2004). Reactions to multicultural counseling competencies debate. *Journal of Mental Health Counseling, 26,* 74–80.

Weinrach, S. G., & Thomas, K. R. (2004). The AMCD multicultural counseling competencies: A critically flawed initiative. *Journal of Mental Health and Counseling, 26*(1), 81–93.

Whiston, S. C., & Quinby, R. F. (2009). Review of school counseling outcome research. *Psychology in the Schools, 46*(3), 267–272.

Are traditional university preparation programs the best way to prepare teachers and administrators to teach diverse student populations?

POINT: Martin Scanlan, *Marquette University*
COUNTERPOINT: Carl Byron Keys, II, *University of Virginia*

OVERVIEW

The essayists in this chapter debate the issue of whether traditional university preparation programs are the best way to prepare teachers and administrators to teach diverse student populations or whether an alternative is needed. The states through their respective departments of education establish standards for school personnel and university preparation programs (Darling-Hammond, 2010). Professional associations also recommend best practices for school personnel who work with diverse populations. State departments of education may set standards for positions in public schools, but market conditions play an important role in the ability of university education programs to attract a diverse faculty and student body. It is not unreasonable to assume that quality educators would have skills necessary to successfully interact with diverse student populations.

After the 1960s' civil rights movement, minorities and women received more employment opportunities outside of education, and many left education for other professions. Further, many elite colleges and universities discontinued their teacher preparation programs. These events caused an overall decline in the quality of the teaching force and a decline of students' test scores by 1980 (Magnuson & Fogel, 2008). For the past 5 decades, Americans have been arguing about how to reform education, but little attention has been paid to how to get more top-quality college students to seek careers in education.

Many have sought to induce market conditions in education with competition between schools such as magnet schools, charter schools, voucher plans, homeschooling, and small schools within schools (Brown, 2003; Brown, 2006). However, these plans do not address improvements in the quality of educators. State standards for licensing teachers and administrators are important, but they address minimum qualifications only. One answer to the question of how to attract higher quality teachers and administrators to education as a career in a capitalist society would be to significantly increase salaries. In short, more money is needed to match reforms. Reforms are cost neutral but alone are not likely to attract more of the best and brightest college students to seek careers in education.

The general systems theory of evaluating organizational output involves (a) inputs (money), (b) thruputs (teaching), and (c) outputs (test scores). Money is the most important of the three components because it can buy superior teachers. Teaching is a process function (thruput) that is common to all states' certification requirements to teach in public schools. Better salaries should also induce elite colleges to establish teacher education programs.

More college students might consider a career in teaching if they could get a starting salary of $65,000 compared to the current starting salary of $39,000, and a minimum salary of $150,000 after 25 years of service compared to the current $67,000 (Eggers & Calegari, 2011, p. 12). Public education is not a system where you can discard low-performing students or recruit better replacements as in industry. Higher salaries are needed to recruit better teachers given that teachers' salaries have declined in terms of spending power during the decade from 1998 to 2008 (NEA, 2008). In the systems theory's evaluation model, money buys excellent teachers that lead to excellence in instruction and high test scores for students.

Reforming school personnel preparation programs such as Teach for America and New Leaders for New Schools are not likely to improve education without higher salaries. These are nonprofit organizations that recruit college graduates from elite institutions by seeking alternative state certification. Both organizations secure millions of dollars from private foundations and the federal government to support their efforts. Likewise, the Broad Foundation spends millions of dollars to prepare noneducators to lead urban schools. However, elite institutions continue their practice of not preparing state-certifiable educators.

Martin Scanlan (Marquette University) argues in the point essay that traditional university preparation programs are the best way to prepare teachers and administrators to serve diverse student populations. Scanlan believes that the federal government's Race to the Top program—designed to promote school choice measures via charter schools, magnet schools, and vouchers, and alternative teacher preparation measures via Teach for America, Urban Teaching Fellows, and the New Leaders for New Schools programs—will do little to improve education for diverse populations. Rather, he concludes that institutes of higher education are central to the goal of preparing teachers and administrators for today's diverse public school.

Carl Bryon Keys, II (University of Virginia) argues in the counterpoint essay that there are other ways to prepare educators to serve diverse student populations by considering different cultures and learning styles. He feels that the way the educational workforce has been, and currently is, trained is in need of revitalization. He notes that education programs have failed to keep pace with the changing demographics of America's schools. Keys concludes that although educational preparation programs have a moral and legal imperative to meet the needs of all students, as it now stands, they lack real efforts to prepare all children.

Both of the authors of the essays in this chapter make excellent points to support their arguments. In reading these essays, you may want to think about several points. Do state standards for teacher certification need to be altered to include criteria for effective teaching of all racial and ethnic groups? Should university preparation programs include more coursework on meeting the needs of diverse learners?

Frank Brown
University of North Carolina at Chapel Hill

POINT: Martin Scanlan
Marquette University

Current initiatives from the federal government (e.g., Race to the Top) and from private foundations (e.g., Bill and Melinda Gates Foundation) are investing significant efforts in nontraditional and alternative routes to train educators, including teachers (e.g., Teach For America) and principals (e.g., New Leaders for New Schools). Debates among proponents and critics of these reform efforts lean toward posturing and positioning rather than respectful exchange, the effect of which is similar to adding green wood to a fire: lots of smoke, little heat. This essay seeks to avoid such polemics while still making clear claims regarding a central question: How do we best prepare teachers and administrators to teach diverse student populations in our elementary and secondary schools? It argues that since education is a profession and educators are professionals, institutes of higher education are the most fertile ground for their preparation.

The focus here is on preparing teachers and principals. Of course, this discussion could easily be expanded to other educators. It first describes the demographic imperative of preparing educators to work with traditionally marginalized students. It then argues for preparing these educators as professionals, and concludes that institutes of higher education are central to this pursuit.

DEMOGRAPHIC IMPERATIVE

Students marginalized by racism, poverty, and exceptionality are most likely to suffer from a dearth of fully qualified educators. Teachers are abundant in some geographic regions and content areas but hard to find in others (Zeichner, 2003). For instance, fields such as bilingual education or science, and geographic areas such as central cities or rural districts, struggle to attract and retain teachers. On the other hand, a middle-class, suburban district has little trouble finding someone to teach a fourth-grade self-contained class of native English-speaking students.

The state of affairs in educational leadership is similar. As Kent Peterson (2002) describes, school districts face "a critical shortage of well-trained principals . . . just as many are realizing the central role of principals in the implementation of better teaching practices that will produce increased learning for all students" (p. 229). Finding highly qualified leaders for urban and rural communities and schools with challenging conditions is exceedingly difficult (Darling-Hammond, LaPointe, Meyerson, & Orr, 2007). In short, recruiting and retaining classroom teachers and school-level administrators is a pressing need, exacerbated in schools serving traditionally marginalized students.

PROFESSIONALIZATION OF THE FIELD

At the same time that the field is clamoring for strong candidates, reform efforts are pushing it in new directions. Kenneth Zeichner (2003) identifies three strands of teacher education reform: professionalization, deregulation, and social justice. Similarly competing dimensions of reform affect the principalship as well (Murphy, 2002). Among competing reform efforts, those focused on professionalism are most comprehensive (Bransford, Darling-Hammond, & LePage, 2005). Simply put, the requisite knowledge base of this profession involves disciplinary understandings that are most abundantly cultivated in institutes of higher education.

Educators as Professionals

The nature of preparing professionals across fields—from architecture to education to medicine—shares certain features (Shulman, 1998). First, professionals share a sense of service to society. Second, the domain of knowledge that defines the field is grounded in empirical and theoretical scholarship that is pursued within institutes of higher education. Third, this knowledge must be applied through the skilled performance or practices of professionals in the field. Fourth, these professionals are members of communities of practice. As Lee Shulman states, "Professions are inherently public and communal. We speak of someone not only being a professional, but being a member of a profession" (p. 520). They learn in these communities of practice to exercise judgment in discerning and applying their knowledge and learning from experiences. Through these communities of practice, quality is monitored and knowledge assimilated, vetted, and promulgated. These four dimensions apply directly to educators.

Service

With all professions, educators serve society (Shulman, 1998). Having developed mastery of distinct skills and knowledge, professionals are not only empowered to practice but also obliged to serve the common good. As Shulman puts it, "The goal of a profession is service: the pursuit of important social ends" (p. 516). The goals of education are contested and shift over time and place, yet consistently serve society. Whether emphasizing education as a public good building citizenry or training workers for the global economy or a private good promoting individual mobility, the field is widely regarded as serving society.

Educators' role of service is vital to eliminating the ubiquitous, persistent gaps in educational opportunities that fester in our communities. These inequities weaken our democracy by inhibiting the formation of reflective and engaged citizenry, and undermine the efficiency of our society by leaving many members unprepared to engage in meaningful work and by arbitrarily opening or foreclosing opportunities for individuals to develop their personal potential.

Schools are central in shaping student learning. Factors external to school—such as socioeconomic background—are clearly relevant to student success. Yet schools in general and teachers in particular have profound effects on this success. Students who work with highly effective teachers, especially those who do so consistently over a series of years, make dramatic gains in learning and overcome barriers to achievement associated with poverty and institutional racism (Bransford et al., 2005). School principals play a central and driving role in organizing schools that reduce educational inequities for the most marginalized of children (Bryk, Sebring, Allensworth, Luppescu, & Easton, 2009).

Knowledge Domains

Second, with other professional fields, education is grounded in a discrete body of empirical and theoretical scholarship (Shulman, 1998). John Bransford, Linda Darling-Hammond, and Pamela LePage (2005) synthesize three domains of knowledge: (1) knowledge of learners, (2) conceptions of curriculum, and (3) understandings of teaching. First, educators must understand theories of learning, including child development and sociocultural dimensions of learning. As Bransford et al. emphasize, this domain focuses on "how people learn, how children develop over time, and how they acquire and use language" (p. 31). Learning is multidimensional, weaving together the individual learner; the particular knowledge, skills, and attitudes that are the goal of the learning; and the assessment of this learning—all situated in a broader community context.

A second domain of professional knowledge in education is a curricular understanding. Content area standards have been developed across subject areas (e.g., www.nctm.org/standards). At the district and school levels, standards and benchmarks are broken into specific curriculum. Here teacher knowledge is central. Bransford et al. (2005) describe the role of teachers as making "a wide variety of curriculum decisions, ranging from the evaluation and selection of materials to the design and sequencing of tasks, assignments, and activities for students, based on their learning needs" (p. 35).

The third knowledge domain in education, Bransford et al. (2005) contend, blends the first two: "Skillful teaching . . . enables learners to access the curriculum" (p. 35). Understanding how to teach involves several dimensions, including knowing (a) pedagogical content, (b) how diverse students learn, (c) multiple forms of assessment, and (d) how to effectively manage teaching and learning environments.

These three knowledge domains focus primarily on teachers, but apply equally to school principals, whose mastery of these domains is essential. A strong command of the foundational knowledge of teaching is necessary (although insufficient) for an effective school principal who aspires to organize a school community for successful teaching and learning. In addition, school principals must know how to articulate organizational vision and create structures that allow for realizing this vision, including the professional development of an array of personnel (Bryk et al., 2009). In sum, educators must master a body of knowledge grounded in empirical and theoretical scholarship.

Applying Knowledge

As professionals, educators not only build knowledge through scholarship; they also apply this knowledge to practice (Shulman, 1998). A key principle here is transfer: taking the knowledge of learners, conceptions of curriculum, and understandings of teaching studied in textbooks and applying this to practice as an educator. The importance of mastering *and* applying domains of knowledge is explicitly stated in standards in the field for both teachers and administrators. These apply to both the state and national levels.

Teachers and principals need to be not only well grounded in the knowledge domains described above, but also on a trajectory to continue to deepen and expand their mastery. Novice educators typically understand the profession in rudimentary manners. For instance, inexperienced teachers might view their job as mechanically transferring information to students. This reflects both inadequate grounding in the requisite knowledge and an inability to apply this knowledge. As noted earlier, masterful educators—in the classroom as teachers and at the school level as principals—make a direct and profound impact on reducing educational inequities. As Bransford et al. (2005) hold, "The findings that teacher knowledge matters are an important reason to treat teaching as a profession, so that, through strong professional education and widespread standards of practice, knowledge about effective learning and teaching is *reliably made available to all practitioners* [italics added]" (p. 15).

Communities of Practice

Professionals develop their knowledge base and learn to apply it in practice by working with colleagues. As Shulman (1998) states, "Professional knowledge is somehow held by a community of professionals who not only know collectively more than any individual member of the community but also maintain certain public responsibilities and accountabilities with respect to individual practice" (p. 520). The concept of communities of practice is useful in describing this aspect of professionalism. Professional fields—from education to architecture—can be thought of as communities of practice, each sharing a common domain of knowledge and comprising members who practice within this domain. Like other professionals, educators participate in multiple communities of practice. These range from tightly knit professional learning communities within schools to broader affiliations within the whole school community to widely spread networks of subject-area specialists. Through conferences and publications, informal gatherings and formal sharing, face-to-face encounters and the virtual communication of blogs and electronic mailing lists—educators learn and grow via these relationships.

In sum, educators are professionals both teaching at the classroom level and administrating at the school level. Institutes of higher education are central to preparing such professionals.

INSTITUTES OF HIGHER EDUCATION

Institutes of higher education (IHEs) are best equipped to cultivate the knowledge, skills, and commitments that characterize expertise in this multifaceted and complex field. Empirical evidence demonstrates that educators who have received formal preparation and certification via IHEs promote stronger learning outcomes. Certified teachers produce significantly stronger student achievement gains than their uncertified counterparts (Clotfelter, Ladd, & Vigdor, 2007). School leaders have positive effects on student learning outcomes by strengthening the instructional climate and supporting teachers' professional growth (Drago-Severson, 2007). Exemplary programs that prepare principals for these roles share features, including a comprehensive curriculum aligned with standards and focusing on instructional leadership; student-centered instructional strategies to integrate theory and practice and stimulate reflection; and structures such as cohorts, mentoring, and internships that scaffold emergent practitioners (Darling-Hammond et al., 2007).

Educators must develop not only mastery of knowledge and skills to apply it, but the moral commitments to service as well. As organizations with explicit missions and visions that support learning and research, IHEs are structured to foster such commitments. IHEs can play a formative role in cultivating reflective practitioners. Moreover, as Bransford et al. (2005) remind us, preparing educators to work in schools is inherently preparing them to work in collegial contexts:

> If improvement in education is the goal, it is not enough to prepare good teachers and send them out to schools. If teachers are to be effective, they must work in settings where they can use what they know—where, for example, they can come to know students and families well; work with other teachers to provide a coherent, well-grounded curriculum; evaluate and guide student progress using information-rich assessments, and use texts and materials that support thoughtful learning. . . . [T]hese conditions are not present in many, perhaps most, U.S. schools. (p. 4)

This underscores the importance of cultivating communities of practice. IHEs are structured to do just this, initiating teachers and principals into the profession with commitments to pursue educational excellence *within the profession* and *grounded in disciplinary understandings.* By way of contrast, approaching the preparation of teachers and school leaders outside of IHEs treats education as an isolated trade, with knowledge, skills, and dispositions that are disconnected from the disciplines of science, mathematics, reading, and so on.

Reforming the Field: Cultivating Expertise

Complimenting my assertion that IHEs are best suited to prepare educators within the four areas of professionalism (service, knowledge, application, and membership in a community of practice) is the fact that IHEs are the focal points promoting research and development in the professions. As in all professions, research and development is requisite to improvement and progress in education. Ongoing and critical analysis of existing practices in how educators are prepared is a pressing demand in the field that can lead to reforms. For instance, recent scholarship suggests the need for more intimate links between IHEs and the diverse school settings in which teachers and principals work. Focusing on linguistically diverse students, Eugene Garcia, M. Beatriz Arias, Nancy J. Harris-Murri, and Carolina Serna (2010) assert that teacher formation for diverse populations is most effective in a setting that crosses "both the school community and the university setting. . . . There is a demographic and intellectual imperative that motivates teacher preparation to become more connected to the schools and communities where [English learners] reside" (p. 139). Reform efforts must facilitate this boundary spanning. Such research, informing substantive reform, reflects the cycle of research and development that IHEs spawn.

Another dimension of reforming the preparation of educators within IHEs involves cultivating interdisciplinary knowledge. While IHEs are optimal sites for building theory and conducting research, they can be limited when faculty members work in disconnected silos. As a profession, the field is consistently spanning new efforts to improve research and development. Again, IHEs play a central role in supporting research that critically addresses the field and develops responses. Trends in recent decades are moving toward more collaborative research and knowledge building between IHEs and schools. By working in close proximity to this scholarship—frequently studying alongside the researchers themselves—teachers and principals are led to see themselves as members of a profession with a knowledge base that is at once established and evolving.

IHEs promote effective research and development by facilitating a comprehensive analysis of the problems befuddling the field. Since schools function within the broader community, reforming them involves reforming the broader context (Zeichner, 2003). Bransford et al. (2005) make a similar point:

> We must attend simultaneously to both sides of the reform coin: better teachers and better systems. Schools will need to continue to change to create the conditions within which powerful teaching and learning can occur, and teachers will need to be prepared to be part of this change process. (p. 5)

CONCLUSION

As alternative routes toward the preparation of educators have emerged, debates have largely focused on the relative efficacy and efficiency of these pathways. These approaches vary widely in structure and quality. Significantly, they do not typically operate in total isolation from traditional IHEs but draw on expertise, coursework, and consultation therein. When considering how to best prepare teachers and administrators to teach diverse student populations, the question is largely not whether, but how, IHEs are involved. The argument of this essay avoids blanket generalizations about the quality and content of these approaches, and instead emphasizes that since the field of education is a professional one, IHEs should play the central role in preparing educators.

It can be argued, as Carl Byron Keys, II does in the counterpoint essay, that IHEs must improve their strategies in numerous ways. Creating a richer pipeline of faculty and students, diverse across multiple dimensions, is a paramount concern. Preparing teachers and school leaders to be culturally responsive educators is related. The charge that traditional teacher and leadership preparation programs in IHEs have failed to create teachers and principals who stem the persistent gaps in achievement that plague our elementary and secondary schools is apt, and without a doubt, many programs would be found guilty as charged.

These important critiques, however, underscore the thesis here: Educators are professionals and need to be prepared as such. Effective teachers and school leaders have developed knowledge, skills, and dispositions that allow them to foster teaching and learning environments in which all students excel. By definition, a masterful educator is one who fosters student learning where the barriers and disadvantages are the greatest. In lay terms, this is what distinguishes a professional from an amateur. IHEs have a central role to play in cultivating such professionals to educate our increasingly pluralistic nation.

COUNTERPOINT: Carl Byron Keys, II
University of Virginia

Annually, faculty and prospective students anticipate the release of reports that purport to rank the merits and overall quality of schools of education. On average, the well-regarded programs stay such, and other programs of education jockey for position. These programmatic trendsetters promote the research and pedagogical standards that the other schools of education attempt to emulate. Acknowledging the variation in qualities for schools of education means giving credence to the variation in quality for teachers and administrators. Ideally, the preparation received in a teacher or educational administration program would equip the novice practitioner to meet the needs of all students and learners. As both research and practice have borne out, however, this is not now (nor has it ever been) the case. There has long been a disconnect between what is espoused in education programs and what actually takes place in classrooms and schools for many students across the United States. In short, the way the educational workforce has been trained is in need of revitalization.

The contexts for America's public schools have changed; schools are full of diverse cultures and learning styles. But in a large way, education programs have failed to keep pace. As a result, teachers and administrators need to be attuned to the pedagogical and philosophical underpinnings guiding their instructional and administrative decisions. Sometimes the changes in school contexts occur rapidly and force educational practitioners to adjust their epistemological vantage points regarding learners from diverse backgrounds. The issue being, have these educators been prepared to amend their paradigms (both personal and professional) to meet the needs of students? The process of disaggregating the data has forced educators to be mindful of the achievement of the diversity of students under their charge.

There is no denying the fact that student demographics have changed. According to the 2000 U.S. Census Data, the national growth for youth aged 5 to 17 was 17%, while the growth for English language learners during the same period was 46% (U.S. Department of Education, 2001).

If I were to paint you a picture of the average American teacher, the teacher would be a 43-year-old White woman with roughly 20 years of classroom experience. She works in a rural elementary school, votes Democrat, and is religious. She'll spend nearly $500 from her pocket on her classroom. What would be the most telling rationale behind her becoming a teacher (aside from an interest in young people and the subject matter) was the influence of a teacher on her life as a student (NEA, 2010). But how was she prepared to instruct her students? What pedagogical influences and rationale does she use to guide her instructional methods? Is she able to adapt to the changes in student populations, both physical and cognitive shifts in student demographics?

David Labaree's work *The Trouble With Ed. Schools* (2006) puts an interesting perspective on the multidimensional issues, both historical and contemporary, facing schools of education. Labaree laments the fact that education schools are held in low regard. Labaree cites the book *The Miseducation of American Teachers* by James Koerner (1963) as pinpointing the "inferior quality of Education faculty" as the reason for not only the lowly status of schools of education but also the poor status of education today. Associated with this belief is a series of telling reports issued by the Holmes Group/ Partnership that form the basis of the education school's greatest dilemmas as well as greatest triumphs.

Tomorrow's Teachers (Holmes Group, 1986) addressed the need for "the professionalization of teaching," "for the development of school-university partnerships (known as professional development schools in *Tomorrow's Schools* [1990]), and for the transformation of ed. schools in *Tomorrow's Schools of Education*" (1995, p. 6).

The last report by the Holmes Group is the weightiest, as it not only delineates problems with traditional programs for teachers and educational administrators but also advocates what steps they need to take to remedy their self-inflicted ills. *Tomorrow's Schools of Education* (1995) critiqued America's schools of education by saying they were "dwelling in a bygone era" (p. 7), "being engaged in practices that cannot be tolerated and will only exacerbate the problems of public education" (p. 6), and "the faculty-unafflicted with an 'enigmatic attitude,' 'lack of will' and 'considerable inertia'" (p. 88).

Lee G. Bolman and Terrence E. Deal's *Reframing Organizations: Artistry, Choice, and Leadership* (2008) builds on the works of previous organizational theorists with their four-frame model for examining organizations. To explain the issues in preparing teachers and educational administrators via traditional university preparation programs, to educate diverse students, the symbolic frame provides the best lens for explicating how I interpret Labaree. The political frame assumes that organizations are rife with conflict that needs to be mediated. Also chief among these assumptions are the following:

- First and primary question for political frame: Who benefits?

- Organizations are coalitions composed of various individuals and interest groups.

- There are enduring differences among individuals and groups in values, preferences, and perceptions.

- Most of the important organizational decisions involve allocation of scarce resources.

- Because of enduring differences and scarce resources, conflict is central to organizational dynamics and power is the key resource.

As a result—an extension, really—the disconnect and mistrust that the collective psyche of the American public has with public officials and bureaucracy has carried over into the classroom and schoolhouse. The teaching profession is relegated to low status, seen as less desirable and inching further away from the realms of a "profession," and quickly becoming a "position." I can recall my own graduate programs not regularly placing teaching candidates in local urban districts because it was not deemed a suitable placement.

DWELLING IN A BYGONE ERA

Diversity in the classroom is generally not at the front of the class. The National Education Association (NEA) regularly conducts a survey titled *Status of the American Public School Teacher*. According to the 1,467 respondents, teachers are getting more education than ever before. From 1960 to 2001, teachers with degrees beyond the bachelor in public education went from 23% of the workforce to 57%. Teachers are staying in the classroom longer than in previous survey periods, with veteran teachers with 20 years or more in the classroom reaching a high of 38% of public school teachers. Wages for teachers have stagnated (NEA, 2010), and many have external sources of income. Teachers have become increasingly aged (over 50 years), White, and female to the tune of 37%, 79% and 90%, respectively. Of the remaining teachers, the next highest percentage (5%) is African American.

Collectively, schools of education have a tumultuous history when it comes to addressing diversity. Perhaps the most glaring aspect of the trouble with education schools is the look of the faculty. Jack H. Schuster and Martin J. Finkelstein (2006) report that "annually about 2% of the aggregate faculty separate from their institutions for reasons other than retirement" and that "these dropouts are likely to be disproportionately women and members of racial and ethnic minorities" (p. 206). Traditional teacher education and educational administration programs tend to treat issues of diversity as novelty, if they are addressed at all. Diversity is a peripheral curricular and practical concern in many programs of study that, if included, will be relegated to a special section or the domain of a guest lecturer (Tillman, 2004).

ENGAGING IN PRACTICES THAT CANNOT BE TOLERATED

Were a student in a teacher or educational administration program to create an instructional toolkit based on the teaching strategies and assessments that he or she has experienced as a graduate student, here's what it would look like. It would primarily consist of direct instruction, with very little experiential learning and complex instruction/constructivist learning. The obvious questions are, What accounts for this? Why do the faculty in postsecondary education, specifically within the field of education, fail to use the pedagogical strategies and modes of assessment that link learning goals with outcomes? Why is there still so much reliance on direct instruction and teacher-centered pedagogy? Given what is commonly understood about learning and cognition, direct instruction is the worst way to educate students; yet it is foundation, frame, and insulation for traditional university teacher education and education administration programs.

The argument can be made that information and studies on K–12 teaching, learning, assessment, and the creation of best practices in that arena should influence higher education pedagogical choices, or that higher education's best practices should hold greater sway over the pedagogical decisions happening in K–12. So, then, why aren't these traditional programs taking their own advice? One of the most basic and fundamental aspects to assessing student knowledge and creating equity is having a public standard that all students can understand

and meet. Coupled with this experience is a nebulous system of assessment that is based on the whims of the instructor who may or may not exercise biases in a manner that will influence grading.

Policymakers and entrepreneurs have seized on this: Programs like Teach For America and Urban Teaching Fellows have filled that void for classroom teachers, while programs such as New Leaders for New Schools and Education Pioneers provide innovative and practical experiences for the preparation school site leadership.

The NEA is widely recognized as the leading authority on teachers, teaching, and schooling. This national organization, along with other respected organizations, recognizes the change in student demographics as having an effect on the operation of schools. The NEA has produced a document that outlines the benefits of cultural competence for educators to meet the needs of an increasingly culturally diverse student population. The definition of cultural competence, as operationalized by NEA, is

> the ability to successfully teach students who come from cultures other than our own. It entails developing certain personal and interpersonal awareness and sensitivities, developing certain bodies of cultural knowledge, and mastering a set of skills that, taken together, underlie effective cross-cultural teaching. (NEA, 2008, p. 1)

LACK OF WILL AND CONSIDERABLE INERTIA

The trouble with education schools is that there is no impetus to change. It is understood that university departments and program areas seek to employ individuals who have similar research methods and interests. Alexander McCormick and Chun-Mei Zhao (2005) describe an unintended consequence of the Carnegie Classification as homogenizing and reinforcing the existing framework of institutional hierarchy. Should there be a correlation between the research interests of professors and those of their departmental colleagues? If there is validity to the idea that multiple voices create richness in academia, why then isn't this notion practiced?

More than 10 years ago, Myles Brand (2000) wrote of the changing faculty roles in research institutions. One proposal mentioned "a small cadre of outstanding researchers would be designated to concentrate their energies where they would be most effective" (p. 45). The better the research reputation/cache of the professors, the more well regarded the institution. I would say very few are aware of how well they are teaching, nor would it matter very much unless they were absolutely horrible. Once tenure has been obtained, some rest on their laurels and do very little to update their syllabus, integrate new technologies, or challenge themselves. New, innovative programs in education avoid granting tenure to faculty. This practice, while controversial, forces instructors to be responsive to their students and their students' experiences in schools. How would addressing glaring inconsistencies in pedagogy by more clearly establishing research-oriented faculty and teaching-oriented faculty at research-intensive institutions affect faculty? What could these new appointments look like? How would this potentially affect salaries?

Returning to the political frame's overarching assumption, conflict is essential to understanding the trouble with traditional university preparation programs. There is competition for the scarce resources of time and money. Faculty members of education schools have the task of changing a profession that is dependent on client participation and take the brunt of the fall for its failings. Schools of education are indeed coalitions of varied disciplines, methods, and agendas that often compete for funding and prominence—and that is just the faculty. To achieve the aims of public education, the attention of faculty will have to turn to improving the quality of the traditional university preparation programs.

Not only has there been a noticeable disconnect with the stated and the enacted in education programs, but there is also a large chasm when it comes to where quality programs send their graduates. It is not to the areas and students most in need of highly trained teachers and administrators.

If we agree that teachers and site administrators are the daily enforcement of learning and socialization for students, then we must address this issue. There was a time when the law regulated the segregated learning experiences of children throughout the country. As a country, if we were to pay attention to the public discourse regarding immigration and diversity, we would easily pinpoint the backlash against the needs of diverse students. Traditional programs have failed to assist in stemming the growing achievement gap. Teachers have failed to find ways to reach these children in any consistent and significant manner. Educational leaders have, in a large way, failed to lead schools with diverse students to maintain any significant and sustained academic growth. Research shows, even taking into consideration the other significant factors, that the more diverse the student population, the worse the students perform. The more things change, the more they stay the same. Educational preparation programs have a moral and legal imperative to meet the needs of all students; as it stands currently, they are lacking in real efforts to prepare all children.

FURTHER READINGS AND RESOURCES

Bolman, L. G., & Deal, T. E. (2008). *Reframing organizations: Artistry, choice, and leadership.* San Francisco: Jossey-Bass.

Boyer, E. (1990). *Scholarship reconsidered.* Princeton, NJ: Carnegie Foundation for the Advancement of Teaching.

Brand, M. (2000). Changing faculty roles in research universities: Using the pathways strategy. *Change, 32*(6), 42–45.

Bransford, J., Darling-Hammond, L., & LePage, P. (2005). Introduction. In L. Darling-Hammond & J. Bransford (Eds.), *Preparing teachers for a changing world: What teachers should learn and be able to do* (pp. 1–39). San Francisco: Jossey-Bass.

Brown, F. (2003). Choice, vouchers and privatization as education reform or the fulfillment of Richard Nixon's southern strategy? In R. C. Hunter & F. Brown (Eds.), *Challenges of urban education and efficacy of school reform* (pp. 65–88). Amsterdam: JAI, Elsevier Science.

Brown, F. (2006). Privatization of elementary and secondary education. In C. Russo (Ed.), *Key legal issues for school business officials* (pp. 33–52). Lanham, MD: Rowman & Littlefield Education.

Bryk, A., Sebring, P. B., Allensworth, E., Luppescu, S., & Easton, J. (2009). *Organizing schools for improvement: Lessons from Chicago.* Chicago: University of Chicago Press.

Clotfelter, C., Ladd, H., & Vigdor, J. (2007). *Teacher credentials and student achievement in high school: A cross-subject analysis with student fixed effects.* Washington, DC: Calder Urban Institute.

Darling-Hammond, L. (2010). *The flat world and education: How America's commitment to equity will determine our future.* New York: Teachers College Press.

Darling-Hammond, L., LaPointe, M., Meyerson, D. E., & Orr, M. T. (2007). *Preparing school leaders for a changing world.* Stanford, CA: Stanford University Press.

Drago-Severson, E. (2007). Helping teachers learn: Principals as professional development leaders. *Teachers College Record, 109*(1), 70–125.

Eggers, D., & Calegari, N. C. (2011, May 1). The high cost of low teacher salaries. *The New York Times,* p. WK12.

Garcia, E., Arias, M. B., Harris-Murri, N. J., & Serna, C. (2010). Developing responsive teachers: A challenge for a demographic reality. *Journal of Teacher Education, 61*(1–2), 132–142.

Holmes Group. (1986). *Tomorrow's teachers.* East Lansing, MI: Author.

Holmes Group. (1990). *Tomorrow's schools.* East Lansing, MI: Author.

Holmes Group. (1995). *Tomorrow's schools of education.* East Lansing, MI: Author.

Koerner, J. (1963). *The miseducation of American teachers.* Boston: Houghton Mifflin.

Labaree, D. F. (2006). *The trouble with ed. schools.* New Haven, CT: Yale University Press.

Magnuson, K., & Fogel, W. (2008). *Steady gains and stalled progress: Inequality and Black–White test score gap.* New York: Russell Sage Foundation.

McCormick, A., & Zhao, C.-M. (2005). Rethinking and reframing the Carnegie classification. *Change, 37*(5), 50–57.

Murphy, J. (Ed.). (2002). *The educational leadership challenge: Redefining leadership for the 21st century* (Yearbook of the National Society for the Study of Education 101). Chicago: University of Chicago Press.

National Education Association (NEA). (2008). *Rankings and estimates.* Retrieved from http://www.nea.org/assets/docs/HE/09rankings.pdf

National Education Association (NEA). (2010, March). *Status of the American public school teacher 2005–2006.* Retrieved November 2, 2011, from http://www.nea.org/assets/docs/HE/2005-06StatusTextandAppendixA.pdf

Peterson, K. (2002). The professional development of principals: Innovations and opportunities. *Educational Administration Quarterly, 38*(2), 213–232.

Schuster, J. H., & Finkelstein, M. J. (2006). *The American faculty: The restructuring of academic work and careers.* Baltimore: Johns Hopkins University Press.

Shulman, L. (1998). Theory, practice, and the education of professionals. *The Elementary School Journal, 98*(5), 511–526.

Tierney, W., & Bensimon, E. (1996). *Promotion and tenure: Community and socialization in academe.* Albany: State University of New York Press.

Tillman, L. C. (2004). (Un)intended consequences? The impact of the *Brown v. Board of Education* decision on the employment status of Black educators. *Education and Urban Society, 36*(3), 280–303.

U.S. Department of Education. (2001). *English language learners and the U.S. Census 1990–2000* (Summary File 3, Table P19). Washington, DC: Author.

Zeichner, K. (2003). The adequacies and inadequacies of three current strategies to recruit, prepare, and retain the best teachers for all students. *Teachers College Record, 105*(3), 490–519.

Can Race to the Top and related programs improve underperforming schools?

POINT: William J. Miller, *Southeast Missouri State University*
COUNTERPOINT: Muhammad Khalifa and Nimo Abdi,
Michigan State University

OVERVIEW

President Obama's Race to the Top (RTT) initiative consists of programs similar to those supported by former Presidents Richard Nixon, Ronald Reagan, George H. W. Bush, and George W. Bush. Those initiatives included school reform programs such as charter schools, magnet schools, private management of public schools, vouchers, and alternative methods of preparing teachers and administrators (Weingarten, 2011). These measures were first introduced to stop or slow court-ordered school desegregation plans (Brown, 2004). The RTT initiatives were introduced in 2009 as part of a larger federal spending bill to stimulate the economy, including the spending of money on public education to reduce the reduction of local school personnel due to the recession. This chapter looks at RTT and other related programs and their effect on underperforming schools.

RTT was part of the American Recovery and Reinvestment Act of 2009 designed to invest in infrastructure and education to help stimulate the economy. The U.S. Department of Education received $5 billion in competitive grants to states to improve education based on the following: common academic standards, a data system, improving teachers and low-performing schools, improvements in science and mathematics, greater use of charter schools, alternative teacher certification programs, and performance-based pay for teachers.

RTT requires states to have charter schools and an increase in the number of charter schools based on the size of the states' population. Research suggests that charter schools have not been more successful in improving low-performing schools compared to traditional schools with similar students (Brown, 2006). Also, charter schools tend to increase racial segregation, which may have a negative impact on students' academic achievement, and charter schools are not required to provide free lunches for children from low-income homes.

RTT supports and funds alternative certification programs for teachers and administrators. Approximately 60,000 teachers have been trained in alternative certification programs and are teaching in public schools, where most are placed in poor urban schools. By state standards, many teachers are not fully certified (Darling-Hammond, 2010). This situation suggests that public education in poor communities is not high on America's list of priorities. This is a problem for urban schools serving largely low-income minority students, whereas schools in wealthier neighborhoods and school districts get to select teachers from among the top teacher education candidates.

RTT also supports merit pay for teachers based on student scores on standardized tests. Teaching is a profession where evaluating individual teachers based on students' test scores is difficult because of the nature of how students are processed through school by grade levels. One question often raised is, who is fully responsible for a student's academic achievement: the teacher in the student's current grade or the teacher in the prior grade? Further, there are many school and home variables that may impact a particular student's capacity to achieve, and finding a comparable control group for research is difficult. Also, low-performing schools have the highest teacher turnover, resulting in a less stable school environment.

RTT programs face many obstacles to improving low-performing schools. First, low-income communities receive less funding from state and local sources because they have fewer experienced teachers, who are paid less than more experienced teachers found in wealthier neighborhoods within the same school district. Second, many low-performing schools tend to accept federal funds for compensatory education under Title I of the No Child Left Behind Act, which requires these schools to have a larger concentration of disadvantaged students (Doyle & Cooper, 1998). Third, low-performing schools tend to have a high teacher turnover rate that leads to a less stable school environment. Fourth, charter schools are likely to be racially isolated schools with inadequate facilities. In general, states do not provide housing for charter schools, and the successful ones often receive supplemental funding from private foundations. Private foundations that support charter schools tend to limit their support for a 5-year period.

Models exist for how to produce excellent results found in almost any wealthy public school; these schools are well funded, with experienced teachers with a low turnover. This would be a good reform model to follow, but it is expensive, and low-performing schools generally do not have the funds to implement such models. This was the original goal under Title I of the No Child Left Behind Act, which mandated that schools receiving Title I funds for low-performing schools must be at the same level as the average school in the district. This mandate was changed over the years. Education quality declined in the 1960s when more talented teachers left the profession and many colleges closed their education programs. Some have argued that now is the time to increase teachers' salaries to attract more college graduates into the teaching profession (Eggers & Calegari, 2011).

In this chapter, William J. Miller (Southeast Missouri State University) argues in favor of the federal RTT initiatives, and Muhammad Khalifa and Nimo Abdi (Michigan State University) argue against these initiatives. Miller contends that if given the chance, RTT can work, even though other programs have failed, because it is built on underlying assumptions that show the potential for long-term success. He acknowledges that it may not be the perfect program but argues that it brings education policy another step in the right direction. Khalifa and Abdi contend that federal educational reforms over the past 3 decades have not helped to improve low-performing schools. They add that RTT and other neoliberal programs have not only failed to reform education and close achievement gaps; they have also contributed to the very problems that they claim to address.

The point and counterpoint essays make excellent statements to support the respective authors' positions. However, given the fact that these initiatives may be temporary or may provide less funding in the future, you may want to consider other questions as you read these essays. How can the federal government recruit more talented teachers and administrators to the education profession? What procedures and policies at the state level are needed to equalize funding between schools in the same district? Will equal funding give each school in the district an equal opportunity to improve?

Frank Brown
University of North Carolina at Chapel Hill

POINT: William J. Miller
Southeast Missouri State University

W hen one wants to discuss the current state of public education performance in the United States, one need look no further than New Jersey for a fiery explanation of the debates currently taking place throughout the country. While Governor Chris Christie has made a name for himself by lambasting union members and sympathizers at various town hall meetings, union leaders have responded in kind by stating, "It's going to take World War III to get rid of Adolph Christie" (Bolduc, 2011, para. 5). In one of the more famous exchanges, Christie faced off with teacher Rita Wilson on May 24, 2010. Wilson argued that if she were paid $3 per hour for the 30 children in her class, she would be earning $83,000 annually (only later to find out she was already making $86,000 plus benefits). As she continued arguing that she was underpaid and unappreciated, Christie simply stated that she did not have to work, then. Continuing on, the governor explained how he would have been able to avoid any cuts to education if the teachers union had agreed to a 1-year salary freeze and a 1.5% increase in employee benefit contributions. Due to that decision, Christie claims that the union's belief that this was "the greatest assault on public education in the history of the state" provides them with "no credibility" (Foster, 2010, p. 5).

While most states are not as embroiled in direct confrontation as New Jersey, there are underlying currents running throughout the nation related to how we—as a society—can best fix public education. When President George W. Bush signed the No Child Left Behind (NCLB) Act in 2002, the most profound criticism revolved around the lack of federal funding issued for the program and the requirement that states comply with all provisions or risk losing their federal funding. As a result, schools argued that they were forced to devote more time (and money) to subjects that were tested under NCLB to assure they were not further penalized. Simply put, educators and policymakers alike preferred not to be threatened by a stick—especially one they did not believe was working to solve the country's current educational dilemmas. Eight years later, President Barack Obama—a month after his inauguration—announced his proposed solution to improving underperforming schools: Race to the Top (RTT). Signed into law as part of the American Recovery and Reinvestment Act (ARRA), the program provides $4.35 billion through a competitive grant program to the states to support investments in innovative strategies that are most likely to lead to improved results for students, long-term gains in school and school system capacity, and increased productivity and effectiveness.

Skeptics will argue (as Muhammad Khalifa and Nimo Abdi do in the counterpoint essay in this chapter) that similar programs fail to improve underperforming schools and can even do more harm than good. In response, however, this essay will discuss how any judgment of RTT is unfair at this time and that, if properly executed, the program provides us the best opportunity to create lasting improvements in underperforming schools throughout the nation. Rather than offering the stick present in NCLB, RTT simply offers programming funding to states that demonstrate success in raising achievement in their K–12 schools and present the best plans to continue making further improvements into the future. Under the current program, there is a large carrot with no noticeable stick.

THE RACE TO THE TOP PROGRAM

On July 24, 2009, President Obama announced a new initiative aimed at aiding America's educational ails. In doing so, he stated,

> America will not succeed in the 21st century unless we do a far better job of educating our sons and daughters. . . . And the race starts today. I am issuing a challenge to our nation's governors and school boards, principals and teachers, businesses and non-profits, parents and students: if you set and enforce rigorous and challenging standards and assessments; if you put outstanding teachers at the front of the classroom; if you turn around failing schools—your state can win a Race to the Top grant that will not only help students outcompete workers around the world, but let them fulfill their God-given potential. (The White House, 2009, para. 5)

An education has become more important to Americans today than at any other point in our history. Manufacturing jobs do not exist in the same quantities they did previously. Even the most basic of positions are now requiring high school diplomas at a minimum. Providing high quality educations to the youth of America helps assure our nation continues its efforts to be a world leader. As the President stated, "In a 21st century world, education is no longer just a pathway to opportunity and success—it is a prerequisite" (The White House, 2011, para. 11).

At the time the program was unveiled in 2004, K–12 education in our country had failed to respond positively to the reforms prescribed by President George W. Bush under NCLB. Roughly one in three students was able to read and do math at their current grade levels, and one in four students dropped out of high school. "In a world where countries that out-educate us today will out-compute us tomorrow, the future belongs to the nation that best educates its people, period"

(Quaid, 2009, para. 8). If we desired to be that nation, President Obama believed some fundamental changes in philosophy and practice were necessary.

To encourage a buy-in to his efforts to overhaul American K–12 education, President Obama offered $4.35 billion in grants through ARRA to states. Since the federal government cannot tell states what to do regarding education policy, the new program aims to reward those states that align themselves with the president's path and goals. Even at the initial rollout of the program, Obama began to answer the question we examine today. While believing that the program would help many states and school districts (including those that were underperforming), he likewise acknowledged that "not every state will win, and not every school district will be happy with the results" (Quaid, 2009, para. 4). RTT was never intended to be the silver bullet for all of America's K–12 education conundrums, but it was expected to be able to help schools do better than they historically have.

THE GOALS OF RACE TO THE TOP

RTT focuses on four central tenets to best spur systematic reform and encourage innovative approaches to fixing the American K–12 education system.

Design and Implementation of Rigorous Standards and High Quality Assessments

RTT asks states to create common academic standards within their jurisdictions that attempt to assure students are prepared for college or careers. These standards should consider both critical knowledge and higher order thinking schools. As such, the goal is not to merely use standardized testing or to have teachers teaching to any particular test. Instead, RTT seeks standards and assessments that show mastery of material along with the capability to critically assess and synthesize information as appropriate for age level.

Attracting and Retaining Great Teachers and Administrators for K–12 Classrooms

Recognizing the importance of good teachers for educational outcomes, RTT seeks to assure effective educators remain in their positions helping young Americans grow and learn. To do so, the program looks to expand support for teachers and principals and to help guarantee proper preparation by (a) revising means of evaluation, compensation, and retention to award effectiveness and (b) ensuring that good teachers are able to work at schools where they are needed the most.

Supporting Data Systems That Holistically Inform Decisions

RTT requires states to fully implement statewide longitudinal data systems that provide the necessary data to drive effective instruction. Further, the data are expected to be made available for key stakeholders throughout the community, state, and country as needed. The goal of longitudinal data allows students to be tracked over time and examined for improvements and growth.

Finding Innovative and Effective Approaches to Turn Around Struggling Schools

Under RTT, states will be expected to demonstrate a viable plan to prioritize and transform schools that have regularly been classified as low performing. While the first three goals discussed assume that a rising tide will raise all boats, this principle requires states to pay special attention to the schools most in need based on previous performance.

Synthesis

In short, RTT is asking states to assure the continued growth of their students by creating standards and assessments that help track their progress as they move toward college or a career. It aims to reward teachers and administrators who have demonstrated success in helping students reach performance goals. RTT asks states to use longitudinal data on teachers and students to guarantee big picture evaluations are possible. And states are asked to specifically target schools that have struggled to reach performance goals previously. Randi Weingarten, president of the 1.4 million–strong American Federation of Teachers, stated that "if it is done right, it can promote innovation and promote promising ideas" (Ross, 2009, para. 3). While individuals may argue against the manner by which these goals are going to be accomplished, at face value, it is difficult to argue against the underlying ideas of these reform efforts.

THE RACE TO THE TOP PROCESS

Money from the RTT program is not an entitlement program to the states. Instead, states must show detailed plans on how they will use the money to meet the program's larger goals. When President Bush announced his NCLB program in the early part of his administration, critics argued that it was an unfunded mandate given that requirements were passed down without any federal funding to support them. Recognizing this concern, RTT instead makes no actual demands of states or schools. Instead, it offers them millions of dollars for showing the ability and willingness to meet the reform goals of the program. While many states have had to alter their policies and programs to maximize their score potential in the competition, they can just as easily continue their current education system without participating in RTT.

Adam Gamoran, director of the Wisconsin Center for Education Research, the largest and oldest university-based research center in the United States, has commented that Secretary of Education Arne Duncan

> orchestrated a funding system so states are required to demonstrate progress and plans to qualify for these funds. His use of funds is aligned with the priorities in it. In my view these goals are very good ideas, so there's a good chance Race to the Top funds will lead to improvements. (Ross, 2009, para. 6)

The grant process favored "bold reform plans from states with proven records of improving student performance" ("Continue the race," 2010, para. 3). States competing in the initial grant process aimed to maximize their scores out of 500 possible points. Points were awarded for myriad factors, including performance-based assessments of teachers and principals, having a statewide reform agenda, and successful conditions for high-performing charters and other innovative schools. From the beginning, President Obama and Secretary Duncan stated that they would hold the money before they funded programs that were not taking the necessary steps to reform their K–12 education systems. Many critics predicted, however, they the Department of Education would eventually cave in and fund mediocre programs. Duncan and Obama held strong. In the first round of awards, only 2 of 41 applications were funded. In the second round, only 10 states were funded.

RACE TO THE TOP EFFECTS

Most of the 12 states that have received RTT grants thus far—along with the more than 30 states that have altered their education policies to help their applications—would have never attempted this magnitude of reform without the promise of federal assistance. States interested in RTT funding were forced to begin critically assessing their K–12 education systems from all angles to determine how they could improve their chances of receiving funding. New York improved its chances by adopting new teacher evaluation systems that take student test performance into account, along with creating an expedited system for firing ineffective teachers. The District of Columbia started a new performance-based contract for teachers, a school turnaround plan, and a new program where not-for-profits from outside the system can come in and operate struggling schools. These new programs and plans were unlikely to have been developed and implemented if not for the incentives of RTT.

The program does not neglect local or state educators as NCLB was accused of doing. States actually gain points by building support among school districts and teacher unions. Governor Christie of New Jersey and his administration lost points on the state's application due to a lack of support from the grassroots level. This support forces teacher unions to make difficult decisions. RTT, after all, does require favorable environments for charter schools to work within a state (including minimum numbers of charter schools within a state's borders). Further, the program will not award money to states that bar performance data from being linked to teacher evaluations. Critics argue that including student performance in teacher evaluations is unfair to the teacher since they have no control over what students they receive and the countless mitigating factors outside of the classroom that can impact student performance. With the use of longitudinal data and holistic assessments, however, states have proved able to account for student performance in teacher evaluations in a nondiscriminatory manner. RTT also supports performance pay, which further fuels the debate over appropriate uses of student performance for teacher evaluation.

Secretary Duncan aimed to create national content standards as part of RTT. Believing these content standards had been "the third rail of education," Duncan lamented the way states and schools had lowered their standards to better position themselves within the framework of NCLB under Bush. Rather than having the federal government create the standards, however, Duncan turned to the National Governors Association and the Council of Chief State School Officers to create common standards. The process was funded primarily through the Bill and Melinda Gates Foundation and the Charles Stewart Mott Foundation. The goal of common standards is to determine nationally what students should learn in English and math each year from kindergarten through high school. A reasonable assumption to work under, the program aims to assure that every third-grader across the country leaves the grade level with the same basic knowledge. Forty-eight states ended up adopting the common standards—especially given the points received in RTT applications for the adoption ("Virginia's stance," 2010).

As with any national education policy proposal, critics have set out to nit-pick many elements of RTT. Some states—particularly Texas and Virginia— have withdrawn from considering RTT funding due to federal interference with their state policies. Unlike under NCLB, however, neither governor had to worry about losing current funding or other negative effects. Instead, they are fully permitted to continue their current policies and be ineligible for additional national funding for education reform. Others have argued that the neoliberal reforms advocated for by RTT have been ineffective in the past. Choice, competition, and accountability—particularly through charter schools—have not found across-the-board success. Yet programs such as the Knowledge Is Power Program (KIPP) and the Harlem Children Zone have had lasting impacts and demonstrated measurable student improvements throughout their existence. While RTT will not provide the funding necessary to duplicate these programs exactly across the country, they will permit districts to move closer to their outcomes.

WHY IT CAN WORK

Secretary Duncan and President Obama never claimed that RTT would cure America's education ailments overnight. Instead, they believed it would help reward states that have taken time to create roadmaps to reform that are embedded in the educational context of their state. By requiring states to pay special attention to schools with histories of not meeting progress standards, underperforming schools will not simply be ignored. With money now awarded, the difficult portion of RTT has begun. Policies must be implemented and plans must become action. There are elements of a high-stakes environment as a result of RTT, but the true battle is being waged between the states, not between the schools.

The underlying assumptions of RTT are difficult to argue against from an outsider's perspective. Why would teachers whose students regularly meet or exceed performance goals not be rewarded? Likewise, why would teachers whose students routinely fail to progress not be subjected to termination? Why should a third-grade student in Alaska not be learning the same information as a third-grade student in Florida? And perhaps most importantly, why would we not use longitudinal data and holistic growth assessments to measure overall student impact rather than relying on single standardized tests? Low-income communities tend to receive less state and local funding due to the lack of experienced teachers in their schools. Under RTT, these schools will be able to retain effective educators through merit pay and other programs. If states believe their current policies are better than RTT, they can simply choose not to apply or participate.

With only two rounds of funding completed and less than 2 years of change under its belt, it is far too early to judge the potential success of RTT on reforming education in America. However, it is clear that this program has been built on underlying assumptions that show the potential for long-term success. Having learned from past education policy failures, President Obama and Secretary Duncan crafted a policy that aims to move K–12 education forward. While only 12 states have successfully laid out plans that merit funding in the eyes of evaluators, thanks to the application process, even states that have not been funded have now crafted detailed road maps to reform and asked questions that likely had not been asked prior to the RTT program. RTT dared to touch the third rail and challenge teacher unions on issues they have long fought against. While RTT may not be the perfect program, it takes education policy another step in the right direction and, with time, will be able to be judged for its actual impact on helping education in America.

COUNTERPOINT: Muhammad Khalifa and Nimo Abdi
Michigan State University

Educational performances in American public education have been dismal, and reforms ineffectual, over the past 30 years. Over one third of the nation's 50 largest cities have graduation rates less than 50%, with former rust-belt cities performing the worst. Many of these trends, along with disparities in school performance based on students' race, have been worsening in recent years. In many suburban and urban districts, for example, Black and Latino students are out performed by their White peers several times in graduation rates, attendance rates, grades, standardized tests, or any other academic measure used. This remains true even for Black and Latino middle-class families and areas. These social constructions of student school performance most heavily inform dialogues on the progress of U.S. schools. But even if there is credence with these constructions, it is often difficult to understand why Americans have embraced the assumptions embedded within the neoliberal and neoconservative approaches to educational reform. Indeed, Race to the Top (RTT) and other neoliberal programs not only have failed to reform education and close achievement gaps but also in many ways have contributed to the very problems that they claim to address.

Some have claimed that broader educational reforms that are coterminous with RTT—such as privatization—were never actually designed to address educational problems (Saltman, 2008) but rather to open public and democratic programs (such as education) to private ownership and interests. Others have questioned the choice theories (e.g., charter schools) under which privatization was designed (Burch, 2009). This essay looks at the failures of reforms in urban environments. It questions, of all of the reforms, why these types of reforms have taken root and remained largely uncontested in professional and political arenas. It is too soon to give complete assessments of RTT. However, in this essay, we argue that similar programs have no real encouraging results for failing Black and Latino students in school; rather, they function in much the same way that White hegemonic structures do with urban, largely Black and Latino communities—a measure of marginalization, power, and control. And finally, as we concede the immense need for educational reform, we offer alternatives. In other words, although ostensibly large numbers of American politicians and educators support these reforms, and although legislation such as the No Child Left Behind (NCLB) Act and RTT were directed at urban, poor, minority students, there are alternative ways of improving education that are sensitive to the unique needs of the people to whom neoliberal reforms were directed.

BACKGROUND ON PROGRAMS

The Race to the Top program is authorized under sections 14005 and 14006 of the American Recovery and Reinvestment Act of 2009 (ARRA). Race to the Top is a competitive grant program to encourage and reward States that are implementing significant reforms in the four education areas described in the ARRA: enhancing standards and assessments, improving the collection and use of data, increasing teacher effectiveness and achieving equity in teacher distribution, and turning around struggling schools. (U.S. Department of Education, 2010, p. 3)

RTT is a competitive grant program that incentivizes implementation of reforms: increased standards and assessment and improvement based on standardized test data, with the flexibility to include other measures. After public complaints of ambiguity, the RTT program further explained that "increasing teacher effectiveness" shall be measured using multiple methods—specifically, that "student growth, not raw student achievement or proficiency data, is therefore the relevant measure on which to focus teacher and principal evaluations" (U.S. Department of Education, 2010, p. 21). This indicates slight changes in the approach—less stringent ways of measuring teacher performance—but the overall thrust of RTT leaves the high-stakes culture unchallenged and intact. This is an explicit acceptance of a number of assumptions that can be challenged: that students, teachers, and administrators are motivated by a high-stakes environment; that positive achievement results can be attained through business and market models of accountability; and now, since sanctions have not worked over the past decade with NCLB, that with RTT, "incentives" will push educators in the direction of reform. It is interesting, as well, that schools would be rewarded for "proposed" and "implemented" reforms, and not for actual results.

Schools, educators, and even district officials seem to be confused about what exactly they are charged with under RTT because it is the state officials who apply for the funding. Then, states are responsible for actually dispersing the monies to local districts. There is an assumption that individual states will act in the best interest of families, students, and teachers at the local level. In other words, if state politicians favor a high-stakes agenda, so too will any changes from RTT. At these early stages, it seems as though RTT leaves untouched the current neoliberal programs of school choice, privatization of school administration, charter schools, and vouchers. Since RTT does not challenge these structures, it essentially reproduces them. RTT and the reproduction of an NCLB-based educational environment are problematic because— even after 10 years—these earlier programs have not been demonstrable of success.

UNDERSTANDING THE CONTEXT OF RACE TO THE TOP

Although the two primary assumptions seem to be that states will act in the best interest of local schools and that schools will attain success if they are incentivized, there are also a number of problematic assumptions related to (school) choice in a free market economy. Regarding charter schools and school choice, scholars have noted the assumptions that (a) there are actually better choices from which parents can choose and that (b) parents will make the right choice. And since both assumptions have been overwhelmingly disputed with recent data, one cannot see the rationale to continue supporting a law based on these assumptions. RTT does not challenge these assumptions. Yet, it is important to note that data from across the country indicate that charter schools, which are primarily unregulated, often perform much worse than similar public schools in the same areas. In their examination of two urban schools, Ron Zimmer and Richard Buddin (2006) found—among countless researchers with similar findings—that charter schools have "mixed" performance results at best, and are usually detrimental for minority students. Yet, these expressions of neoliberalism, which assumes that free market choice of consumers (read: parents) will lead to increased competition (read: school performance and results), has not proven true for schools. In fact, if one looks at current data, it becomes clear that not only are the charter schools performing much worse on standardized test scores, but they are also siphoning off crucial dollars that could be directed toward struggling public schools that are actually producing modest improvements.

Another major neoliberal trend that RTT does not challenge—and therefore runs the risk of reproducing—is the trend toward privatizing education. Proponents of privatization of education argue that private (i.e., for-profit) companies "could operate public schools better and cheaper than the public sector" (Saltman, 2008, p. 270). Patricia Burch (2009) offers a more generalized argument, in which she suggests that supporters of privatization claim that public employees actually operate in self-interest rather than in public interest. The assumption, therefore, is that private companies will act in the best interest of consumers, because that will be in their own best interest. But Burch ultimately dismisses this argument, pointing out a number of problems with privatization, not the least of which is lower oversight, lower quality education, and increased inequalities in education. Thus, the belief that private companies could actually operate public schools better than pubic school employees is without merit. In the 10 years since the passage of NCLB, poor-performing schools continued on their trajectory of poor performance. Meanwhile, ubiquitous representations of these same low-performing schools are used as justification to vigorously push forth privatization reforms.

In point of fact, it is rarely asked how policymakers came to the conclusion that *business* modeled programs would solve educational problems. There are a number of very serious public problems in education, which is likely why these programs receive even greater public and political validation when movies such as *Waiting for "Superman"* and school projects like the KIPP Academies or the Harlem Children Zone are publicized. This is not a criticism of any good that comes from such projects, but as scholars such as Richard Rothstein (2004) and Martin Carnoy, Rebecca Jacobsen, Lawrence Mishel, and Richard Rothstein (2005) demonstrate, the successes of such publicly referenced programs are exaggerated, if not misleading. The Harlem Project, for example, has several thousands of dollars of additional aid and forms of support per student, and this is what undoubtedly contributes to the successes of that project. KIPP Academies target and admit students who already come from motivated families that, according to Carnoy et al. (2005), significantly contribute to the successes of students there. The academies have highly selective admission policies and stringent admission requirements. And so the question becomes, if typical public schools in, say, Chicago, Atlanta, Los Angeles, or Newark, do not have the opportunity to serve the same types of parents or receive similar additional supports, or even freedoms to restrict whom they admit, then why are they measured up to schools that do? If it is not possible for the schools to achieve similar outcomes without these additional supports, then rationales for neoliberal approaches to education are brought into serious doubt.

POSITIVE RESULTS, PLEASE?

Despite the heavy pushes, constant redefinitions, and refashioning of neoliberal reforms, they have not produced results. Diane Ravitch (2009) says that since the passage of the most significant neoliberal reform in the recent past, "the number of failing schools grows each year" (p. 4). It is no wonder why Ravitch, once a stalwart supporter and designer of neoliberal programs, has since rebuked such programs and has lobbied for their repeal. Eric Hanushek, John Kalin, Steven Rivkin, and Gregory Branch (2006) found that school quality in Texas's charter schools is not significantly different from that in the local public schools. In fact, when parents in their study decided to leave charter schools, it was precisely because of the quality of the school. These findings are not surprising given that often the persons administering such schools are neither trained educators nor trained school leaders.

Even more broadly, examination of such reforms has few positive results. In a major report funded by the Harvard Civil Rights Project, Jaekyung Lee (2006) raises serious concerns about the intended impact of NCLB, and this appears to hold true of all high-stakes programs. RTT's reinforcement of these programs—by incentivizing instead of challenging them—will likely get similar results. Lee states,

> Past and current NAEP reading and math achievement trends, however, raise serious concerns about the unrealistic performance goal and timeline and the possible consequences for schools that repeatedly fail to meet their performance target. If the nation continues to make the same amount of achievement gains as it did over the past 15 years, it may end up meeting only less than half of the reading proficiency target and less than two-thirds of the math proficiency target by 2014. These projections become much gloomier when it comes to closing the achievement gaps for disadvantaged minority students who are even more left behind in reading and math proficiency. (p. 56)

Policymakers and politicians have not explained why they have chosen to buttress current practices in light of the fact they have not achieved much. In fact, Lee also explains that many of the advances in closing the racial achievement gaps realized in the 1970s and 1980s have not continued into the current NCLB period. It is not clear how RTT will subvert, or even address, these underlying problems that neoliberal legislation seems to pose of academic achievement.

EXPANDING INEQUITY

More than 3 decades ago, Samuel Bowles and Herbert Gintis (1976) argued that though schools are touted as "great equalizers," they actually reproduce societal class structures. Recent research suggests that neoliberal approaches not only reproduce racial and class inequities in education but also exacerbate these disparities. One example is an examination of North Carolina's charter school systems. Robert Bifulco and Helen Ladd (2006) demonstrated that because of increased student racial isolation as a result of charter schools, the Black–White achievement gaps increased. This is true because of the lack of culturally relevant pedagogies in the classroom.

Gloria Ladson-Billings (1995) forwarded a theory of culturally relevant pedagogy, in which she argued that teaching and K–12 educational curricula are essentially designed to address the learning needs of middle-upper-class White students. This has excluded the learning and school environmental needs of students of color and other marginalized student populations. When teaching styles, along with culturally relevant classroom and school cultures, are accommodating for students of color, those students perform much better in school. Perhaps most pertinent for the discussion here, however, is the crafting of a culturally relevant curriculum. If RTT continues to emphasize similar standardized testing measures, and emphasizes a high-stakes environment where schools are rewarded only for their commitment to these hegemonic practices, then it will serve to reproduce these inequities. This is true because teachers will continue to teach specifically to a curriculum that continues to suppress and ignore the cultural learning needs of marginalized student populations. Most schools, which operate under an overwhelming pressure to perform well on high-stakes tests, focus completely on high-stakes measures of achievement and the standardized, top-down curriculum. This leaves little room for educators to teach in ways that are responsive to children's lives. Thus, the needs of African American, Latino, and poor students are often unmet in classrooms, and they consequently fall even further behind their more educationally validated peers.

FINAL CONSIDERATIONS OF RACE TO THE TOP

While we may theoretically agree that social and economic reforms are needed for effective educational reforms, educators—particularly those serving in challenged areas—do not have the luxury of waiting for such reforms to happen. If recent economic policies portend forthcoming behaviors, we accept that economic and social reforms are unlikely to happen anytime soon. Indeed, projects like the Harlem Children Zone bolsters Rothstein's (2004) argument of coupling educational and other, broader reforms. But most public school educators, for example, do not have the luxury of waiting for private foundations to commit to building a $150 million endowment replete with a program offering all-inclusive parental services; nor do they have the option to be highly selective about which students they admit. But politicians can place trust in teachers by giving them classroom autonomy and simultaneously mutually agreeing on results; they can also strive to make education a relevant learning experience for all. We elaborate on these ideals as follows.

Teacher Autonomy/Expected Results

When contextualizing neoliberal approaches to education, it is important to note the overwhelming accomplishments of Americans—the Industrial Revolution, the computer, space exploration, and biomedical engineering, just to name a few—that occurred without high-stakes environments and standardized testing. Teachers were entrusted with the imaginations and intellects of children, and students then discovered who they were, and who they could become, as learners. In the schools the authors have visited across the country, baby-boomer teachers complain that they can no longer do this (i.e., be innovative and creative) with their children; teachers under 35, who have taught *only* in high-stakes environments, haven't any point of reference. Indeed, we recognize that schools need to improve and education needs to be reformed. But after years of implementation, there is no evidence that fashioning our schools in light of our business models, or comparing our children's school performance to those in other countries, will lead to better schools. We argue for an equalization of stakeholder voice, with particular emphasis on elevating parent voice and teacher voice. If teachers are allowed to inform the reform process, and parents are allowed to offer their vision of education—and not merely have parents and teachers comment on politically charged models that are already in process—they are more likely to take ownership of education. Teachers would understand that, yes, they have classroom autonomy, but that after they all agreed on goals, they are responsible. These decisions can be made at a local level, and in this digital age, curricula can be tailored down to the individual teachers in each classroom.

Culturally Relevant Pedagogy

Schooling practices—including but not limited to teaching style, curriculum, and normative school cultures—must respond to the unique needs of the student population. Neoliberal programs prevent this from happening in favor of generic, text-rich approaches to education; these programs have had dismal positive results for people who are not from the dominant hegemonic American culture. But what does show tremendous promise are the educational approaches that use educational artifacts and approaches that have already been familiar to children in their home and neighborhood lives. Let us use the example of the pervasive existences and influences of hip-hop music and culture. From a curriculum point of view, teachers can ask how major concepts can be taught using styles, symbolisms, and characteristics of hip-hop culture. A number of scholars demonstrate how this is possible (e.g., see Hill, 2009). In this example, it is actually not necessary for teachers or principals to enact unauthentic, impersonating hip-hop performances. Students will see the missing authenticity and "real-ness" in such enactments. What principals and teachers *can* do, however, is to create spaces in school, and opportunities in classrooms, for these students to enact their own culture.

PURPOSE OF SCHOOLS?

Finally, when considering RTT, one must ask, what is it all for? And more broadly, what is the purpose of schooling? Is it for the benefit of the student, or society, or perhaps both? If both, can these two stakeholding entities be at odds with one another? If education is to benefit the student first and society second, why are schools built on business models? If education is to benefit society first through improved schooling, and assumptions are made that this can best happen by mimicking business models, then how might politicians explain this in light of recent economic downturns and ominous business outlooks? We argue that the ultimate goal of education should be to produce people who can critically think and contribute to their world—global or local—in a positive way. Even if a student does well on his or her school's standardized test, and their state procures millions in RTT funding, what will this mean to his or her community? How will the student contribute? If the answer is one of bewilderment, then we question the very premise on which RTT and similar programs stand.

FURTHER READINGS AND RESOURCES

Bifulco, R., & Ladd, H. (2006). School choice, racial segregation, and test-score gaps: Evidence from North Carolina's charter school program. *Journal of Policy Analysis and Management, 26*(1), 31–56.

Bolduc, B. (2011, June 16). Union leader dubs Governor "Adolph Christie." *National Review.* Retrieved from http://www.nationalreview.com/corner/269815/union-leader-dubs-governor-adolph-christie-brian-bolduc

Bowles, S., & Gintis, H. (1976). *Schooling in capitalist America: Educational reform and the contradictions of economic life.* New York: Basic Books.

Briscoe, F. (2008). Discipline. In D. Gabbard (Ed.), *Knowledge and power in a global economy* (pp. 199–205). Mahwah, NJ: Erlbaum.

Brown, F. (2004). Nixon's "southern strategy" and forces against *Brown. Journal of Negro Education, 73*(3), 191–208.

Brown, F. (2006). School choice and educational equity under No Child Left Behind in the post-*Brown* era. In F. Brown & R. C. Hunter (Eds.), *Advances in educational administration: Vol. 9. No Child Left Behind and other federal programs for urban school districts* (pp. 37–60). Amsterdam: Elsevier.

Burch, P. (2009). *Hidden markets: The new education privatization.* New York: Routledge.

Carnoy, M., Jacobsen, R., Mishel, L., & Rothstein, R. (2005). *The charter dust up. Examining the evidence on enrollment and achievement.* Washington, DC: The Economic Policy Institute.

Coleman, J. (1966). *Equality of educational opportunity.* Baltimore: Johns Hopkins University Press.

Continue the race. (2010, August 28). *The New York Times.* Retrieved from http://www .nytimes.com/2010/08/29/opinion/29sun2.html

Darling-Hammond, L. (2010). *The flat world and education: How America's commitment to equity will determine our future.* New York: Teachers College Press.

Doyle, D. P., & Cooper, B. S. (1998). *Federal aid to the disadvantaged: What future for Chapter I?* New York: Falmer Press.

Eggers, D., & Calegari, N. C. (2011, May 1). The high cost of low teacher salaries. *The New York Times,* p. WK12.

Foster, D. (2010, August 4). Chris Christie: The scourge of Trenton. *National Review.* Retrieved from http://www.nationalreview.com/articles/243599/chris-christie-scourge-trenton-daniel-foster

Hanushek, E., Kain, J., Rivkin, S., & Branch, G. (2006). Charter school quality and parental decision making with school choice. *Journal of Pubic Economics, 91*(5), 823–848.

Hill, M. C. (2009). *Beats, rhymes, and classroom life: Hip-hop pedagogy and the politics of identity.* New York: Teachers College Press.

Ladson-Billings, G. (1995). Toward a theory of culturally relevant pedagogy. *American Educational Research Journal, 32*(3), 465–491.

Lee, J. (2006). *Tracking achievement gaps and assessing the impact of NCLB on the gaps: An in-depth look into national and state reading and math outcome trends.* Cambridge, MA: Harvard Civil Rights Project. Retrieved from http://www.eric.ed .gov/PDFS/ED491807.pdf

Mathison, S. (2008). Assessment. In D. Gabbard (Ed.), *Knowledge and power in a global economy* (pp. 161–172). Mahwah, NJ: Erlbaum.

Quaid, L. (2009, July 24). Obama offers "Race to the Top" contest for schools. *The Guardian.* Retrieved from http://www.guardian.co.uk/world/feedarticle/8625198? FORM=ZZNR7

Ravitch, D. (2009). Time to kill "No Child Left Behind." *Education Digest, 74*(1), 4–6.

Ross, B. (2009). Can Race to the Top save struggling schools? Retrieved from http://www.education.com/magazine/article/pros-cons-race-to-the-top

Rothstein, R. (2004). *Class and schools: Using social, economic and educational reform to close the Black–White achievement gap.* New York: Teachers College Press.

Saltman, K. (2008). Privatization. In D. Gabbard (Ed.), *Knowledge and power in a global economy* (pp. 269–281). Mahwah, NJ: Erlbaum.

U.S. Department of Education. (2010). *Race to the Top guidance and frequently asked questions.* Retrieved from http://ed.gov/programs/racetothetop/faq.pdf

Virginia's stance against national standards is a blow for students. (2010, June 5). *The Washington Post.* Retrieved from http://www.washingtonpost.com/wp-dyn/content/article/2010/06/04/AR2010060404807.html

Weingarten, R. (2011, April 25). Markets aren't the solution: Top-performing countries revere and respect teachers, they don't demonize them. *The Wall Street Journal,* p. A15.

The White House. (2009, July 24). *Remarks by the president on education.* Retrieved from http://www.whitehouse.gov/the_press_office/Remarks-by-the-President-at-the-Department-of-Education

The White House. (2011, March 28). *FACT SHEET: Winning the future: Out-educating our global competitors by improving educational opportunities and outcomes for Hispanic students.* Retrieved from http://www.whitehouse.gov/the-press-office/2011/03/28/fact-sheet-winning-future-out-educating-our-global-competitors-improving

Zimmer, R., & Buddin, R. (2006). Charter school performance in two large urban districts. *Journal of Urban Economics, 60*(2), 307–326.

COURT CASES AND STATUTES

American Recovery and Reinvestment Act, Pub. L. No. 111–5, 123 Stat. 115 (2009).

No Child Left Behind Act, 20 U.S.C. §§ 6301–7941 (2006).

5

Is aid to schools under Title I the best way to close the achievement gap between students who are economically disadvantaged and those who are not?

POINT: Paul E. Pitre and E. Lincoln James,
Washington State University
COUNTERPOINT: James E. Lyons,
University of North Carolina at Charlotte

OVERVIEW

Title I was established under the Elementary and Secondary Education Act of 1965, designed to close the achievement gap between poor and wealthier students (Doyle & Cooper, 1998). It was reauthorized by and is now part of the No Child Left Behind (NCLB) Act of 2001. Title I–funded compensatory education programs are designed to help disadvantaged students catch up academically with their more economically advantaged peers (Brown, 1976, 1982). This chapter examines the issue of whether Title I has helped close the achievement gap between students who are economically disadvantaged and their wealthier peers.

The original intent of Title I was to close the achievement gap between low-income students and more economically advantaged students by using Title I funds to supplement local funds. Although Congress did not intend for Title I funds to supplant local revenues, in the early years, many school districts did just that rather than augment local funding. Thus, many districts made compensatory education decisions that were inconsistent with the intent of Title I. In 1970, Congress amended Title I to ensure that Title I schools received state funding comparable to the average school in the district.

There is a connection between race and poverty in the United States (Stricker, 2007; Wilson, 2009). Poor minorities would have little hope of becoming well educated and reaching their full potential as adults, without equal funding between schools within each district (Brown, 2006). A national study of Title I effectiveness in 1966, a year after its original enactment, proved to be premature since the program had not been effectively implemented. However, later studies concluded that students in Title I programs performed no better academically than comparable cohorts of equally disadvantaged students—but that Title I programs did no harm. Title I programs create conditions that require local and state level educational agencies to strive toward closing the education gap between poor and more advantaged students. State departments of education are responsible for the management and allocation of Title I funds to local school districts and oversee their use. Most state departments of education tend to allow school districts to manage these funds in good faith.

In spite of its lofty goals, Title I has not achieved all of its objectives. Many Title I students fail to meet state proficiency standards, and there is little evidence that the achievement gap between White students and minority students is closing. As the essays in this chapter show, most school districts targeted for Title I funding still do not provide enough academic assistance and support services to significantly improve students' achievement. Further, not all disadvantaged students are served by Title I because these funds must go to schools with the most disadvantaged students. To complicate matters, Title I schools often have fewer experienced teachers and may be racially segregated. Some Title I schools are successful, but their successes have not always been transferred to other schools.

In this chapter, Paul E. Pitre and E. Lincoln James (Washington State University) argue that federal Title I funds under NCLB can close the achievement gap between disadvantaged and advantaged students. Pitre and James argue that Title I continues to be the best funding mechanism for providing aid to students and communities affected by poverty and contend that without compensatory education programs, racial and ethnic minorities living at or below the poverty line would have little hope of becoming educated and reaching their full potential. Although they acknowledge that there are concerns, they posit that Title I has pointed school systems in the right philosophic direction, which is equitable treatment for all students. These authors feel that a federal watchdog may be needed to guard against a misuse of Title I funds but are convinced that it is helping to close the gap between economically disadvantaged and advantaged students.

James E. Lyons (University of North Carolina at Charlotte), on the other hand, argues that Title I is not a good program to achieve this goal. Lyons contends that Title I has not achieved its objective of providing compensatory education for the economically disadvantaged students necessary to close the academic achievement gap with their economically advantaged peers. He states that little evidence can be found to indicate that the achievement gap between White students and minority students, particularly between both African American and Native American students and White students, is closing; the indication is that these students are not catching up with their White peers.

As you read the essays in this chapter, you may want to consider the questions that follow. Should only Title I students in a particular school participate in Title I activities? Would Title I programs better help close the achievement gap if current funding by the federal government was increased? Would a system that rewards schools for success provide an incentive for improvement?

Frank Brown
University of North Carolina at Chapel Hill

POINT: Paul E. Pitre and E. Lincoln James
Washington State University

T he 20th century was characterized by an intensive struggle for Black civil rights. This community, disenfranchised by law, through *Plessy v. Ferguson* (1896), started attaining civil rights, beginning with the abolition of a dual education system in 1954 through the landmark ruling in *Brown v. Board of Education.* White resistance to integration notwithstanding, nation-wide civil unrest and public consciousness of the ways in which Blacks and the impoverished had been ill-treated in the past, facilitated the passage of the Civil Rights Act in 1964. The Elementary and Secondary Education Act (ESEA) was passed the next year under the Johnson administration and reinforced the march toward equality by providing funding for elementary and secondary education. Johnson's War on Poverty took aim at the social structures that marginalized individuals and groups and prevented them from gaining access to the middle class. Education and ESEA were cornerstones in the war's strategy. ESEA also provided help for professional development, instructional resources, and promotional material for parents. Title I, a key fiscal component of the act, provided funds for specific K–12 programs in high-poverty school districts. The intent of ESEA of 1965 was to close the achievement gap between low-income students and others. Indeed,

> The overall purpose of ESEA was to improve educational opportunities for poor children. This was not meant as a general package of aid to all schools; the allocation formulas directed assistance to the local education agencies (LEAs) with the greatest proportions of poor children. The funds were purposely distributed through state education agencies (SEAs) to avoid the perception that the federal government was intervening in the rights and obligations of states to provide public education and also to use the funds as leverage to upgrade the capabilities of SEAs themselves. (Allison, 1966, p. 786)

For the first several years following the passage of the statute, weaknesses in the Title I language allowed schools to spend newly acquired federal funds mostly on infrastructure, materials, and salaries, and not so much on the needy, as was the intent. So in many school districts, Title I funds were being misused to supplant rather than augment state funds.

Early in the implementation stages of the ESEA policy, the Title I program ran into difficulties in meeting its goals. Many individuals at the "street level" of the policy process made funding decisions that ran contrary to the intent of the policy. To curb this bad habit and sharpen the focus of this important program, the Department of Education specified strict guidelines under which states would receive Title I funding. In 1970, Congress passed the Title I Comparability Law (Section 105 (a)(3)); in essence, schools in low-income districts should receive federal funding for programs and projects that would bring them up to the standards comparable to that of the average school in that district. The basic tenets of the Comparability Law remain almost intact today.

So, is aid to schools under Title I the best way to close the achievement gap between students who are economically disadvantaged and those who are not? The authors of this essay argue that Title I continues to be the best funding mechanism for providing aid to students and communities affected by poverty. In arguing for the necessity of Title I, this essay sets forth with a discussion on poverty and its relationship to the achievement gap in education. The authors provide evidence of the inextricable connection between race and poverty in the United States. Much like the notion of reproduction developed by Pierre Bourdieu and Jean-Claude Passeron (1977) asserting that schools and education reproduce the social inequality, this essay affirms the position of these authors and goes a step further to show that Title I and its school funding mechanisms have provided the scaffolding for equal educational opportunity, and without it, racial and ethnic minorities living at or below the poverty line would have little hope of becoming educated and reaching their potential. As the largest source of federal funding to our nation's public K–12 education system, it is also the educational lifeline for improving academic achievement and equality. If implemented and managed correctly, Title I has the power to level the educational playing field for those children from poverty who are, overwhelmingly, racial and ethnic minorities. Title I continues to be the catalyst for educational opportunity for an underclass that comprises minorities disproportionately. While it is clear that Title I is the answer, it is not the perfect answer, and this essay points to areas of this key policy that need improvement.

POVERTY AND THE ACHIEVEMENT GAP

Black and Hispanic individuals, families, and children living in poverty exceed the national average by far. In 2009, 25.8% of Blacks and 25.3% of Hispanics were poor, compared to 9.4% of non-Hispanic Whites and 12.5% of Asians (U.S. Bureau of the Census, 2010). According to recent U.S. Census data in 2008, some 15.5 million children in the United States are living below the poverty line—these numbers have climbed since the economic downturn beginning in 2008. Children, making up only 25% of the total population, are 35% of the poor population (U.S. Bureau of Census, 2010). Most of these poor children are Black (35.4%) or Hispanic (33.1%).

The importance of funding educational programs for students living in high-poverty areas was highlighted in the Coleman Report (1966). The Coleman Report was one of the first empirical studies to legitimize the existence of an achievement gap between low-income (mainly Black) and other students (mainly White) in the public education system. Not only did the report present evidence of an achievement gap, but it also argued that family rather than school quality accounted for the difference in the achievement of these students. Since that time, it has been suspected that this disparity in achievement is due to socioeconomic status (SES), poor home environment, weak parental involvement, poor teaching, unequal opportunity, cultural differences, and even genetic predispositions.

Indeed, current data show that Blacks, Latinos, and low-income students in general graduate from high school at a lower rate than Whites and perform at a lower level than Whites on all standardized tests, especially in reading and math skill. They are more likely to drop out from school, be assigned to special education classes, or be expelled from school. In sum, a preponderance of the evidence shows that there is a wide disparity in the performance of Blacks, Latinos, and low-income students on all education success measures, which results in low graduation rates (Lee, 2006; Rothert, 2005).

Title I provides aid to these low SES individuals in an effort to help reduce the disparity in educational achievement between the haves and the have-nots. Without such help, poor children would not have a fair opportunity to acquire the important educational skills needed in today's society. We know well that economically deprived children tend to perform poorly in schools because they come from families that are preoccupied with survival and thus do not have the supporting family background where education is a top priority. When they do attend school, economically deprived students tend to live in economically deprived areas with equally deprived schools. Many schools tend to be poorly funded with inadequately trained teachers, and within districts, disparities still exist. Those public schools with superior funding due to demographics of their student populations stand to gain additional educational benefits.

Disparities exist in state and local level funding that goes to high-minority/high-poverty districts. Even within districts, often less money goes to schools that have the highest need due to the low-income high-minority concentration of their student population. Fair and equitable distribution of funds for education still continues to be a problem across school districts in states and even across schools in individual districts.

Large school districts are still working on ways to equitably distribute funds between schools within a single school district. The disparities that exist in our schools based on the unequal distribution of resources across school districts cannot be denied, and the micro-level politics that contribute to resource inequality cannot be ignored. Title I and its focus on disenfranchised populations has gone a long way toward alleviating these conditions and improving the life chances of children by mandating that teachers attain highest levels of competence and making the schools accountable for the performance of students. Thus, by providing grants for remedial teaching and other programs for poor children, and by tying funding to performance, Title I has created conditions that force local and state level educational agencies to strive toward closing the education gap between poor students and others. In our current high-stakes educational environment, Title I serves as a lifeline for those students who attend schools in areas with a high concentration of minority and low-income families. Without it, our educational system would continue to reproduce the status inequalities that already exist in our broader society.

TYPES OF AID PROVIDED BY TITLE I

As mentioned previously, school funding can quickly take on a political tone. Title I attempts to move past the internal politics of state school systems and individual school districts to deliver funds, when possible, to racial and ethnic minority and low SES students. This important piece of legislation authorizes key sources of aid for the purpose of "improving the academic achievement of the disadvantaged."

The NCLB states that the primary focus of Title I is

(2) meeting the educational needs of low-achieving children in our Nation's highest-poverty schools, limited English proficient children, migratory children, children with disabilities, Indian children, neglected or delinquent children, and young children in need of reading assistance;

(3) closing the achievement gap between high- and low-performing children, especially the achievement gaps between minority and nonminority students, and between disadvantaged children and their more advantaged peers. (NCLB, 20 U.S.C. § 6301)

The types of aid provided by Title I can be classified into eight categories. These categories provide a summary yet comprehensive view of critical areas necessary to close the achievement gap. The categories provided below are extrapolated from the 12 provisos authorized in Part A of Title I that ESEA aid helps fund

1. teacher training so that schools hire quality teachers who have passed the state exam and can present evidence of knowledge in their teaching content area;

2. aid to states for conducting annual assessments measured by norm-based criterion tests that evaluate a student's performance against national and state standards;

3. funds for schoolwide or targeted assistance for at-risk low-income individuals (aid may take the form of in- or out-of-class tutoring by state-certified tutors familiar with the content area);

4. aid to hire tutors for individuals with reading difficulties;

5. funds for creating programs for migrant children, children with limited English proficiency, Native American children, and neglected or delinquent children;

6. identifying and eliminating or turning around low-performing schools after they have failed to meet standards in 5 consecutive years, along with moving students from these schools to high-performing schools;

7. allocating funds for enriched and accelerated programs to accommodate providing children an enriched and accelerated educational program; and

8. providing funds for promotions that stimulate parent participation in the education process.

This section gives evidence of the broad, sweeping reach of Title I and the key areas of education to which it lends help and hope. Without Title I, many students, families, and communities would suffer more educational deprivation than they already do. It is clear that Title I has become an integral piece of the U.S. educational system, and its impact is far reaching. Even so, there is a need to sharpen the focus of this policy and its provisions.

AREAS OF IMPROVEMENT FOR TITLE I

Critics of NCLB are legion. Even though they acknowledge the positive intent of the legislation, they single out particular aspects for criticism: aspects such as standardized testing and the sanctions imposed on failing schools. While there is merit to some of their concerns, Title I in general has pointed our system of education in the right philosophic direction, which is equitable treatment for all students and bringing the historically ignored up to levels comparable to state and national standards. There are indeed some continuing issues with funding streams in education. Title I grants are the largest stream of funding for both NCLB and the current Race to the Top. In fiscal year 2010, over $12 billion was dedicated to Title I Grants to Local Educational Agencies, the largest NCLB program (New American Foundation, 2010b). Four types of grants are used to allocate funds to school districts. These are Basic Grants, Concentration Grants, Targeted Assistance Grant, and the Education Finance Incentive Grants—with the poorest schools receiving highest priority. Indeed,

> The Basic Grant formula allocates funding to school districts based on the number of poor children they serve. Any school district with at least 10 poor children and 2 percent of its students in poverty receives funding through the Basic Grant formula, so almost all school districts, even very affluent school districts, get at least some Title I funding through this formula. In fiscal year 2010, $8.6 billion, or 52 percent of all Title I funding, will be distributed through the Basic Grant formula. (New American Foundation, 2010a)

According to the New American Foundation (2010a), school districts must have the lesser of 15% or 6,500 poor student to receive Concentration Grant funds, which are in addition to the Basic Grant funding. Those districts with 14.9% poverty and 6,499 students receive no Concentration Grant money.

> Under both the Basic Grant and Concentration Grant formulas, once school districts pass the threshold percentage of poor children required to receive funding, they receive the same amount of money per poor child regardless of how many poor children they serve. In other words, a school district with 15 percent of children in poverty gets the same amount of money per poor child as a school district with 99 percent of children in poverty—despite considerable evidence that it costs more to educate students in schools with high poverty rates.... [Thus] the number weighting alternative is favorable to large districts, especially low-poverty suburban districts. (New American Foundation, 2010b)

This funding approach is an inherent weakness of Title I funding, which has the potential to do a much more effective job of closing the achievement gap. This aspect of Title I grant aid needs to be revamped since it has the potential to perpetuate that which it was intended to solve. As Bourdieu and Passeron (1977) would say, in this instance, schools would simply be reproducing status inequality. The other two types of grants, Targeted Assistance and Education Finance Initiative, tie allocation to school districts' poverty rates and fiscal responsibility performance measures, respectively. Also, because of state laws on fundraising, very often the only other stream of funding available to public education is property tax levies. School districts do not get the full benefit of property taxes because of the way property taxes are collected and distributed by states. The greater portion of property taxes goes into state general funds, and wealthier communities contribute more to local tax levies, which are not disbursed equitably.

Other issues that need to be addressed to make Title I more effective in closing the achievement gap include closer scrutiny for misuse of funds. There is a clear and present danger that Title I could simply become a slush fund for schools with low SES students in their general population given the recent economic downturn and the funding shortages faced by many schools and school districts. The way schools use Title I monies should be better monitored especially given the fact that those advocating flexibility in funding want freedom to spend on programs not aimed at the neediest students.

A federal watchdog may be in order here, which raises a second issue as to whether or not America's poorest children are receiving their fair share of federal education funds. There is a need for closer scrutiny of misuse. There is also a need to evaluate current inverse structures where good teachers teach at the best schools and the worst teachers teach at the worst schools. Then there is the matter of segregation in housing patterns that mirror inequities in public schooling and corollary funding. As Gary Orfield and Nancy McArdle (2006) have noted, "Housing determines a family's location, and because of that housing is the fulcrum of opportunity, linked to many factors" (p. 3). The fact of the matter is that there is always room for improvement with any project. Title I efforts have gone a long way toward fulfilling the dream of ESEA. It is indeed helping in closing the gap between students who are economically disadvantaged and those who are not. So, with the struggle the United States is in to remain relevant and competitive in the global arena, the question that truly needs to be answered is, without Title I, where would the U.S. system of education be?

COUNTERPOINT: James E. Lyons
University of North Carolina at Charlotte

Title I was radically changed under the No Child Left Behind (NCLB) Act, as it ushered in an unprecedented era of heightened accountability for

America's public schools. The act set in motion the machinery to greatly encourage and assess the academic performance of students in each of the 50 states, the District of Columbia, Puerto Rico, and other U.S. territories. The principal goals of NCLB were to foster stronger accountability for student performance; provide more flexibility to states and communities; encourage proven, research-based educational practices; and provide more options to parents. Specifically, the NCLB's stated fundamental purpose was to close the achievement gap between poor and minority students and their more advantaged peers and assure that no students would be academically left behind. By participating in Title I, states were charged to bring these students up to proficiency levels in language arts, mathematics, and science by the year 2014. Moreover, the act included progressively severe sanctions for schools that repeatedly fail to make adequate yearly progress (AYP) as measured by the academic performance of subgroups of students served. Arguably, the most crucial factor vis-à-vis accountability in NCLB was the requirement that each school provide disaggregated test scores for all racial/ethnic subgroups and the students collectively. This requirement greatly impacts the number of schools that make AYP in the various states.

PROGRESS TOWARD CLOSING THE GAP

The achievement gap between poor disadvantaged students, most of whom are members of minority groups, and their more advantaged peers, most of whom are White, has been a vexing, challenging, and continuing problem for educational policymakers, school leaders, teachers, and educational researchers, particularly during the past 50 years. Perhaps this is why closing the gap is a hallmark goal of NCLB. An examination of the empirical research on this phenomenon leads one to conclude that the results to date are mixed and inconclusive. For the most part, since Title I was enacted, the collective body of research indicates that on a national basis, there was a period in the early 1970s through the 1980s when the gap was narrowing in reading and mathematics, although very slowly. However, from the 1990s to the present, the gap has generally wobbled up and down and experienced periods when there was no change. Paul E. Barton and Richard J. Coley (2010) note that "there are decades since the late 1980's in which there has been no clear trend in the gap, or sustained period of change in the gap, one way or another" (p. 2). Nationally, from 2003 to 2009, fourth-grade reading performance for both lower income and higher income students edged up slightly, but the gap separating these groups did not change (Rowan, Hall, & Haycock, 2010). Unfortunately, as Barton and Coley explicitly note, reasons for achievement gap changes or lack of changes have not been pinned down with solid evidence.

A 2010 report by the Schott Foundation for Public Education provides one of the most illuminating examples depicting the magnitude of the achievement gap dilemma. Titled *Yes We Can: The Schott 50 State Report on Public Education and Black Males 2010*, it presents the high school graduation rates for all 50 states and for all school districts enrolling more than 10,000 Black males for 2007. It reveals that the national average graduation rate for Black males in the United States is a low 47%. Nineteen states had graduations rates of less than 50%. The following states all had Black male graduations rates of less than 40%: New York (25%), Florida (37%), Louisiana (39%), and South Carolina (39%). New Jersey was the only state that had a significant Black male population with a graduation rate greater than 65%. The study concluded that the overwhelming majority of U.S. school districts and states are failing to make targeted investments to provide the core resources necessary to determine what works for Black male students. Given these statistics, it is clearly evident that substantial improvement is needed to assist Black males in getting through high school, not to mention attending college.

One factor that may be thwarting the effort to close the achievement gap is the manner in which students are assigned to schools in the United States. Pervasive evidence exists to show that a disproportionate number of poor, disadvantaged, and minority students often attend urban, mostly segregated, or rural schools. This is frequently the case in large urban districts where there are large concentrations of poor, disadvantaged students. Most frequently, these schools have the most new and inexperienced teachers, and there is usually high teacher and principal turnover. Linda Darling-Hammond (2007) has noted that schools serving large concentrations of minority students feature lower budgets, larger class size, lower quality curriculum, and less-qualified teachers and school leaders in most states across the nation. These factors undoubtedly have a profound impact on the quality of the school environment. There is some evidence that these schools have a tendency to lose their effective teachers due to the job securities that higher achieving schools offer in comparison to low-achieving schools that may be labeled "low performing," increasing the level of pressure and stress on the staff (Jimerson, 2005). In the majority of cases, these are Title I schools that serve mostly low SES students who frequently begin school from a lower starting platform than do more advantaged students and often remain behind them throughout their school experiences. Joshua S. Wyner, John N. Bridgeland, and John J. Diiulio (2007), in their report titled *Achievement Trap: How America Is Failing Millions of High-Achieving Students From Lower-Income Families*, argue that there are millions of students from low-income families who are or can be high-achieving students. They note that there are approximately 3.4 million of these children from low-income households who are capable of ranking in the top quartile academically. They note further that this population of students is larger than the individual population of 21 states. Unfortunately, they contend that these students are very capable, but they start grade school behind their peers, fall back during high school, and complete college and graduate school at lower rates than those from higher income families. Regrettably, they note that many of these students, through no fault of their own, never reach their full potential.

The teachers in the schools these children attend frequently have low expectations for them, do not assign them challenging work, and fail to recognize their potential. Kati Haycock (2001) noted that often teachers assign these students boring, drilling work that causes them to lose interest in school. She noted that Educational Trust staff who observed some of these schools was surprised to see how much coloring teachers required their students to do in middle school rather than giving them challenging assignments in reading and mathematics. Even at the high school level, the staff observed teachers giving students coloring assignments. Low-level expectations for disadvantaged students invariably lead to low academic achievement and certainly will not assist in narrowing the achievement gap.

In spite of the efforts to reduce the achievement gap, it persistently continues to exist. One study noted the following:

> On average, black and Latino students are roughly two to three years of learning behind white students of the same age. This racial gap exists regardless of how it is measured, including both achievement (e.g., test score) and attainment (e.g., graduation rate) measures. Taking the average National Assessment of Educational Progress (NAPE) scores for math and reading across the fourth and eighth grades, for example, 48 percent of blacks and 43 percent of Latinos are "below basic," while only 17 percent of white students are, and this gap exists in every state. A more pronounced racial gap exists in most large urban districts. (McKinsey & Company, 2009, pp. 9–10)

Others have noted that the achievement gap is so pronounced that several national tests found that by the end of high school, African American and Latino students scored at roughly the same levels in reading and mathematics as White eighth graders (Haycock, 2001). Similarly, in an in-depth examination of the achievement gap conducted by the Civil Rights Project at Harvard University, the author concluded that the disparities between Black and White students and Hispanic and White students remained unchanged in both reading and math in both grades 4 and 8, essentially the same 4 years post-NCLB as they were pre-NCLB (Lee, 2006). The author further concluded that few states have been able to narrow the racial and socioeconomic gaps while improving overall achievement levels at the same time, and that that if the nation continues to make the same amount of achievement gains as it did during the last 15 years, it will likely end up meeting only less than half of the reading proficiency target and less than two thirds of the math proficiency target by 2014. She notes that the prospects are even gloomier when it comes to closing the achievement gaps for disadvantaged minority students who are even more left behind in reading and math.

Another major factor deeply incorporated into school practice serves to thwart efforts to reduce the achievement gap. It is what is frequently referred to as *summer effect hypothesis* or *summer setback*, which has been largely ignored by school officials in their attempt to reduce the achievement gap (Borman & D'Agostino, 1996). Summer setback occurs when students return to school after summer vacation with diminished reading skills, principally due to lack of reading during the summer. The research indicates that the reading skill of poor children as a group declines during the summer while the readings skill of children from advantaged families holds steady or increases modestly. It is generally believed that this summer setback has a cumulative detrimental effect on poor children and serves to negate efforts to reduce the achievement gap. Many poor children do not have access to age-appropriate reading materials and the necessary support and assistance at home to engage in stimulating learning activities during the summer. Thus, many of these students return to school in the fall having regressed 3 or 4 months from where they were when school closed for the summer break. Because of tight budgets, few school districts are able to provide free summer school so that these students might continue to develop their reading and math skills during summer breaks. Neither is Title I funding sufficient to provide funding to support summer schools for students served in Title I schools. Hence, the summer experiences of poor disadvantaged students usually depend on parental/guardian, family structure, household, and neighborhood factors.

Perhaps a recent report by the Center on Education Policy (2010), titled *A Call to Action to Raise Achievement for African-American Students*, best summarizes the status of the achievement gap. It presents the following key points:

- Since NCLB was enacted in 2002, African American students as a group have made gains on state tests in both reading and math and have narrowed achievement gaps with White students in most states. Despite this progress, many African American students are not achieving at the high levels needed for future success in college and careers, and achievement gaps remain large.

- The African American subgroup was the lowest-performing racial/ethnic subgroup in 2008 in the majority of grade levels and subjects analyzed (grades 4, 8, and high school in reading and math). In the nine states that together enroll more than half of the nation's African American students, the African American subgroup also had the lowest percentage proficient among racial/ethnic subgroups in reading and math with few exceptions.

- States in which African Americans were the lowest-performing racial/ethnic subgroup in both reading and math at all tested grades in 2008 tended to be those in which relatively high proportions of students attend racially isolated schools (those in which African American students comprise 90% or more of the enrollment).

CONCLUSION

During the last 45 years, hundreds of billions of dollars have been expended through the Title I program to help poor, disadvantaged, and migrant children. Given the nation's enormous investment, the question must be asked, has the Title I program served its intended purpose and achieved its stated goals? While NCLB has very noble goals and is intended to bring all students up to expected proficiency levels in the respective states, the current trajectory of the recent academic performance of poor and minority students suggests that the achievement gap will unlikely be closed in the foreseeable future and that it will be nearly impossible for all students to meet expected proficiency standards by 2014. The goal is laudable, but it is unrealistic and foolhardy to think that it will be accomplished by the target date.

Although the academic achievements of poor, disadvantaged, and minority students have, for the most part, been slowly improving, one is hard pressed to find evidence that the gap is consistently closing when these students' performance is compared with that of more advantaged White students. Principally, this is because, based on NAEP scores, which serve as the best national tool for comparative purposes, the scores of White students have also risen (Barton, 2008). Thus, after operating Title I for 45 years, investing hundreds of billions of dollars and significantly raising accountability expectations mandated under NCLB, little can be said beyond what Geoffrey D. Borman and Jerome V. D'Agostino concluded in 1996: Title I has not fulfilled its original expectation of closing the achievement gap between advantaged students and disadvantaged participants, but "it appears to have contributed to achievement growth" (p. 324).

Title I programs are unlikely to have a consistent positive effect on the education of the students they are intended to serve unless and until policymakers and educational leaders revise some of the existing regulations and practices that govern this federal school improvement initiative. Moreover, given the relative small federal investment in public education (approximately 10%), the major responsibility for improving the plight of poor, disadvantaged, and minority students will continue to rest at the state and local levels. Nevertheless, to remedy this problem, it will require some bold, focused changes at every level, federal, state, and local. To name a few:

- Continuing to try to educate poor, minority, migrant, and homeless children in under-resourced, high-poverty schools staffed by teachers and principals who are the least qualified, competent, and experienced in the district is unlikely to improve their performance.

- Lowering proficiency standards to make AYP on NCLB makes states, districts, and schools look better but will not help students.

- Failing to serve numerous students who need additional academic support through Title I programs or other equivalent programs may greatly reduce their chances for becoming productive, contributing citizens.

- Failing to provide poor and disadvantaged students summer learning experiences greatly reduces their chances for staying on grade level.

- Holding low expectations for poor and minority students and giving them busywork, low-level school assignments will not help them become high achievers.

- Failing to recognize that many poor and minority students can become high achievers with effective teachers and high expectations will stymie their efforts to reach their full potential.

RESPONSE TO POINT ESSAY

The authors of the point essay, Paul E. Pitre and E. Lincoln James, correctly noted that there is still a wide gap between disadvantaged students and their more advantaged peers. Moreover, while they argue that Title I has the potential to level the playing field between these two categories of students, the empirical evidence to date shows that this has not yet occurred. In short, the most reliable evidence to measure the gap, NAEP scores, do not show that the gap is consistently closing over time.

FURTHER READINGS AND RESOURCES

Allison, G. E. (1966). ESEA: Title I at work in Orange County, Florida. *Audiovisual Instruction,* p. 786.

Barton, P. E. (2008). The right way to measure growth. *Educational Leadership, 65*(4), 70–73.

Barton, P. E., & Coley, R. J. (2010). *The Black–White achievement gap: When progress stopped.* Princeton, NJ: Educational Testing Service.

Borman, G. D., & D'Agostino, J. V. (1996). Title I and student achievement: A meta-analysis of federal evaluation results. *Educational Evaluation and Policy Analysis, 18,* 309–326.

Bourdieu, P., & Passeron, J. C. (1977). *Reproduction in education, society and culture.* Beverly Hills, CA: Sage.

Brown, F. (1976). Title I: Is it compensatory or just a partial equalizer? *Emergent Leadership, 1*(1), 10–14.

Brown, F. (1982). Improving schooling through Title I: A model for change. *Education and Urban Society, 15*(1), 125–142.

Brown, F. (2006). Educational equity, globalization and the No Child Left Behind Act. In F. Brown & R. C. Hunter (Eds.), *Advances in educational administration: Vol. 9. No Child Left Behind and other federal programs for urban school districts* (pp. 309–320). Amsterdam: Elsevier.

Center on Education Policy. (2010). *A call to action to raise achievement for African-American students.* Washington, DC: Author.

Darling-Hammond, L. (2007). *The Wallace Foundation's national conference.* New York: The Wallace Foundation.

Doyle, D. P., & Cooper, B. S. (1998). *Federal aid to the disadvantaged: What future for Chapter I?* New York: Falmer Press.

Haycock, K. (2001). Closing the achievement gap. *Educational Leadership, 58*(6), 6–11.

Jencks, C., & Phillips, M. (1998). America's next achievement test: Closing the Black–White test score gap. *The American Prospect, 40,* 44–53. Retrieved from http://www.prospect.org/cs/articles?article=americas_next_achievement_test

Jimerson, L. (2005). Placism in NCLB: How rural children are left behind. *Equity and Excellence in Education, 38*(30), 211–219.

Lee, J. (2006). *Tracking achievement gaps and assessing the impact of NCLB on the gaps: An in-depth look into national and state reading and math outcome trends.* Cambridge, MA: Harvard Civil Rights Project. Retrieved from http://www.eric.ed.gov/PDFS/ED491807.pdf

McKinsey & Company. (2009). *The economic impact of the achievement gap in America's schools.* Retrieved from http://www.mckinsey.com/app_media/images/page_images/offices/socialsector/pdf/achievement_gap_report.pdf

New American Foundation. (2010a). *Federal education budget: Background and Analysis: No Child Left Behind Act—Title I distribution formulas.* Retrieved from http://febp.newamerica.net/background-analysis/no-child-left-behind-act-title-i-distribution-formulas

New American Foundation. (2010b). *Federal education budget: Background and Analysis: No Child Left Behind funding.* Retrieved from http://febp.newamerica.net/background-analysis/no-child-left-behind-funding

Orfield, G., & McArdle, N. (2006). *The vicious cycle: Segregated housing, schools and intergenerational inequality.* Retrieved from Joint Center for Housing Studies Harvard University website: http://www.jchs.harvard.edu/publications/community development/w06-4_orfield.pdf

Rothert, C. (2005). Achievement gaps and No Child Left Behind law highlights problems and spurs effective new efforts. *Youth Law News, 26*(2), 1–3.

Rowan, A. H., Hall, D., & Haycock, K. (2010). *Gauging the gaps: A deeper look at student achievement.* Washington, DC: The Education Trust.

Schott Foundation for Public Education. (2010). *Yes we can: The Schott 50 state report on public education and Black males 2010.* Cambridge, MA: Author.

Stricker, F. (2007). *Why America lost the War on Poverty—and how to win it.* Chapel Hill: University of North Carolina Press.

U.S. Bureau of the Census. (2010). *Income, poverty, and health insurance coverage in the United States: 2009* (Current Population Reports, P60-238, Table B-2, pp. 62–67). Washington, DC: U.S. Government Printing Office.

Wilson, J. W. (2009). *Why the poor stay poor: Being Black and poor in the inner city.* New York: W. W. Norton.

Wyner, J. S., Bridgeland, J. M., & Diiulio, J. J., Jr. (2007). *Achievement trap: How America is failing millions of high-achieving students from lower-income families.* Lansdowne, VA, & Washington, DC: Jack Kent Cooke Foundation & Civic Enterprises.

COURT CASES AND STATUTES

Brown v. Board of Education, 347 U.S. 483, 495 (1954).

Elementary and Secondary Education Act of 1965, 20 U.S.C. § 6301 *et seq.* (1965).

No Child Left Behind Act, 20 U.S.C. §§ 6301–7941 (2006).

Plessy v. Ferguson, 163 U.S. 537 (1896).

6

Is aid to schools under Title I an appropriate strategy for closing the achievement gap between minority and majority students?

POINT: Richard C. Hunter, *University of Illinois at Urbana-Champaign and Bahrain Teachers College, University of Bahrain, Kingdom of Bahrain*
Clare Beckett-McInroy, *Bahrain Teachers College, University of Bahrain, Kingdom of Bahrain*
COUNTERPOINT: James E. Lyons,
University of North Carolina at Charlotte

OVERVIEW

This chapter is the second in this volume to address the federal Title I program. Title I was first established in 1965 under the Elementary and Secondary Education Act (ESEA) to close the academic achievement gap between poor and the economically advantaged students. The name of the statute has changed over the past 50 years and, as amended, is currently known as the No Child Left Behind (NCLB) Act. Title I funds compensatory education programs to help boost the academic achievement of disadvantaged students. Title I services are available to disadvantaged students in private schools, as well as public schools, if such services are requested by private school officials. Services to private schools must be provided by the local public school district that accepts Title I funds (Brown, 1976, 1982, 2006). Title I is the largest funding component of NCLB.

In the American economic system, racial and ethnic minority students are often at the bottom, mainly because minority groups cannot adequately protect themselves in the American political marketplace. Minorities may vote and may influence political decisions, but they cannot, as a group, decide the final state and federal political outcomes. This chapter focuses on poor minority students, many of whom are located in racially segregated schools and neighborhoods. Being poor and minority is not the same as being poor and White in the United States (Stricker, 2007; Wilson, 2009). There are more opportunities to escape poverty for Whites than for racial minorities. It is common knowledge that there is an academic achievement gap between minority students and White students.

States delegate to local school boards the authority to administer schools. But the state still has the responsibility to secure equal schooling for all children regardless of poverty and wealth. Title I encourages schools to employ more highly qualified teachers, but its success has been limited so that minority children often are educated in schools that attract less qualified teachers. After the 1960s, America saw a decline in the quality of college students pursuing education; more students began enrolling in other professional fields. Also, elite colleges and universities closed their education programs, leaving teacher preparation programs to lower ranked institutions. This resulted in an overall decline in test scores for all racial and economic groups after 1980. Due to this decline in teacher quality, reform efforts promoted by the federal government and private foundations over the past 30 years have not yielded success (Brown, 2006; Weingarten, 2011). America has witnessed both a decline in the quality of its teaching force and teacher salaries (Eggers & Calegari, 2011).

NCLB included a greater focus on standardized tests and school accountability. Interventions included pre-kindergarten programs, reductions in class sizes, small schools, curricular reform, alignment of different key stages, and increased teacher expectations. However, it should be noted that NCLB accountability measures are based on each state setting its own standards for students. These standards must be applied to disaggregated subgroups such as Black, Hispanic, low-income, and educationally handicapped students. But the number of such subgroups is left to the discretion of each state and school district. These subgroups were established for schools to meet expectation for each subgroup.

NCLB requires that student test data be collected by all racial subgroups in a school and not just by the average academic achievement for a particular school. For a school to be deemed successful, all subgroups must meet expectations. This expectation serves to determine if any subgroup of students is left behind in terms of achievement. This requires that all groups perform successfully or else a school as a whole does not meet annual expectations. Again, each state is allowed to establish its own academic and content standards.

Richard C. Hunter (University of Illinois at Urbana-Champaign and Bahrain Teachers College, University of Bahrain, Kingdom of Bahrain) and Clare Beckett-McIroy (Bahrain Teachers College, University of Bahrain, Kingdom of Bahrain) in the point essay in this chapter state that Title I is an appropriate strategy for closing the achievement gap between minority and majority students. Hunter and Beckett-McIroy cite results from the National Assessment of Educational Progress that support the argument that the achievement gap has closed in part because of Title I. The data from this assessment shows a narrowing of the academic gaps between minority and White students at the elementary school level but not at the middle and high school levels.

Conversely, in the counterpoint essay, James E. Lyons (University of North Carolina at Charlotte) argues that Title I is not an appropriate strategy for closing the achievement gap between minority and majority students. Lyons buttresses his argument with an extensive review of Title I under NCLB, which requires that student test data be collected by all racial subgroups. Under the NCLB, all schools that enroll any appreciable number of students from a minority subgroup must show that they are performing reasonably well to meet expectations. Lyons concludes that the aggregate studies and research do not show that the NCLB is a catalyst to substantially reduce if not close the achievement gap between minority and White students, and it is unlikely to do so in the foreseeable future.

In reading this chapter, it may be helpful to consider two questions. First, does Title I target the conditions that cause the achievement gap in the first place? Second, if not, what needs to be done to fix the problem?

Frank Brown
University of North Carolina at Chapel Hill

POINT: Richard C. Hunter
University of Illinois at Urbana-Champaign and Bahrain Teachers College, University of Bahrain, Kingdom of Bahrain

Clare Beckett-McInroy
Bahrain Teachers College, University of Bahrain, Kingdom of Bahrain

It is important to answer this very fundamental and basic question: Why does the achievement gap exist? Studies have shown there are many factors that influence student performance in school that are both sociocultural and structural. Maureen Hallinan (2000) suggests that academic achievement is more closely tied to race and socioeconomic status. In contrast, Richard J. Hernstein and Charles Murray (1994) claim that a genetic variation in average levels of intelligence is a major factor. The latter theory is a very unpopular conclusion, and one that has not been universally accepted. Some researchers have found that minorities are disadvantaged, even before they enter the field of education, due to cultural differences. For example, Black parents may not provide early education for their young children because they do not fully understand the benefits of early academic skill development or lack the resources to send their children to preschool. This means that cultural differences cause many Black students to begin their formal schooling with a smaller vocabulary than their White counterparts (Jencks & Phillips, 1998). This resonates with the work of Annette Lareau (1985), who suggests that students who lack middle-class cultural capital and have limited parental involvement are likely to have lower academic achievement than their better-resourced peers. It follows that poverty can be a confounding factor, and differences that are assumed to be from racial or cultural factors may be socioeconomically driven. Therefore, children who are poor (despite their race) come from homes that lack adequate childcare in terms of quality and quantity, adequate nutrition, and medical care. All of these factors contribute to less academically developed public school children. In turn, these children begin school with less knowledge and experience and may enter public schools with an achievement gap, as a result of a lack of experience of objectified cultural capital (Bourdieu, 1984) in the form of books and language acquisition, which create different understandings and expectations in the classroom context (Hart & Risley, 1995).

Moreover, a staggering 13.1% of the entire U.S. population lived below the poverty line in 2004. Additional studies have shown that when parents assist their children with homework, they do much better in school (Suarez-Orozco & Suarez-Orozco, 1995); yet, many minority students lack this support due to the large number of single-parent households and the increase in non-English-speaking parents. Minority students often feel less motivated to achieve educationally because they do not believe it will pay off in the long term with a better job and upward social mobility (Roscigno, Tomaskovic-Devey, & Crowley, 2006). More research shows that good teaching and good leadership in schools can help close the achievement gap (Gordon, Kane, & Staiger, 2006). However, schools in lower income school districts tend to have teachers who are less well qualified, and the schools have fewer educational resources (Roscigno et al., 2006).

FEDERAL PROGRAMS AND THE ACHIEVEMENT GAP

The federal government has attempted to address the historic achievement gap between White, minority, and poor students in public schools through policy legislation or actions of the U.S. Supreme Court. Public school desegregation is one of the most important actions of the federal government that has impacted the achievement gap between White and minority-group students in the public. This essay is not about public school desegregation, and this topic will not be fully discussed here. However, the impact it has had on education of Black and Hispanic students in the United States is too great to not mention it in a discussion of the achievement gap for the minority and poor students (Orfield, Schley, Glass, & Reardon, 1993). The Elementary and Secondary Act of 1965 (ESEA) and its reauthorizations, the subject of this essay, were enacted to specially close the achievement gap between White, poor, and minority student in the public schools of the United States.

ELEMENTARY AND SECONDARY EDUCATION ACT OF 1965

Lyndon B. Johnson, the 36th U.S. president (1965–1968), concentrated on civil rights, poverty, and barring discrimination on the basis of race, color, or national origin in all programs receiving federal aid through the landmark Civil Rights Act of 1964 and the Economic Opportunity Act of 1964. In line with his War on Poverty under his Great Society agenda, President Johnson increased federal aid to education. Existing aid had proven insufficient to meet the growing needs of most disadvantaged students. The U.S. Office of Education produced a major report titled *Compensatory Education for*

Cultural Deprivation (Bloom, 1964), and in the same year, only three states (Massachusetts, California, and New York) offered state aid to local compensatory education programs. Johnson appointed a presidential task force to improve educational opportunities and achievement of students attending schools in areas of both urban slum and rural deprivation, with high rates of unemployment and low per capita income or educational achievement (Jeffrey, 1978). The ESEA followed and amended the previous law of 1950, and its first title, Title I, focused on the needs of the poorest students. It aimed to improve educational opportunities and outcomes for disadvantaged children, refocusing the spotlight on children, not schools. Funds were now spent on textbooks, teachers, and technology in classrooms. Despite federal officials being hesitant to push for evaluations, fearing the act was not working, there was talk of regular evaluations to ensure that federal aid was producing measurable gains in student achievement. Funds reached the schools in 1965–1966, but concerns regarding the most effective way to equalize educational opportunities were evident. Some argued that compensatory education might hinder desegregation and equal educational opportunities where a concentration of poor children (and Black children) maximized eligibility of federal grants. This prompted a study of the dilemmas of compensatory education or racial integration by Johns Hopkins University in 1966. James Coleman concluded that racial integration, as such, is unrelated to student achievement to the extent that the data can show a relationship and that compensatory education was unlikely to improve achievement (Jeffrey, 1978). Title I was implemented in 1965 to enable the achievement gap to be reduced, and the Coleman Report (1966) supported the initiative by suggesting that school factors, as well as home and community factors, have an impact on the academic achievement of students and contribute to the achievement gap. There was interplay between socioeconomic groups (income) and its correlation with educational achievement. The Coleman Report was controversial, which encouraged Harvard University researchers to reanalyze the data—and they reached similar conclusions.

President George W. Bush, the 43rd U.S. president (2001–2009), was responsible for the reauthorization of the ESEA. He renamed it the No Child Left Behind (NCLB) Act of 2001, which for some moved ESEA, Title I into the 21st century along with bilingual education grants for innovation and other programs. NCLB focused on standards, aligned tests, school accountability, and the goal that all students should have the same educational opportunities. Other interventions were also implemented in various schools, districts, and states including pre-kindergarten programs, reductions in class sizes, small schools, curricular reform, alignment of different key stages, increased expectations, and improvements in teacher education programs. A "big picture" was established, and it encompassed all students' performance in reading, mathematics, and science at the proficient level by 2014; adequate yearly progress (AYP) benchmarks were established and were applied to several disaggregated groups, including Black, Hispanic, low-income, and educationally handicapped students. Severe consequences were established for schools that did not make AYP for each of the student groups for 3, 4, and 5 consecutive years. The use of scientifically based educational research to find solutions to underachievement was advocated through the Education Sciences Reform Act of 2002. Testing was a way to prove that fiscal funds were working effectively and were improving educational equity for students, even those from disadvantaged backgrounds. Even though assessments varied from state to state, they added value and could be used by the federal government to measure if the program was effective or not.

HAS THE ACHIEVEMENT GAP CLOSED?

This section provides two examples of statistical data and analysis to support the argument that the achievement gap has closed in part because of ESEA, Title I. As can be seen below from the National Assessment of Educational Progress (NAEP) data, while there has been some significant narrowing of the gaps, especially at the elementary school level, gaps in middle and high school remain wide. To solve this, NCLB requires all students of all groups to perform at grade level on all tests, and they must demonstrate continual improvement from year to year. However, schools with the highest number of poor and minorities generally face the greatest challenges to meet these goals.

Raw data of average reading scores in 1971 and 2008 are listed in Table 6.1.

Table 6.1

A comparison of brick-and-mortar school and virtual school cost items

Year	Age	Average Reading Score		
		Black	White	Score Gap
1971	9 years	170	214	44
2008	9 years	204	228	24
1971	13 years	222	261	39
2008	13 years	247	268	21
1971	17 years	239	291	52
2008	17 years	266	295	29

Source: Data from U.S. Department of Education, National Center for Educational Statistics, National Assessment of Educational Progress (2009, pp. 14–15).

As can be seen, Black and White students of all ages achieved higher reading scores in 2008 than in previous years. In 1971, 9-year-old White students
had an average score of 214, and Black students in the same age group
attained 170. In 2008, the average score for 9-year-olds was 228 for White
students and 204 for Black students. The achievement gap between Black and
White 9-year-old students narrowed from 44 in 1971 to 24 in 2008. For
13-year-old students, the achievement gap narrowed from 39 to 21 over the
same period; for 17-year-olds, it narrowed from 52 to 29. Assessment of the
data indicates that most of this reduction in the achievement gap occurred
during the 1970s and 1980s. Since the 1990s, the gap between Black and White
students has remained fairly steady, but reading scores of Black students continue to improve. The NAEP report shows a comparable achievement gap
between Black and White students in the area of mathematics. In addition,
there is a similar but smaller gap between White and Hispanic students in
reading and mathematics. Despite efforts to improve the education system for
all, minority students fall behind White students.

WHITE–HISPANIC ACHIEVEMENT GAP

When academic performance among African American, Hispanic, and White
students on standardized assessments are compared, reading scores for
17-year-olds narrowed significantly for both African American and Hispanic
students from 1975 to 1988. From 1990 to 1999, these gaps either remained
constant or grew slightly in both reading and mathematics. NAEP data show
that by the time minority students reach grade 12, they are about 4 years
behind other students. There are also gaps between the highest levels of educational attainment for various groups at all levels. Hispanic and African
American high school students are more likely to drop out of high school in
every state. Of these high school graduates, college matriculation rates for
African American and Hispanic high school students remain below those of
White high school graduates, although they have risen in recent years.
Furthermore, Hispanic and Black young adults are only half as likely to earn a
college degree as White students. However, a 2004 American Community
Survey found that 83.9% of the U.S. population aged 25 years and over graduated from high school, which means that they have at least 12 years of educa-
tion (U.S. Census Bureau, 2011).

CONCLUSION

It is clear that to close the achievement gap, those students who are the furthest
behind need increased opportunities to learn to enable them to catch up. Aid

to schools under ESEA, Title I of NCLB has closed the achievement gap in part between minority and majority students because it has provided challenges to previously high-performing schools where they have not met AYP and have been labeled low performing. They may have previously been "coasting" and failing to address the learning needs of the students in various groups. Establishing high performance benchmarks encourages schools to be accountable and, with disaggregated scores, provide equal opportunities for all students. The benefits of allowing more flexible use of ESEA, Title I funds lead to a positive future and help to ensure administrators use the funds effectively and as intended. Promoting and ensuring scientifically based research for school programs is an excellent requirement to end a culture of using educational fads and intuition to determine strategies for school improvement. In effect, money and time should no longer be wasted, as they have been in the past, on implementing unproven programs (Schmoker, 1999). The authors acknowledge a need for early intervention in addition to what is happening in schools. Quality state-supported full-day preschool and kindergarten provisions can provide effective intervention and enriched student language development. This should be linked to the implementation of policies to assess early reading and math and to provide an intervention programs to bring them up to expectations. Increased focus on data for teachers, principals, and superintendents, bearing in mind that most states had existing requirements for school districts prior to NCLB, as well as transparent district report cards, has caused administrators to target strategies for improvement. ESEA, Title I has provided more resources to support school improvement, and federal funds have increased. NCLB allows parents to be more aware of their child's progress, and it also makes the school's progress report available to families and communities, therefore ensuring more accountability. Parents are entitled to transport their children to a better school and supplementary education if their child's school does not meet its benchmarks for 2 consecutive years and/or if the school is persistently dangerous. The same applies for annual testing, which enables principals and teachers to evaluate and restructure their curriculum to make it accessible to every child's needs, as schools have been allowed to be more creative in how they spend their funds in line with best practices. Furthermore, schools are receiving more funds than ever before, although this may still not be enough. Highly qualified teachers should teach children; however, demographics influence teachers' choice for employment.

REBUTTAL

Aid to schools under Title I is an appropriate strategy for closing the achievement gap between minority and majority students. As James E. Lyons, the author of the counterpoint essay on this topic, has indicated, Black and other low-income students have made progress during the implementation of Title I and have done so even during the latter years, since *A Nation at Risk* (National Commission on Excellence in Education, 1983). This demonstrates that Title I has been an effective program, one that has efficacy for improving selected student achievement and for closing the achievement gap. Lyons also indicated the greatest progress for Black and other minority student achievement took place during the active school desegregation years in the 1970s and 1980s. During this period, two effective programs were operating: public school desegregation and Title I. It is unfortunate that the Reagan and Bush administrations have guttered school desegregation. We can only speculate what the achievement gap would be today if both of these programs had been implemented effectively. Clearly, less student achievement progress has been made for Black and other low-income students without the effort that was being invested by the nation on school desegregation during the 1970s and 1980s. Consider the possibility that the achievement gap between White, Black, and other student groups would now be closed had we, as a nation, continued these two effective educational strategies. Failure to continue with school desegregation does not mean that Title I is not an effective strategy to close the achievement gap for Black and other low-income students; it has simply made the job more difficult.

COUNTERPOINT: James E. Lyons
University of North Carolina at Charlotte

When Title I was reauthorized and substantially refocused by then U.S. President George W. Bush and the U.S. Congress as the No Child Left Behind (NCLB) Act, it was made explicit that an essential purpose of the act was to improve the performance of minority students. In fact, President Bush noted that NCLB was designed to end the "soft bigotry" of low expectations frequently held for minority students. To assure that state and local school officials would be held accountable for the performance of minority students, one of the critical indicators of student performance included in NCLB was the yearly achievement of all subgroups of students enrolled in a school. Specifically, this was to end the practice whereby schools and school districts could mask the poor performance of subgroups of students, particularly minority students, in a school if its overall test results were generally good. Under this system, if a sufficient number of students scored well enough on standardized tests to produce overall grade level or school scores deemed to meet expectations, the general performance of the school was deemed to be good or better. To successfully meet the adequate yearly progress (AYP) expectations of NCLB, all schools that enroll any appreciable number of students from a minority subgroup must show that they are performing reasonable well.

A report issued in August 2010 by the Center on Education Policy provides a broad summary of the schools that did not make AYP in the various states. It notes that about one third of the schools in the United States did not make AYP in 2008–2009. In nine states and the District of Columbia, at least half of the public schools did not make AYP. In a majority of the states (34 including Washington, D.C.), at least one fourth of the schools did not make AYP. The percentage of public schools not making AYP varied greatly by state, from 5% in Texas to 77% in Florida.

Another report issued by the U.S. Department of Education (2009) clearly shows that there are great variations between states in terms of measuring student performance. *Title I Implementation—Update on Recent Evaluation Findings* shows the comparison between proficiency levels achieved between student performance on state and National Assessment of Educational Progress (NAEP). Since the NAEP test is the same for all samples of students tested across the country, it is a better tool for comparing students in the various states. This report vividly shows that student performance on state exams is inconsistent with their performance on NAEP assessments, demonstrating the variation in state standards.

THE MINORITY–WHITE STUDENT ACHIEVEMENT GAP

Anna Habash Rowan, Daria Hall, and Kati Haycock (2010) contend that the most common way of measuring the achievement gap is by simple subtraction: The performance of White students minus the performance of African American students equals the African American–White achievement gap. If the resulting number is decreasing over time, the gap is closing; if that number is stagnate or growing, then the gap is not closing. They further note that how the gap is closing is important, as it is crucial to examine if both African American and White students are improving. For it is possible to close the gap if African American students are improving and White students are remaining stagnate. Alternatively, it is also possible for the gap to narrow if scores for both African

American and White students decline, if scores for the higher score group decline more than that of the lower group.

Numerous studies and reports have been done during the last several decades on the African American–White achievement gap as well as the minority–White achievement gap. In addition to examining African American–White achievement gaps, the latter studies often examine the Latino–White gaps, Native American–White gaps, and, to a lesser extent, Asian–White gaps. Of these various comparison studies, however, the African American–White achievement gap has received the most attention. Perhaps this is because in the public schools across the United States since the 1950s and the U.S. Supreme Court's *Brown v. Board of Education* decision in 1954, African Americans have been the dominate minority group most broadly represented in the public schools across the country. While Latinos have been enrolled in America's public schools a very long time, they have been principally concentrated in school districts in a relative small number of states, including California, Arizona, Florida, New York, and Texas (Kober, Chudowsky, Chudowsky, & Dietz, 2010). During the last several decades, however, the percentage of Latino students has been rapidly increasing in many other states. Thus, increasingly, comparisons are now frequently made between the performance of Latino students in comparison to Whites and between Latino students and other minority groups.

When studies and reports done during the last decade of the African American–White achievement gap are examined in the aggregate, the results are mixed, uneven, and, frequently, contradictory. The authors of one of the most comprehensive studies of state test score trends through 2008–2009, titled *Slow and Uneven Progress in Narrowing Gaps* and sponsored by the Center on Education Policy, concluded that achievement gaps are still large and persistent (Kober et al., 2010). They reported that in many states, the percentage of African American students scoring proficient on state tests was 20 to 30 points lower in 2009 than the percentage proficient for White students, and the gap ranged from a high of 50 points in one state to a low of 8 points in another state. The gaps between Native American and White students were similarly wide like the gap with African American students, and the gaps between Latino and White students often amounted to 15 to 20 percentage points.

In a similar report, published by the Educational Testing Service, Paul E. Barton and Richard J. Coley (2010) tracked NAEP scores from 1973 to 2008 to determine the direction of the achievement gap between Black and White students. They found that much of the progress in closing the achievement gap occurred during the 1970s and 1980s. However, from 2004 to 2008, there was little change in the gap in math, and only modest progress in closing the gap in reading for 9- and 13-year-old students. Ironically, the latter period was during the time that NCLB would have been operational for 7 years. Thus, in comparison with the 1970s and 1980s, progress in closing the gap essentially stopped during the decade of the 2000s. Barton and Coley concluded that the achievement gap has alternated between small declines and small gains, interspersed with periods of no change.

In the main, little evidence can be found that shows that the achievement gap between White students and minority students, particularly between both African American and Native American students and White students, is persistently closing, which would indicate that these students are catching up with their White peers. Although some studies show that the performance of African American students is improving, there is scant trend-line evidence that the gap with White students is closing to a substantive level. Based on the trajectories by which the gap is moving, there is very little possibility that the gap between minority and White students will close by 2014, which is a hallmark goal of NCLB.

AN UNCERTAIN FUTURE

As one ponders the uncertain future of NCLB, the question must be asked, Under its current policies, goals, and regulations, will the current iteration of Title I, which is NCLB, reduce the achievement gap between minority students and their White peers? Based on the current funding, funding formulas, existing guidelines, current regulations, and operating procedures, it is unlikely that this Title I program, which is the federal government's largest compensatory educational initiative, will achieve its target goal by 2014. There are some impediments to NCLB that, unless addressed, will very likely derail this laudable goal. These issues are addressed in the following section.

IMPEDIMENTS TO THE SUCCESS OF TITLE I

Specifically, Title I was intended to serve as a vehicle for increasing educational opportunities for disadvantaged, poor, and minority students, particularly African American students and more recently Latino students. Although there was a period during the 1970s and 1980s when there was slow progress, during the last 2 decades there has not been any consistent trend in closing the gap. Thus, one is led to conclude that Title I alone is unlikely to be the panacea that will close the achievement gap between minority and White students. Research on the achievement gap suggests that the following are some factors that may be serving to inhibit the effectiveness of Title I.

Inadequate Funding

Given the paucity of federal funding that is allocated to public elementary and secondary education in America, the amount of money is too small to have a substantive effect on schools and students. Since the average public school district in the United States only receives about 7% of its funding from the federal government, the amount of funding is insufficient to have a profound impact. In developing NCLB, Congress gave the federal government substantial authority over public education and increased expectations, including imposing increasingly severe sanctions on schools and school districts that fail to have all subgroups of students make the expected AYP. With the small amount of Title I funding that districts receive to serve the students or schools targeted by the funding, the majority of districts do not have adequate Title I funding to provide the academic assistance and support needed to dramatically improve student achievement. In short, the amount of funding is not equivalent to the expected academic results that local school districts are expected to produce. Arguably, better funding might produce better results in terms of student performance and success in closing the achievement gap. This would allow school officials to employ the staff to provide targeted students more small-group and individualized instruction, tutorial assistance, support services, and so on.

Deserving Students Not Served

Based on options that school districts have for selecting the schools that will be eligible to receive Title I funding, most districts have disadvantaged/poor students assigned to schools that are not designated as Title I schools; in these cases, these students generally are not served through Title I. This is because Title I has a complicated funding system that requires that local school districts select the schools that will be designated as Title I schools and receive Title I funding. In short, it requires that districts rank all their schools at a grade band level that serve a poverty percentage of students greater than 75%. Once all schools at that grade band level with a poverty percentage above 75% have been designated as Title I schools, the district may then identify and serve those with a poverty percentage below 75% by either continuing with the districtwide ranking or grade band grouping (i.e., K–5, 6–8, 9–12). Under this procedure, most districts use up their Title I allocation before they get to all schools with a substantial number of low-income students. Since schools just below the cutoff are similar to those just above the cutoff, this means that students in some schools are served by Title I while other very similar students are not served because their schools are not designated as Title I schools (Weinstein, Stiefel, Schwartz, & Chalico, 2009). As a consequence of this, many students who could benefit from Title I are not served because they do not attend a school that has been designated as a Title I school.

Increasing Percentage of Poor Students

There is concrete evidence that shows that the percentages of students who are poor are increasing in the public schools across the United States. According to a 2010 report by the Southern Education Foundation titled *The Worst of Times: Children in Poverty in the South and Nation*, the number of children who are poor has increased substantially both in the South and across the nation during the last decade (Suitts, 2010). It notes that the number of children who are now categorically classified as poor constitutes 45% of the children enrolled in the public schools, nearly half of all students. This poverty rate, which is based on the number of students who are eligible for free and reduced lunch based on family income, shows that more than 5.7 million children were living in extreme poverty in 2008. While these children who are classified as poor are represented in every state, the report notes that they are heavily concentrated in 15 states of the American South. It further notes that this rising child poverty rate stems from the fact that the U.S. economy has been in great distress, and many poor and formerly middle-class families are now hurting. This means that, more and more, school districts find that they must serve and address the needs of growing numbers of poor students, 66% of whom are minority (Suitts, 2010). Thus, from the perspective of NCLB, school districts are trying to close the achievement gap for students who are increasingly becoming more poor and disadvantaged.

Weak and Inexperienced Teachers

Studies that have compared the quality of teachers in schools that enroll a majority of poor students and schools that enroll small percentages of poor students clearly show that the best and most qualified teachers are not evenly distributed across all kinds of schools and students (Haycock & Crawford, 2008). In particular, the research shows that the students who attend schools where the poverty rate is highest are taught by the least qualified and experienced teachers. In contrast, the research shows that students who attend schools where the poverty rates are lowest are taught by the most qualified and experienced teachers. Frequently, the research indicates that these weak and inexperienced teachers fail to bring students up to mastery level before moving on to the next lessons. Since a large percentage of these high-poverty schools enroll primarily African American and Latino students, it is clearly evident that the vast majority of poor, disadvantaged, and minority students are not being taught by the most qualified and experienced teachers. Given the magnitude of this unequal distribution of teachers, it is little wonder that little significant progress is being made in closing the achievement gap. Since there is compelling research that shows that teacher quality has an enormous affect on student learning, this unequal distribution of teachers is likely serving to negatively affect the primary purpose of Title I.

Segregated Schools

Another factor that is likely thwarting the effort to close the achievement gap is the manner in which students are assigned to schools in the United States. Pervasive evidence exists to show that a disproportionate number of poor, disadvantaged, and minority students often attend urban, mostly segregated and rural schools. This is frequently the case in large urban districts where there are large concentrations of poor, disadvantaged students. As the Southern Education Foundation has noted, African American and Hispanic students make up 78% of the total enrollment of the 100 school districts in the United States with the highest levels of extremely poor children (Suitts, 2010). Most frequently, these schools have the most new and inexperienced teachers, and there is usually high teacher and principal turnover. As Gary Orfield and Chungmei Lee (2004) and others have noted, America's schools today are increasingly becoming more segregated rather than integrated. By concentrating poor minority students in these schools, in which teacher and principal turnover is disproportionately high, school districts may be establishing the conditions for school failure and, in the process, negating the impact that Title I might have in reducing the achievement gap.

Instructional Capacity of Schools

If the achievement gap is to be substantially and consistently improved, those schools that serve large percentages of minority and poor children will have to develop the instructional capacity to help them learn. Based on the data currently available, there is little evidence that the necessary instructional capacity is broadly represented in schools that primarily serve these students. While there are a number of schools that enroll mostly poor and minority students that are making good progress as measured by standardized achievement tests, these schools are often the exception rather than the rule. In fact, they are often seen as anomalies, outliers that are making good strides in spite of the odds, and perceived as oddities (see, e.g., Morris, 2004). Frequently, researchers attribute the success of these schools to the dynamic and often inspirational leadership of the principal who has been able to elicit the collective efforts of the staff to develop and implement effective teaching practices that foster student learning in the school. However, these effective practices do not appear to be readily transferable to other schools—even within a district. Often, when this principal is transferred, promoted, or resigns, the school regresses back to its previous performance level vis-à-vis student achievement. These schools can best be described as idiosyncrasies, and these principals may best be described as idiosyncratic leaders, possessing individualistic qualities that are difficult to define and identify. Hence, district officials often find themselves, through trial and error, trying to find these "turnaround" principals to place in low-performing schools.

CONCLUSION

When Title I was reauthorized by NCLB, it was lauded as a vehicle that would serve to close the gap between minority and White students in America's schools. Specifically, it was envisioned that NCLB would serve as a catalyst to substantially reduce, if not close, the achievement gap between minority and White students. As of 2011, the aggregate studies and research do not show that this is likely to occur by 2014 or in the foreseeable future beyond it. While there is evidence that shows that minority students, especially those who are Black and Latino, have generally been making progress as measured by their performance on standardized state tests, other evidence shows that little progress is being made on closing the achievement gap. The latter evidence is based on student performance on NAEP tests, which are a more reliable and valid comparison of student performance on a nationwide basis. Therefore, at this time, there is not conclusive and compelling evidence to show that Title I is substantially closing the achievement gap between minority and White students in America's schools.

REBUTTAL

Richard C. Hunter and Clare Beckett-McInroy, the authors of the point essay, argue that if school integration had pervasively occurred, the achievement gap would have narrowed. Even in schools that are integrated, the evidence shows that gaps continue to exist between White and minority students. No comprehensive studies could be found by this author that showed the achievement gap consistently narrows in schools that are integrated. Further, the authors correctly note that the gap remains wide in middle and high schools.

FURTHER READINGS AND RESOURCES

Barton, P. E., & Coley, R. J. (2010). *The Black–White achievement gap.* Princeton, NJ: Educational Testing Service.

Bloom, B. (1964). *Compensatory education for cultural deprivation.* Educational Resources Information Center. Retrieved from http://www.eric.ed.gov/ERICWebPortal/record Detail?accno=ED001717

Bourdieu, P. (1984). *Distinction: A social critique of the judgment of taste.* London: Routledge and Kegan Paul.

Brown, F. (1976). Title I: Is it compensatory or just a partial equalizer. *Emergent Leadership, 1*(1), 10–14.

Brown, F. (1982). Improving schooling through Title I: A model for change. *Education and Urban Society, 15*(1), 125–142.

Brown, F. (2006). Educational equity, globalization and the No Child Left Behind Act. In F. Brown & R. C. Hunter (Eds.), *Advances in educational administration: Vol. 9. No Child Left Behind and other federal programs for urban school districts* (pp. 309–320). Amsterdam: Elsevier.

Center on Education Policy. (2010, August). *How many schools did not make AYP under the No Child Left Behind Act?* Washington, DC: Author.

Coleman, J. (1966). *Equality of educational opportunity.* Baltimore: Johns Hopkins University.

Eggers, D., & Calegari, N. C. (2011, May 1). The high cost of low teacher salaries. *The New York Times,* p. WK12.

Gordon, R., Kane, T. J., & Staiger, D. O. (2006). *Identifying effective teachers using performance on the job.* White Paper 2006-01. Washington, DC: Brookings Institution, Hamilton Project.

Gorey, K. M. (2009). Comprehensive school reform: Meta-analytic evidence of Black–White achievement gap narrowing. *Education Policy Analysis Archives, 17*(25), 1–15.

Hallinan, M. (2000). Tracking: From theory to practice. In R. Arum, I. Beattie, & K. Ford (Eds.), *The structure of schooling: Readings in the sociology of education* (2nd ed., pp. 188–192). Mountain View, CA: Mayfield. (Reprinted from *Sociology of Education, 67*(2), 79–91, 1994)

Hart, B., & Risley, T. (1995). *Meaningful differences in the everyday experiences of young children.* Baltimore: Paul H. Brookes.

Haycock, K., & Crawford, C. (2008, April). Closing the teacher quality gap. *Educational Leadership, 65*(7), 14–19.

Hernstein, R. J., & Murray, C. (1994). *The bell curve: Intelligence and class structure in American life.* New York: The Free Press.

Jeffrey, R. (1978). *Education for children of the poor: A study of the origins and implementation of the Elementary and Secondary Education Act of 1965.* Columbus: Ohio State Press.

Jencks, C., & Phillips, M. (1998). America's next achievement test: Closing the Black–White test score gap. *The American Prospect.* Retrieved from http://www.prospect .org/print/V9/40/jencks-c.html

Kober, N., Chudowsky, N., Chudowsky, V., & Dietz, S. (2010). *Improving achievement for the growing Latino population is critical to the nation's future.* Washington, DC: Center on Education Policy.

Lareau, A. (1985). *Social class and family–school relationships in two communities.* Paper presented at the American Educational Research Association, Chicago, IL.

Morris, J. E. (2004). Can any good come out of Nazareth? Race, class, and African-American schooling and community in the urban South and Midwest. *American Education Research Journal, 41*(1), 69–112.

National Commission on Excellence in Education. (1983). *A nation at risk: The imperative for educational reform.* Washington, DC: Author.

Orfield, G., & Lee, C. (2004). *Brown at 50: King's dream or Plessy's nightmare?* Boston: The Civil Rights Project at Harvard University.

Orfield, G., Schley, S., Glass, D., & Reardon, S. (1993). *The growth of segregation in American schools: Changing patterns of separation and poverty, since 1968.* Alexandria, VA: National School Board Association.

Roscigno, V., Tomaskovic-Devey, D., & Crowley, M. (2006). Education and the inequalities of place. *Social Forces, 84*(4), 2121–2145.

Rowan, A. H., Hall, D., & Haycock, K. (2010). *Gauging the gap: A deeper look at student achievement.* Washington, DC: The Education Trust.

Schmoker, M. (1999). *Results: The key to continuous school improvement.* Alexandria, VA: Association for Supervision and Curriculum Development.

Stricker, F. (2007). *Why America lost the War on Poverty—and how to win it.* Chapel Hill: University of North Carolina Press.

Suarez-Orozco, C., & Suarez-Orozco, M. (1995). *Immigration, family life, and achievement motivation among Latino adolescents.* Stanford, CA: Stanford University Press.

Suitts, S. (2010). *The worst of times: Children in poverty in the South and nation.* Atlanta, GA: The Southern Education Foundation.

U.S. Census Bureau. (2011). *American community survey.* Retrieved from http://www .census.gov/acs/www

U.S. Department of Education. (2010). *Race to the Top fund.* Retrieved from http:// www2.ed.gov/programs/racetothetop/index.html

U.S. Department of Education, National Center for Educational Statistics, National Assessment of Educational Progress. (2009). *The nation's report card: Trends in academic progress in reading and mathematics 2008.* Retrieved from http://nces.ed.gov/ nationsreportcard/pdf/main2008/2009479.pdf

U.S. Department of Education, Office of Planning, Evaluation, and Policy Development, Policy and Program Studies Service. (2009). *Title I implementation—Update on recent evaluation findings.* Washington, DC: Author.

Weingarten, R. (2011, April 25). Markets aren't the solution: Top-performing countries revere and respect teachers, they don't demonize them. *The Wall Street Journal,* p. A15.

Weinstein, M. G., Stiefel, L., Schwartz, A. E., & Chalico, L. (2009). *Does Title I increase spending and improve performance?* New York: Institute for Education and Social Policy, New York University.

Wilson, J. W. (2009). *Why the poor stay poor: Being Black and poor in the inner city.* New York: W. W. Norton.

COURT CASES AND STATUTES

Brown v. Board of Education, 347 U.S. 483 (1954).

Civil Rights Act of 1964, Pub. L. No. 88–352, 78 Stat. 241, codified in 42 U.S.C. § *et seq.* (2006).

Economic Opportunity Act of 1964, Pub. L. No. 88–452, 42 U.S.C. § 2701.

Education Sciences Reform Act of 2002, Pub. L. No. 107–279, 20 U.S.C. § 9516 *et seq.*

Elementary and Secondary Education Act of 1965 (ESEA), 20 U.S.C. § 6301 *et seq.* (1965).

No Child Left Behind Act (NCLB), 20 U.S.C. §§ 6301–7916 (2006).

Given school dropout rates, especially among poor and minority students, should college attendance be the norm for all U.S. students?

POINT: Saran Donahoo, *Southern Illinois University Carbondale*
COUNTERPOINT: Valerie Hill-Jackson, Brandon Fox, and Rachel Jackson, *Texas A&M University*
Marlon C. James, *Loyola University Chicago*

OVERVIEW

Given the very high dropout rate for public high school students in the United States, should college attendance be the norm for all U.S. students? First, how many students have dropped out of high school in the United States? According to a report by the U.S. Department of Education's National Center for Educational Statistics (NCES, 2010b), 4.2% of high school students dropped out during the 2007–2008 school year, and approximately 25% of high school students do not graduate on time. There is a disproportionate number of African American and Hispanic young people who are part of these statistics. Moreover, there are serious consequences for dropping out of high school.

First, it is much more difficult for dropouts to find employment, especially since the military does not want to accept people who have not completed high school. This is because the military has advanced considerably and now uses complicated technologies that require more educated citizens than in the past. Further, young people who do not graduate from high school have a higher rate of prison incarceration, as opposed to those who graduated. They also are often the first to be laid off in an economic downturn and earn less money in their lifetimes than high school graduates.

According to the U.S. Constitution, public education is not a primary responsibility of the federal government but is the province of state government. This means there are 50 different educational policy agendas for the country, or we could say 51, when the federal government's agenda is considered. The federal government is a major player in public education and has become so by annually providing billions of dollars, by legislating educational policy, and through actions of the executive and judicial branches of government.

Nevertheless, it is clear that state governments have created local public school districts and promulgated legislation, which has established compulsory attendance laws for school-age citizens. Universal high school for the nation's public school students was a laudable goal, and the focus on requiring school-age Americans to attend high schools has been successful. Moreover, the goal of making high school education available to all citizens has been satisfactorily implemented, as most students of different racial and ethnic groups are now attending high school. This has been achieved by states requiring students to attend public schools until they reach the age of 16, while several states require students to attend schools until they are 17, and eight states require attendance until age 18.

What has happened with overall educational attainment in the United States? Well, it increased during the 1950s, 1960s, and 1970s for adults age 25 to 29, from 50% in the 1950s to 90% today. Also, 85% of the country's adult population have completed high school, and 27% of them have earned a university bachelor's degree. Also, the United States has a reading literacy rate at 99% for people age 15, but is ranked below the average for developed countries in science and mathematics. Additional data tell us that in 2005, the vast majority of the population (85.2%) finished high school, and nearly a quarter (22%) completed a bachelor's degree. And the percentage of college and high school graduates has continued to increase since 2000. The number of women who have completed secondary and postsecondary education have exceeded the number of men. In 2005–2006, the percentage of women earning associate degrees was 62%, while 58% earned bachelor's degrees, 60% earned master's degrees, and 48.9% earned doctorates. It is projected that women will earn 64.2% of associate's degrees, 59.9% of bachelor's degrees, 62.9% of master's degrees, and 55.5% of doctorates in 2016–2017 (NCES, 2011). The educational attainment for all races increased during the 1990s. Also, the educational gap between African Americans and non-Hispanic Whites decreased slightly. Nevertheless, severe differences between the races remain, especially among those with a bachelor's degree or higher. It should be noted that Asian Americans had the highest educational attainment. Whites had a higher percentage of high school graduates but a lower percentage of college graduates than Asian Americans, and the educational attainment of Hispanics was the lowest of all groups.

The previous information offers a strong argument for compulsory attendance in public education, but how has it affected students from different racial and ethnic groups who are now attending high school in large numbers? Getting young people to attend high school is only part of the solution. The other part is getting them to remain in school and to graduate, and more work needs to be done to address the dropout problem. The question for this chapter is, given school dropout rates, especially among poor and minority students, should college attendance be the norm for all U.S. students? The data seem to indicate that making education compulsory for various racial and ethnic groups in K–12 education has increased both the number of high school and college graduates for all groups (Beeghley, 2004; Gilbert, 2002; Thompson & Hickey, 2005).

Will the same policy work for college education? The authors of the essays on this subject fully discuss, debate, and offer arguments to support both sides of the question. In the point essay, Saran Donahoo (Southern Illinois University Carbondale) contends that today's young adults have little hope of succeeding in the labor market if they do not acquire some education and training beyond high school. She notes that even though not all jobs require a college degree, having some postsecondary education or training broadens individuals' employment opportunities. Further, having a college degree increases workers' earnings potential. In the counterpoint essay, Valerie Hill-Jackson (Texas A&M University), Brandon Fox (Texas A&M University), Rachel Jackson (Texas A&M University), and Marlon C. James (Loyola University Chicago) maintain that college attendance for poor learners of color should not, and cannot, be the norm if educationalists are unwilling to provide a new narrative of high school reform. In pointing out that educationalists have neglected to see the value of alternative secondary programs, such as career and technical education programs, the counterpoint authors conclude that these programs provide a feasible method to support students of color on the secondary level, while serving as bridge to postsecondary education.

Richard C. Hunter
University of Illinois at Urbana-Champaign and
Bahrain Teachers College, University of Bahrain,
Kingdom of Bahrain

POINT: Saran Donahoo
Southern Illinois University Carbondale

For both economic and political reasons, the United States is facing an increasingly uncertain future. The economic downturn that began in 2007 is a recent reason for young adults to fear that they will have a difficult or even impossible time living as well as their parents. Adding to this is the fact that high schools (due to many factors that are outside of their control) no longer provide the type or level of education that allows most young people to earn a living wage. Yet, even as all of this uncertainty bombards the nation and its youth, the rising global economy suggests that we should encourage young people to get more education, not less. While it is not always clear where it will take them or the types of returns they will receive, attending college still provides young people with more opportunities to survive and support themselves in an ever-changing economy. As such, regardless of why students elect to drop out of high school before obtaining a diploma, most of them will still need to both earn a secondary credential and pursue some postsecondary training to succeed in the global economy.

DROPPING OUT

According to the Department of Education's National Center for Education Statistics (NCES, 2010a), approximately 2.9 million students enrolled in grades 9 to 12 during the 2007–2008 school year. Yet, the Alliance for Excellent Education (2007) estimates that 7,000 students drop out of high school on a daily basis, which means that 1.2 million will not complete high school in the traditional time and manner. This translates to a national dropout rate of around 25% (Tyler & Lofstrom, 2009). Disaggregating this data according to race reveals that while White students have a dropout rate of 6%, African American and Latino students occupy much more of this population with rates of 12% and 20%, respectively. Being low income further increases the likelihood that students will leave high school without a diploma since 17% of young people 16 to 24 years of age lack any type of secondary credential whatsoever (Bloom, 2010; Cataldi, Laird, & KewalRamani, 2009). Clearly, U.S. public education has a school dropout problem. Even so, the fact that about 40% of secondary students at some point take time off from high school does not mean that the nation should begin to deemphasize the importance or value of postsecondary training, certificates, and degrees. Regardless of when and how students complete high school, the financial structure of the global economy now mandates the need for more formal education and training beyond secondary school.

THE NEED FOR POSTSECONDARY TRAINING

Students who drop out of high school experience a diminished quality of life in a variety of areas. Considered from the perspective of the global economy, failing to complete high school and attend college negatively affects the quality of life, employability, employment options, and earnings potential available to dropouts.

Quality of Life

Although not absolute, people who complete high school generally enjoy a better quality of life than those who never obtain a diploma or equivalency credential. Based on the educational levels of most inmates, individuals who finish high school are less likely to end up in prison. Likewise, 50% of all single mothers who end up using public assistance also lack a high school diploma, thus making it more difficult for them to transition into a better financial circumstance for themselves and their children (Tyler & Lofstrom, 2009). From a personal perspective, attending college helps to position individuals to avoid negative financial and social experiences (Danziger & Ratner, 2010). Viewed from a societal standpoint, attending college moves most young people from fiscal liabilities to taxpaying contributors. Not only are high school completers and the college educated less likely to end up in prison or use the public welfare system; they also pay more than twice as much income tax than those who drop out (Danziger & Ratner, 2010; Tyler & Lofstrom, 2009). In this way, finishing high school significantly influences the quality of life available to both individual citizens and the nation as a whole.

Employability

Whether students complete a secondary education with a traditional diploma or a GED, many are not prepared to enter adult life after high school. Although the U.S. Bureau of Labor Statistics projects that only 30% of jobs do or will require a college degree, the agency also finds that completing training beyond high school provides some protection from unemployment as these people now occupy 59% of the workforce (Ramey, 2010; Roderick, Nagaoka, & Coca, 2009). The fact that people who attend college or receive some postsecondary training have both greater employment opportunities and less unemployment clearly illustrates the need for all students to complete some college.

Looking globally, a college education appears to serve as a positive first step toward both surviving and maximizing economic changes. Even as the United States works to embrace the notion of a global economy during the worst recession since the 1930s, individuals who lack a high school diploma experience triple the unemployment rate of those who hold college degrees (Farrell, 2010). The decline of the high-wage manufacturing era has been particularly hard on those who lack a college education since the jobs now most readily available to this segment of the population pay far less and often lack the unionized benefits and security associated with industrial-based employment (Greenhouse, 2003; Hartley & Mowry, 2010; Milkman, 1997). While costly to high school dropouts and their families, this low educational attainment also negatively influences the nation's ability to compete in the global marketplace since these individuals have a difficult time gaining employment in other areas and often experience significant pay cuts to avoid complete unemployment. Recognizing that pursuing a college degree is not economically feasible for people of all ages due to financial obligations and pending retirements (whether by choice or mandate), young adults will have little hope of succeeding in either the current or future labor market if they do not acquire some education and training past high school.

Employment Options

In addition to making individuals more attractive to potential employers, completing some college coursework and earning a degree broadens the employment options open to educated persons. Even though all jobs do not require a college degree, completing a degree does make individuals eligible for both a larger variety and a greater number of positions. While the recession continues to limit employment opportunities, research conducted by the National Association of Colleges and Employers (NACE, 2010) suggests that students who graduate from college in 2011 will experience increased chances of obtaining employment since employers indicated that they will hire 13.5% more new college graduates than in 2010. Indeed, college increasingly serves as an attractive place to wait out bad economic times since low-income youth are particularly more likely to at least pursue 2-year college degrees when employment rates rise above 10% (Bozick, 2009). Examining college enrollments reported in the fall of 2009, the Bureau of Labor Statistics (2010) found that a historical record 70.1% of recent high school graduates were enrolled in a postsecondary institution on at least a part-time basis. Essentially, individuals who lack a college education have a more difficult time weathering poor job markets because they are not as attractive to some employers and lack the skills and training needed to pursue careers in fields that are looking to hire new personnel. Although attending college during an economic downturn provides only a temporary resolution to workforce limitations, the new skills and credentials attainable through postsecondary training and degree completion improve the job outlook for most.

Earnings Potential

Beyond encountering a better job outlook, young people who attend college will also improve their earnings potential. Even without attending college, simply completing high school strongly increases the wages that individuals can earn. For example, women who drop out of high school earn only 65% as much as those who hold diplomas, and men earn 70% of those who possess diplomas (Tyler & Lofstrom, 2009). Yet, a high school diploma will not allow most young people to match or meet the standard of living set by most of their parents. As illustrated in Tables 7.1 and 7.2, the ability of most Americans to earn high incomes now depends heavily on the level and type of education that individuals complete.

Table 7.1

2006 Earnings for Females, Ages 25 and Up

Level of Education	2006 Mean Income	Difference From Dropouts	Percentage Earned by Dropouts
Female dropouts	$24,136	—	—
Female HS grad/GED	$30,251	$6,115	79.79
Female some college	$37,730	$13,594	63.97
Female associate's	$41,414	$17,278	58.27
Female bachelor's	$54,398	$30,262	44.37
Female master's	$63,597	$39,461	37.95
Female doctoral	$91,733	$67,597	26.31
Female professional	$100,892	$76,756	23.92

Source: Based on earnings data from Postsecondary Education Opportunity (2007a).

Table 7.2

2006 Earnings for Males, Ages 25 and Up

Level of Education	2006 Mean Income	Difference From Dropouts	Percentage Earned by Dropouts
Male dropouts	$32,943	—	—
Male HS grad/GED	$44,598	$11,655	73.87
Male some college	$51,247	$18,304	64.28
Male associate's	$52,978	$20,035	62.18
Male bachelor's	$77,868	$44,925	42.31
Male master's	$97,218	$64,275	36.09
Male doctoral	$125,393	$92,450	26.27
Male professional	$144,069	$111,126	22.87

Source: Based on earnings data from Postsecondary Education Opportunity (2007b).

For both males and females, the earnings gap in the United States is increasingly an education gap. While dropping out of high school may appear to be an appropriate short-term solution to social, academic, and family financial problems, leaving high school and neglecting to attend college creates the foundation for many negative long-term consequences. Indeed, the modern labor market makes it virtually impossible for young adults who hold only a high school diploma to achieve or maintain financial self-sufficiency (Danziger & Ratner, 2010). Although it does not provide guaranteed protection from unemployment or an economic downturn, earning a college degree has become a fiscal necessity for the 21st century.

STRIVING FOR MORE EDUCATED MINORITY AND LOW-INCOME YOUTH

The nature of the global economy not only encourages more education and training after high school, but also makes postsecondary education an absolute necessity. To make this matriculation process both easier and more appealing, we need to make high school more useful and applicable to preparing all students for the challenges of adult life. While this will entail ensuring that all students have access to the academic content and courses needed to gain access to college, this should also include life skills education topics such as banking, budgeting, personal credit, job searching, interviewing, and effective work habits. This will allow high schools to communicate information to students that they can use both immediately and over the course of a lifetime.

Likewise, we need to provide students with more accurate information about higher education and the degree completion process. After years of promoting college access, students of all races now enter higher education at virtually the same rate (Deil-Amen & Tevis, 2010). What we now need to concentrate on is helping young minority students to succeed in college and complete degrees before leaving campus. Some information that can help in this effort includes publicizing dual-credit programs that allow high school students to get some college credits while working toward their diplomas often at little or no costs, attending community college to complete certificates and associate degrees that lead to employment with less financial and time investment than a traditional 4-year degree, completing an associate's degree at a community college before moving on to a 4-year institution for a bachelor's degree, and establishing and maintaining an appropriate school/work balance that will allow students to support themselves while achieving academic success.

The common goal for much of the second half of the 20th century was to get more students—especially women and racial minorities—into higher education. Having made college more accessible to people from all backgrounds, income categories, and levels of academic performance, the primary goal for the 21st century needs to shift. Instead, the theme for the 21st century should be one of college completion and success. Similar to access in the recent past century, the theme of college completion and success will and should vary from one person to the next. The goal is not for everyone to get the same or highest degree available. Rather, we need to concentrate on communicating the message and making it possible for each student to get the training that he or she needs to obtain adequate employment and succeed in the ever-changing labor market.

REBUTTAL

Admittedly, individuals who drop out of high school do not have full control over many of the circumstances that structure and influence the education that they access and receive. Even so, similar to students and their families, schools are also only partially responsible for the education of anyone regardless of age, income level, or other factors.

Another point emphasized in the counterpoint essay is increasing access to career and technical education to improve the applicable skills taught to low-income students. While these opportunities provide some advantages to students, their families, and society as a whole, it will be difficult to implement this as a solution to dropping out. Among other factors, the structure of the modern labor market places the emphasis and access to these programs at the community college level, meaning that most interested students will still need to attend postsecondary school to access these programs.

Realistically, students and parents must take initiative and responsibility for identifying, seizing, and making the most of their educational opportunities. Whether economically, politically, socially, or emotionally, students and their families will experience the most damaging consequences as a result of dropping out. As such, we should encourage them to emulate wealthier parents by learning to be more proactive and involved rather than rely exclusively on schools to solve their problems for them.

COUNTERPOINT: Valerie Hill-Jackson, Brandon Fox, and Rachel Jackson
Texas A&M University

Marlon C. James
Loyola University Chicago

The merits of college attendance for poor learners of color cannot effectively be debated in isolation from matters about who is liable for America's dropout crisis and possible high school reform efforts that may remedy the problem. In this essay, the phrase "of color" is used to refer to all non-White ethnic groups. Further, scholars and practitioners who assume that the high dropout rate in the United States is within the control of the dropouts themselves have accused families, peer groups, and the wanting cultural habits of poor learners of color for their academic underachievement (Lewis, James, Hancock, & Hill-Jackson, 2008). The expanding body of literature establishes that poor children of color have not been adequately served by the nation's educational system (Cross, 2007; Kozol, 2005). The United States has an educational system whereby wealthier communities have resources to support their students' higher education aspirations while impoverished communities do not. In a sense, the community's schools and socioeconomic conditions act as arbiters to student achievement.

If the American educational systems in effect fail to provide poor children of color with realistic aspirations for college, then what options might educationalists employ to prevent these students from dropping out and help them seek and complete higher education? The authors maintain that college attendance for poor learners of color should not, and cannot, be the norm until educationalists can provide a new narrative of high school reform. This response is one that advances the call for secondary reform for those in jeopardy of dropping out by (a) underscoring the actual genesis of the dropout conundrum, (b) heralding Career and Technical Education (CTE) as one possible mechanism for college preparation while wrestling with the ideological debates of encouraging poor learners of color into vocational training, and (c) agreeing with the position that college completion, not attendance, must be the goal for learners of color and yields economic benefits for them. However, the authors maintain that alternatives to status quo secondary approaches must be part of the dropout solution.

THE REAL CAUSES OF THE DROPOUT DILEMMA

Those who critically assess the landscape of the so-called dropout crisis understand that these young Americans are not dropouts, but rather push-outs or left-outs. Martin Haberman (2005) explains,

> Being a drop-out or a push-out dooms people to dead-end jobs, living in unsafe neighborhoods, and never being able to fully provide adequate health care for themselves and their families. It also means that those who are miseducated never develop the individual potentialities that would give their lives greater meaning and society the benefit of their participation and productivity. (p. 98)

Peter McLaren (2010) echoes the same type of dire circumstances for America's push-outs:

> When students feel the game of school success is rigged from the start, they tune out, sometimes lash out, or are more frequently pushed out (structural constraints include . . . unsafe neighborhoods with gang violence, poverty, lack of study space, disparities in per-pupil expenditures between states and within states due to local tax bases, homelessness, . . . schools with high teacher attrition, . . . decaying buildings, and lack of equipment). (p. xiii)

Pedro Noguera (2003) concurs and paints a scathing image of the public school environment in which most push-outs can be found and where a lack of options for high school reform are accepted without challenge:

> In the absence of genuine alternatives, even failing public schools retain a dependent although disgruntled constituency base because they are typically the only social institution that provides a consistent source of stability and support to impoverished families. . . . Politicians who often lead the chorus of criticism have largely failed to devise policies to address the deplorable conditions present in many inner-city schools and communities. . . . Most of the popular educational reforms enacted by states and the federal government . . . fail to address the severe social and economic conditions in urban areas that invariably affect the quality and character of public schools. (p. 6)

These scholars converge to illuminate a disturbing truism in America's educational system: Structural exclusion policies have created educational conditions in which marginalized learners are forced to endure. Structural exclusion policies (e.g., No Child Left Behind) for the underserved encourage an emphasis on irrelevant skills and reproduce existing social and economic inequalities, leading to increased dropout rates, an erosion in the quality of education, and a disconnect between educational need and provision. A rebirth of school and learner accountability pressures has advanced the dropout and college readiness canon while preventing the secondary school system from constructing new opportunities to transform the high school experience.

CAREER AND TECHNICAL EDUCATION AS AN OPTION FOR UNDERSERVED LEARNERS

CTE schools, also known as *vocational training schools,* have evolved to educate all of America's learners and as a means to assist those who do not fit the mold of mainstream educational institutions. There is considerable research suggesting that CTE schools reduce dropout and absenteeism rates (McCombs, 2000). Vocational education has a nearly 240-year history in the United States, marked by four key periods of awakening, independence, vocational age, and "coming of age." While all four periods are important, it is the latter that lauds itself as the mechanism for American education that reaches out to the disadvantaged and to the particular needs of ethnic and diverse groups (Barlow, 1967). These programs are also ideal for low-income areas as they teach students valuable skills and make learning more relevant to students' lives. Vocational programs also assist in developing skills that students could use in future jobs and also promote intrinsic motivation that would help them to succeed in their core curriculum subjects (Slaats, Lodewijks, & van der Sanden, 1999).

In a recent survey of high school dropouts, participants confessed that they felt alienated at school and that no one even noticed if they failed to show up for class. High school dropouts also complained that school did not reflect the real world. Over half of respondents said that the primary rationale for dropping out of high school was that they felt their classes were not interesting and relevant. Others leave because a lack of connection to the school environment, a perception that school is boring, feeling unmotivated, academic challenges, and the weight of real-world events—81% of students who dropped out said that "more real world learning" may have influenced them to stay in school (Bridgeland & diIulio, 2006).

Today's CTE programs provide students with the following: academic subject matter taught with relevance to the real world; employability skills, from job-related skills to workplace ethics; career pathways that link secondary and postsecondary education; second-chance education and training; and education for additional training and degrees, especially related to workplace training, skills upgrades, and career advancement (Association for Career and Technical Education, 2008). Although the benefits of CTE are undeniable, the disputes over its value for underprivileged populations have a long history.

Resistance to CTE for the Underserved

Ideological debates over CTE as an alternative system for poor learners of color ensued among vocational training reformers and scholars such as Booker T. Washington and W. E. B. Du Bois, and John Dewey and Charles Prosser. The Washington–Du Bois debates highlighted the segregated and social class issues of vocational training. Initially, education in the manual arts was meant to free people from their social class. Many argued that "class, gender and racial disparities in occupational status have a history of being reproduced through vocational programs" (Ainsworth & Roscigno, 2005, p. 259). Washington believed that through the manual arts and labor, socially oppressed people, like African Americans, could transcend to higher "financial and social spheres." In contrast, Du Bois believed that only by mastery of the mind could African Americans and other disadvantaged groups move up the corporate and social ladders and avoid social predestination to the vocational realm (Gordon, 1999).

The Dewey–Prosser debates tackled the issue of a dual-system approach. After elementary education, children would continue on to trade school and apprenticeship. Dewey believed this dual system approach to be too "utilitarian" and that the overwhelming emphasis on technical training would make education an "instrument of perpetuating unchanged the existing industrial order of society, instead of operating as a means of its transformation." He instead proposed vocational exploration in which the student could apply academic principles and "acquire practical knowledge." Prosser believed that school should accommodate industry by giving students opportunities to "practice and [think] about practice" and to "[do] and think about doing" (Gordon, 1999, p. 32). In other words, students will be indoctrinated into the ethical standards and values of a "dominant society."

The Smith-Hughes Act, possibly the most notable landmark vocational training legislation, was passed in 1917. This piece of legislation provided national support and aid for trade schools and vocational training programs (Smith, 1999) and suggested that Washington's and Prosser's ideologies prevailed in a contemptuous progressive era of high school reform. Poor and immigrant students attended these schools in droves, while wealthier families sent their children to 4-year institutions (Neckerman, 2007). Many people in the United States associated secondary education with academic work exclusively, to the point where it caused many to separate themselves from those who did manual labor or connected to the vocational field.

The resistance to vocational programs and schools is emblematic of a long-standing spirit of elitism in which person power is deemed of less worth than brainpower in a nation that values white-collar over blue-collar careers. Those who resist vocational training may also do so because of a lingering legacy of locating vocational schools in city districts and not suburban ones, and because they view vocational tracking as a means to keep children from low-income families in low-income jobs. Traditionally, high school students have had limited options between choosing an academic pathway leading to college or a pathway to work or technical studies after high school completion, which are usually viewed as mutually exclusive.

The legislation of the 1990s signifies a national recommitment of vocational education in a technically advancing society. The Carl D. Perkins Vocational and Applied Technology Education Act of 1990 emphasized "integration of academic and vocational education, articulation between segments of education engaged in workforce preparation, and closer linkages between school and work" (Gordon, 1999, p. 88). As the first act of Congress that intertwines vocational training with traditional education, there has been opposition from the states and local agencies. The Applied Technology Education Act, also known as Perkins II, financially bypassed the states and specified allocation of funds to certain areas of educational interest; prompting many states and local agencies not to comply. Also, in Perkins II, Congress attempted to "legislate methodology," which had long-term diminished quality-related consequences.

Over the last 2 decades, more legislation has been signed into existence to mitigate academic rigor issues and the effects, or ineffectiveness, of Perkins II for such programs as School-to-Work Opportunities Act of 1994, the Personal Responsibility and Work Opportunity Act of 1996, and the Carl D. Perkins Career and Technical Education Act of 2006 (Perkins IV). School-to-Work stipulations included collaborative partnerships between schools and the labor market, integrated curriculum, and comprehensive career guidance. School-to-Work also "advocated . . . work-based learning, including job shadowing, mentoring, internships and apprenticeships" (NCES, 2000, p. 5). Clearly the advocates of college attendance and completion for learners of color are unfamiliar with the tremendous gains made in the CTE movement.

RESPONSE TO POINT ESSAY

Saran Donahoo in the point essay of this chapter offers another perspective on the dropout/push-out crisis that rests in alignment to the authors' counterpoint argument as we concede that the focus for educating learners of color should center on *completing* college, not just *attending* college in a global economy. We also agree that secondary education affords one (a) a better quality of life, (b) greater employability, (c) diverse employment options, and (d) improved earnings potential. However, progressives in secondary education fail to push more critical approaches to combat the United States' push-out challenge.

The Association for Career and Technical Education (ACTE, 2008) shares several exemplary programs and makes the case for CTE as another option for underserved students and postsecondary attainment. The ACTE research report on the value of CTE cites the following facts:

> CTE students enter postsecondary education at approximately the same rate as all high school graduates. . . .
>
> The National Center for Education Statistics (NCES) in 2000 discovered that vocational graduates were more likely than their traditional education peers to obtain a degree or training certificate within two years after high school, in spite of the fact that many vocational graduates have employment while in school.

Another NCES (2000) study found that 71.2% of all subbaccalaureate students (two years or less) have vocational majors.

The National Assessment of Vocational Education (2004) claims that CTE student college attendance increased by nearly thirty-two percent between 1982 and 1992. (para. 5)

The research demonstrates that vocational schools can lead students to, not away from, college (Hillmert & Jacob, 2003). While not a perfect option, which needs more enhancement and improved integration of the arts (Carl D. Perkins, 2006), 21st-century CTE programs and schools appear to offer another route toward a college degree, one that couples technical and workplace skills with academic sensibilities.

CONCLUSION

The authors maintain that college attendance for poor learners of color should not, and cannot, be the norm if educationalists are unwilling to provide a new discourse of high school reform so "that [students] are conscious of powers, passions, and tastes which the [traditional] school does not recognize" (Kantor, 1986, p. 409). Policymakers, scholars, and practitioners mistakenly point a collective finger at poor learners of color for their underachievement and not structural exclusion policies that have, in effect, created an American educational system with an inequitable distribution of resources. Society and educationalists find scapegoats by blaming the victim for the American dropout predicament, but both are culpable for the academic outcomes that burden poor learners of color while ignoring possible alternative solutions. To be sure, our nation is faced with a dropout/push-out crisis, but our "crisis of options" should be a more immediate concern.

Many educationalists have neglected to see the value of alternative secondary programs, similar to CTE programs, which can link academics and technical study to provide a rigorous and relevant education with multiple means of self- and career exploration for the underserved. The evidence of CTE schools as a feasible method to support students of color on the secondary level, and as bridge to postsecondary education, is overwhelming.

Conventional wisdom posits that postsecondary attendance and completion must be the expectation for learners of color and that it offers many economic benefits for them. But we may have neglected to have a critical discussion on the options for getting there.

FURTHER READINGS AND RESOURCES

Ainsworth, J. W., & Roscigno, V. J. (2005). Stratification, school-work linkages and vocational education. *Social Forces, 84*(1), 257–284.

Alliance for Excellent Education. (2007, October). *The high cost of high school dropouts: What the nation pays for inadequate high schools.* Washington, DC: Author.

Association for Career and Technical Education (ACTE). (2008, March). Research report: The value of CTE. *Techniques,* pp. 50–53. Retrieved from http://www.acteonline.org/uploadedFiles/Publications_and_Online_Media/files/files-techniques-2008/Research-Report-March-2008.pdf

Barlow, M. (1967). *History of industrial arts in the United States.* Peoria, IL: Charles A. Bennett.

Beeghley, L. (2004). *The structure of social stratification in the United States.* Boston: Pearson, Allyn & Bacon.

Bloom, D. (2010). Programs and policies to assist high school dropouts in the transition to adulthood. *The Future of Children, 20*(1), 89–108.

Bozick, R. (2009). Job opportunities, economic resources, and the postsecondary destinations of American youth. *Demography, 46*(3), 493–512.

Bridgeland, J., & DiIulio, J. (2006). *The silent epidemic: Perspectives of high school dropouts.* Washington, DC: Civic Enterprises.

Bureau of Labor Statistics. (2010, April 27). *College enrollment and work activity of 2009 high school graduates.* Washington, DC: Author. Retrieved September 6, 2010, from http://www.bls.gov/news.release/hsgec.nr0.htm

Cataldi, E. F., Laird, J., & KewalRamani, A. (2009). *High school dropout and completion rates in the United States: 2007* (NCES 2009-064). Washington, DC: U.S. Department of Education, Institute of Education Sciences, National Center for Education Statistics. Retrieved August 30, 2010, from http://nces.ed.gov/pubsearch/pubsinfo.asp?pubid=2009064

Cross, B. E. (2007). Urban school achievement gap as a metaphor to conceal U.S. apartheid education. *Theory Into Practice, 46*(3), 247–255. doi:10.1080/00405840701402299

Danziger, S., & Ratner, D. (2010, Spring). Labor market outcomes and the transition to adulthood. *The Future of Children, 20*(1), 133–158.

Deil-Amen, R., & Tevis, T. L. (2010, Winter). Circumscribed agency: The relevance of standardized college entrance exams for low SES high school students. *The Review of Higher Education, 33*(2), 141–175.

Farrell, C. (2010, June 24). Failing U.S. education will dumb down economic growth. *Bloomberg BusinessWeek.* Retrieved September 8, 2010, from http://www.businessweek.com/investor/content/jun2010/pi20100624_409585.htm

Gilbert, D. (2002). *The American class structure in an age of growing inequality.* Belmont, CA: Wadsworth.

Gordon, H. R. (1999). *The history and growth of vocational education in America.* Boston: Allyn & Bacon.

Greenhouse, S. (2003, September 13). As factory jobs disappear, workers have few options. *CommonDreams.org.* Retrieved September 8, 2010, from http://www.common dreams.org/headlines03/0913-09.htm

Haberman, M. (2005). *Star teachers: The ideology and best practice of effective teachers of diverse children and youth in poverty.* Houston, TX: Haberman Educational Foundation.

Hartley, D., & Mowry, B. (2010, June 15). Could low educational attainment be slowing the recovery? *Economic Trends.* Retrieved September 8, 2010, from http://www .clevelandfed.org/research/trends/2010/0710/01labmar.cfm

Hillmert, S., & Jacob, M. (2003). Social inequality in higher education: Is vocational training a pathway leading to or away from university? *European Sociological Review, 19*(3), 319–334.

Kantor, H. (1986). Work, education, and vocational reform: The ideological origins of vocational education, 1890–1920. *American Journal of Education, 94*(4), 401–426.

Kozol, J. (2005, September). Still separate, still unequal: America's educational apartheid. *Harper's Magazine, 31*(1), 41–54.

Lewis, C., James, M., & Hancock, S., & Hill-Jackson, V. (2008). Framing African American students' success and failure in urban settings: A typology for change. *Urban Education, 43*(2), 127–153.

McCombs, B. L. (2000). Reducing the achievement gap. *Society, 375*(247), 29–36.

McLaren, P. (2010). Foreword. In V. Hill-Jackson & C. W. Lewis (Eds.), *Transforming teacher education: What went wrong with teacher training and how we can fix it* (pp. xi–xvii). Sterling, VA: Stylus.

Milkman, R. (1997). *Farewell to the factory: Auto workers in the late twentieth century.* Berkeley: University of California Press.

National Association of Colleges and Employers (NACE). (2010). *Job outlook 2011 fall preview.* Bethlehem, PA: Author. Retrieved September 6, 2010, from http://www .naceweb.org/Publications/Spotlight_Online/2010/0901/College_Hiring_ Rebounds_13_5_Percent_for_Class_of_2011.aspx

National Center for Education Statistics (NCES). (2000). *Vocational education in the United States: Toward the year 2000* (NCES 2000–029). Washington, DC: U.S. Government Printing Office.

National Center for Education Statistics (NCES). (2010a). *Public school graduates and dropouts from the common core of data: School year 2007–08.* Washington, DC: U.S. Department of Education. Retrieved from http://nces.ed.gov/pubs2010/2010341.pdf

National Center for Education Statistics (NCES). (2010b). *The condition of education.* Washington, DC: U.S. Department of Education. Retrieved August 29, 2010, from http://nces.ed.gov/programs/coe/2010/section1/indicator02.asp

National Center for Education Statistics (NCES). (2011). *Projections of education statistics to 2020.* Washington, DC: U.S. Department of Education. Retrieved from http:// nces.ed.gov/pubs2011/2011026.pdf

Neckerman, K. M. (2007). *Schools betrayed: Roots of failure in inner-city education.* Chicago: University of Chicago Press.

Noguera, P. (2003). *City schools and the American dream: Reclaiming the promise of public education.* New York: Teacher College Press.

Postsecondary Education Opportunity. (2007a). *Education and training pay for females.* Oskaloosa, IA: Author. Retrieved September 6, 2010, from http://www.postsecondary .org/commondetail.asp?id=1624

Postsecondary Education Opportunity. (2007b). *Education and training pay for males.* Oskaloosa, IA: Author. Retrieved September 6, 2010, from http://www.postsecondary .org/commondetail.asp?id=1624

Ramey, A. (2010). *Analysis of education and training data.* Washington, DC: U.S. Bureau of Labor Statistics. Retrieved August 30, 2010, from http://www.bls.gov/emp/ep_ education_training.htm

Roderick, M., Nagaoka, J., & Coca, V. (2009). College readiness for all: The challenge for urban high schools. *The Future of Children, 19*(1), 185–210.

Slaats, A., Lodewijks, H. G. L. C., & van der Sanden, J. M. M. (1999). Learning styles in secondary vocational education: Disciplinary differences. *Learning and Instruction, 9*(5), 475–492.

Smith, N. B. (1999). A tribute to the visionaries, prime movers and pioneers of vocational education, 1892 to 1917. *Journal of Vocational and Technical Education, 16*(1), 67–76.

Thompson, W., & Hickey, J. (2005). *Society in focus.* Boston: Pearson, Allyn & Bacon.

Tyler, J. H., & Lofstrom, M. (2009). Finishing high school: Alternative pathways and dropout recovery. *The Future of Children, 19*(1), 77–103.

COURT CASES AND STATUTES

Carl D. Perkins Career and Technical Education Improvement Act of 2006, 20 U.S.C. § 2301 *et seq.* (2006).

Does incorporating elements from popular culture, such as hip-hop, on school campuses help public schools serve diverse student populations?

POINT: Latish Reed, *University of Wisconsin–Milwaukee*
Natalie A. Tran, *California State University, Fullerton*
Christopher N. Thomas, *University of San Francisco*
COUNTERPOINT: Dana Griffin, *University of North Carolina at Chapel Hill*

OVERVIEW

The ebb and flow of public education places teachers and administrators in the position of always looking to or answering questions about the latest curricula, technology, and instructional approaches as they continually work to devise effective ways of educating all of the children in their schools. Whether as a response to external pressure or a professional desire to improve academic achievement, public education professionals spend considerable time identifying and examining new teaching methods and educational strategies to increase test scores and other performance indicators.

Incorporating popular culture into public education has proven to be one such method; it has been used recently in the United States as a means of increasing cultural relevance for students. In the 1880s, the McGuffey readers helped provide a common curricular base for public schools. At the same time, these texts communicated morals, ethics, and a common patriotic American identity that helped to assimilate immigrants and their children into their new home country.

During the 1920s, the growth of print media not only increased national literacy but also generated a greater variety of texts for the public to consume. Along with the expansion of print media, the rise of radio helped create mass culture by creating a common cultural narrative, context, and collection of events, which people all across the nation experienced in a like manner. Within education, the desire to gain employment in lucrative industrial jobs and the wish to participate in mass society sparked expanded emphasis on English language acquisition for immigrant children and high school participation, especially in more industrialized labor markets.

Later, in the 1940s and 1950s, the cultural mechanisms that helped cultivate popular support and mobilization during World War II also seeped into public education. After enduring the suppression of the Great Depression, many parents of children growing up in the post–World War II era worked aggressively to give their offspring a true childhood by allowing them to grow up unconcerned with the everyday issues that affect adult life. In doing so, the 1950s nurtured the growth of adolescence as a true developmental phase between childhood and adulthood. Accordingly, these adolescents developed unique language, views, and cultural elements separate from that of both their parents and their younger siblings. As represented and promoted by the media, adolescents brought aspects of their culture with them to school, thus influencing the relationship shared with teachers, administrators, and other school professionals.

Furthermore, the influence of adolescent culture on public education increased during the 1960s, 1970s, and 1980s. Spurred on by the protest movements of the 1960s, the culture of adolescents and young adults moved from simply altering the ways in which these students approached their educational activities to more influential positions by having a direct impact on the courses and overall structure of schooling. This continued on into the 1970s and 1980s as the end of legalized racial segregation ushered in new public attention to the culture and considerations of African Americans. Indeed, attending to the previously neglected African Americans led to revisions in the books assigned as American literature, the narratives taught as U.S. history, and the general ideas emphasized in various areas of the curricula.

Cultural changes of the 20th century created the context from which emerged the concept of culturally responsive pedagogy. Drawing on the lessons of the past, culturally responsive pedagogy calls on educators to identify the cultural

perspectives and needs of their students; craft lessons and teaching strategies that meet students in the cultural space, language, and context with
which the students are most comfortable; and merge elements of students'
home culture into their school activities. To that end, culturally responsive
pedagogy aims to provide a comprehensive approach to teaching and learning, to validate multiple perspectives, to empower students to take a more
active role in their education, and to transform the classroom from an authori-
tative setting to an environment that allows all participants to grow as a result
of these experiences.

Culturally responsive pedagogy attempts to combine every aspect of students' lives into their educational experiences. Rather than attempt to establish
and maintain a barrier between school and other elements outside of the
school day, students are encouraged to use experiences and knowledge from
their everyday lives as the foundation for developing academic skills.

Another goal of culturally responsive pedagogy is to validate multiple perspectives. While educational policies require that all students have access to
the same academic information, this does not preclude teachers from allowing
students to acquire this knowledge in different manners. To that end, the paradigms of culturally responsive pedagogy encourage teachers to foster learning
development in students in ways that produce the desired outcomes without
expecting all students to approach their educational activities from the same
point of view.

Additionally, this multiple perspectives approach has been viewed as
empowering students to exercise personal responsibility over their learning.
Within this context, students can choose how to combine elements of their
home life within their school activities. In this way, according to advocates of
culturally responsive pedagogy, learning transitions from something that students do because they are told into something that they participate in actively,
purposely, and willingly.

Using elements of popular culture, such as hip-hop, in public education can
be considered an element of culturally responsive pedagogy. Within this vein,
the point essay in this chapter, written by Latish Reed (University of Wisconsin–
Milwaukee), Natalie A. Tran (California State University, Fullerton), and
Christopher N. Thomas (University of San Francisco), argues that using
hip-hop in public education can help students gain access to many of the
advantages that are, by definition, associated with culturally responsive pedagogy. Noting that there is evidence that hip-hop can be used as a tool to
facilitate student learning, the authors posit that it can be an ally in educating
traditionally marginalized youth. In this respect, the authors contend that by
using culturally responsive pedagogy as a tool, educators can connect with

students while using their cultural and linguistic knowledge to facilitate effective teaching and learning.

Conversely, the counterpoint essay by Dana Griffin (University of North Carolina at Chapel Hill) cautions against reliance on hip-hop and other elements of popular culture to foster learning since this is not always the most effective way of reaching all students. Griffin acknowledges the research that indicates that using elements of popular culture can be an effective teaching technique and that culturally relevant pedagogy is needed, but she feels that incorporating elements of hip-hop into lessons is not the way to go. In particular, Griffin is concerned that hip-hop may have the unintended effect of perpetuating negative stereotypes.

Saran Donahoo
Southern Illinois University Carbondale

POINT: Latish Reed
University of Wisconsin–Milwaukee

Natalie A. Tran
California State University, Fullerton

Christopher N. Thomas
University of San Francisco

M any educators and scholars pause when they consider the value of incorporating elements from popular culture such as hip-hop into the curriculum or any other aspects of formal schooling. Adults express a fear of advocating for what many perceive as the worst part of popular culture— promoting negative stereotypical images of youth from low socioeconomic backgrounds. This scenario could not be farther from the truth. Today, hip-hop culture is far-reaching and has become a strong force of influence among youth.

In recent years, we have witnessed a proliferation of the various theoretical approaches aimed to heighten educators' understanding of the importance of the incorporation of culturally relevant pedagogy (CRP) in the classroom settings. Using this framework, Gloria Ladson-Billings (1995a) describes three critical components of successful teaching: academic achievement, cultural competence, and sociopolitical consciousness. She explains that teachers who implement these components in their practice are just doing what "good teachers" should do. Consequently, when teachers do not validate students' experiences as a whole person, they fail to make adequate inroads that are relevant to student learning. From this perspective, we argue that the incorporation of hip-hop is important to facilitate an educational experience that promotes higher learning for all students.

Today, hip-hop culture represents a multibillion-dollar industry and touches every aspect of youth culture from music, art, fashion, mass media, sports, to advertisement. While hip-hop has great appeal to youth on both the U.S. and international landscapes, educators have yet to fully understand its movement, recognize its impact on popular youth culture, and use its influence in school settings. This lack of understanding and acceptance not only prevents educators from connecting with youth but also prevents educators from using students' cultural and linguistic knowledge to facilitate effective teaching and learning. To effectively integrate hip-hop in the classroom, it is critical that educators understand the following: the historical context of the hip-hop culture, the ways in which it has been used to facilitate teaching learning in the classrooms, and how educators have successfully integrated hip-hop in their schools to improve classroom climate and student performance.

Despite its long-standing opposition, hip-hop exerts an undeniably strong influence on the popular youth culture. As Carl S. Taylor and Virgil Taylor (2004) have noted,

> Hip-Hop, like Rock and Roll before it, is not only a genre of music, it is also a complex system of ideas, values, and concepts that reflect newly emerging and ever-changing creative, correlative, expressive mechanisms, including but not limited to song, poetry, film, and fashion. (p. 251)

Bakari Kitwana (2002) describes hip-hop as "more than just a new genre of music, hip-hop since inception has provided young Blacks a public platform in a society that previously rendered them mute. It has done the same for youth for other cultures as well" (p. xiii). Given the astronomical economic gain from rap and hip-hop culture, it is clear that hip-hop reaches far beyond the African American community. Its popularity is undeniable, with Whites purchasing 70% of the 81 million compact disks that were sold in 1998 (Chang, 2003). Despite the negative images associated with hip-hop culture including misogyny, explicit sexual lyrics, violence, and crime, educators can no longer ignore the impact that this cultural movement has on the lives of our youth. For better or worse, hip-hop is not "entertainment alone; it's also a voice of the voiceless" (Kitwana, 2002, p. xiii).

Despite its widespread influence in popular youth culture, hip-hop maintains its peripheral role in mainstream settings. The schism between mainstream and hip-hop culture, along with waxing and waning societal values, continues to force hip-hop culture to the margins of society. To illustrate this point, an ongoing debate regarding who has the authority to determine the validity of popular music continues to be a contested terrain. In the media, we have witnessed how hip-hop spawned opposition from prominent Black leaders like Rev. Dr. Calvin Butts and U.S. Congressional Representative Maxine Waters from South Central Los Angeles. During the early 1990s, Rev. Butts staged a symbolic decimation of rap music by gathering his congregation's rap tapes and CDs and rolling over them in a steam roller. About this same time period, during congressional hearings on music lyrics, Rep. Maxine Waters publicly voiced her opposing stance against not only the rap artists but also the record companies who produce them.

This rejection of hip-hop culture is also observed in education. There are opposing views in the current debate among educators and scholars concerning hip-hop and its role in youth's social and academic development. This tension is evidenced in the distancing among academics and professionals in referencing hip-hop culture in their practice and scholarly activities. The mere mention of hip-hop in an academic setting elicits laughter or doubt of valid content. This divide must not be taken lightly as hip-hop not only represents the collective voice of young people but also the experiences of other marginalized groups.

WHY HIP-HOP IN EDUCATION?

Strong evidence exists to support that claim that hip-hop can be used as a tool to facilitate student learning. First, researchers investigating literacy development among youth have turned to music found in the hip-hop culture to identify factors that influence youth's engagement and literacy development. For example, in her ethnographic work, Korina M. Jocson (2006) illustrates how innovative curriculum, derived from music and popular culture, allowed students to broaden their understanding of literacy through reading, writing, and spoken word poetry exhibitions—all elements found in the hip-hop culture. Hip-hop provides a unique opportunity for instruction, particularly to improve phonological awareness and decoding skills that are connected to reading fluency, mastery of new vocabulary, and comprehension. Other literature has suggested that out-of-school literacy practices such as writing poetry, song lyrics, and prose could affect youth's engagement and achievement in school. Factors associated with students' engagement in literacy practices included helping students make connections between the content knowledge and their everyday experiences, develop a sense of control over their own work, and finding opportunities to revise their work—all of which can inform educators about creating environments that optimize student learning in the classroom (Weinstein, 2007).

Opponents of hip-hop argue that it helps spread violence, poverty, and other social ills among youth. Contrary to this belief, research has shown that students can benefit from exposure to hip-hop. Jabari Mahiri and Erin Conner (2003) examined Black youth's perspectives on violence and the extent to which their perspectives are linked to their exposure to hip-hop and rap music. They found that students have an understanding of violence and how it is portrayed. This knowledge comes from everyday experiences and other sources of influence such as the media and the music they listen to. More importantly, students learn to critique the messages of violence and develop coping mechanisms for greater challenges within their environments. This critique is important since exposure to hip-hop can help students develop skills and abilities needed to respond to changes in their environments.

We must also acknowledge the extent to which adults can mediate the influence of hip-hop on students' beliefs, attitudes, and development. While it may seem that students exhibit opposition to the values imposed by adults, yet they need adults' support and understanding to make sense of the information presented in their surroundings. Since hip-hop music plays an integral role in students' lives, it is essential that adults not only become familiar with hip-hop culture but also remain informed about its influence on students' academic and social development. Indeed, hip-hop music can be used to guide students in thinking critically about the connection between music in popular culture and literature read in the classroom, and the extent to which these elements reflect the reality of everyday life, as experienced by students. David Stovall (2006) argues that

> the infusion of hip-hop culture can provide the context for students to develop a critical lens in approaching subject matter and its relevance to their daily lives. Hip-Hop culture, as relevant to the lives of many high school students, can provide a bridge to ideas and tasks that promote critical thinking and understanding. (p. 589)

However, these connections are not possible without the support and assistance of capable adults.

As described above, some teachers and researchers do value hip-hop's contribution to the students' learning and development. Educators who understand and appreciate the role of hip-hop are able to incorporate elements of the hip-hop culture into the formal curriculum. By doing so, they extend their hands to students who would be left behind and offer a critical voice for these marginalized students.

Our argument for incorporating hip-hop into the curriculum does not call for every educator or educational scholar to become an expert in hip-hop. Rather, our goal is to offer a different perspective on what hip-hop is, the role it plays in our society, and, perhaps most importantly, what it means to the children we seek to educate. Even though our nation has adopted rhetoric about leaving no child behind, many students are left behind. Aside from providing students with opportunities to learn, we leave their voices behind when we fail to integrate their experiences in the classroom. Hip-hop is the voice for people, regardless of age, race, creed or nationality. Not considering hip-hop as part of the educational experience of our youth is to take away their voice and not validate their experiences. Given the controversial issues on hip-hop, our goal is to raise awareness of the important role that hip-hop plays in youths' lives and explore the ways in which hip-hop can serve as an ally in our efforts to educate traditionally marginalized students.

We acknowledge that hip-hop carries multiple connotations. On the one hand, it is associated with misogyny, explicit sexual lyrics, violence, and crime. On the other hand, it serves as a voice for individuals in marginalized groups. While the controversy around hip-hop continues to persist in various aspects of our society, hip-hop can serve as an effective instructional tool used to facilitate students' social and academic development.

RESPONDING TO COUNTERPOINT ESSAY

In the counterpoint essay for this chapter, Dana Griffin notes in her introduction that she has been able to achieve great success without popular culture or hip-hop being infused in her academic program. While this was the case for her, we wonder if this lack of cultural connection has negatively affected the learning experiences of other students. Teachers' blatant failure to connect with their students' culture and values has attributed to student disengagement and academic failure. That is, when students are disengaged, the prospects of academic achievement are slim to none. She further notes, "There are other ways to incorporate elements of different cultures into the learning environments that allow for students to transcend their cultural socialization and pursue academic excellence, which hip-hop cannot do." As educators, our responsibility is not to place value on students' family and community socialization. Our job is simply to educate them. As our colleague has referenced, the integration of popular culture and/or hip-hop can actually yield academic success for students.

Our colleague indicates that scholars who advocate for CRP do not specifically include hip-hop as a medium to engage students. We challenge this narrow perspective and argue that CRP is a framework that advocates for academic achievement, cultural competence, and sociopolitical consciousness; therefore, it surpasses any particular culture and can be used to transcend culture and practices. In fact, since academic success is the first component of the CRP tripartite, all teaching strategies should be geared toward ensuring academic success. The incorporation of hip-hop that we advocate for is only that which will lead to academic success. We acknowledge that hip-hop is not the only way in which we can incorporate CRP in the educational settings, but it is a tool that can be used to engage students in the classroom context.

Our colleague notes that our job "is to prepare students to face the outside world." She indicates that we do students "a huge disservice if they are only taught to be able to relate to 'their' world, as opposed to knowing how to succeed as a minority in an oppressed and discriminating society." We argue that when elements of popular culture such as hip-hop are introduced in school settings, we are teaching them not simply to relate to their own world but also to use their world as a starting place for understanding the world at large. Furthermore, our colleague asserts that "students of color may have different negative social experiences that may hinder academic development." We posit that the widespread influence of hip-hop stretches far beyond students of color. Hip-hop offers a critical lens for all students to interpret their social experience, regardless of race.

Finally, our colleague offers some empirical evidence to support the use of various cultural attributes within the educational context. She refers to the work of Kathryn Au and Cathie Jordan (1981) who examined the extent to which linguistic patterns found in native Hawaiian culture was used to facilitate student learning. Using cultural competence or tools from students' contexts led to academic achievement. That said, why would a teacher not use 2Pac lyrics to connect with Nathaniel Hawthorne's *Scarlet Letter* if it would result in higher academic achievement? Hester Prynne's alienation from her community is a theme to which many of today's youth can relate. The works of hip-hop artists like 2Pac speaks to youth experiences on the margins of their communities. By using 2Pac's contemporary commentary, students can connect their experiences to the broader "outside world."

COUNTERPOINT: Dana Griffin
University of North Carolina at Chapel Hill

Incorporating elements from popular culture, such as hip-hop, on school campuses does not help public schools serve diverse student populations. However, there is a plethora of research that argues against or counters this position. For example, Stovall (2006) asserts that hip-hop could be a transformative element in the development of teaching and thinking. Indeed, literature addressing culturally relevant pedagogy often includes hip-hop, or popular culture, as a method to promote critical analysis and address issues of race, gender, and class, and provide educational relevance to students of color. Nonetheless, while well-known scholars in the field of education such as Paulo Freire (1971), bell hooks (1994), and Gloria Ladson-Billings (1994, 1995a, 1995b) have all advocated for the use of pedagogy that centers on issues and concerns of minority students, this does not have to be interpreted as using hip-hop as a tool for promoting academic and social development of students of color.

Being an African American woman who grew up dealing with race, gender, and class barriers to academic success, and listening to 2Pac, Biggie Smalls, Nice & Smooth, Niggaz With Attitude (NWA), Ice Cube and Ice T, Public Enemy, 2 Live Crew, Digital Underground, Salt & Pepa, Heavy D, Big Pun, Queen Latifah, and Naughty by Nature (you down with OPP?), just to name a few, I hesitate in taking a stand against hip-hop as a form of culturally relevant pedagogy. However, my work as a school counselor and marriage and family counselor found that this type of music taught young Black men and women, Black boys and girls, that it is acceptable to use words like *nigga, bitch, ho*; for men to objectify women's body parts; and for women to let them do so. It also taught them that having a life a crime is an easy way out of poverty, out of racism, out of oppression, out of hopelessness. Although the music they listened to was never processed through a critical lens, or used to address issues central to life inside and outside of the school, even without infusing hip-hop as culturally relevant pedagogy into their classes, countless of these students of color and low-income students were able to overcome barriers to academic success and find academic victory. These students were able to understand Shakespeare and Faulkner, comprehend geometry and calculus, and set the stage for a great future in education and beyond.

Before continuing, it must be disclosed that in my work as a counselor who primarily worked with low-income African American students, hip-hop and other popular culture were used in individual and group counseling sessions with adolescents and families. However, using popular culture, or hip-hop, as educational material to help meet the needs of diverse student populations should not be considered. However, culturally relevant pedagogy should be. This argument stipulates that there is a marked difference between culturally relevant pedagogy and the use of hip-hop as culturally relevant pedagogy.

When educators infuse teaching practices with hip-hop and other popular culture, and feel that students can be better reached through these techniques, it sends a message that students of color can do better if we introduce things that are familiar and surround them outside of school, namely, hip-hop. However, the job of educators is to prepare students to face the outside world, outside of their community and into larger society domains and we do them a huge disservice if they are only taught to be able to relate to "their" world, as opposed to knowing how to succeed as a minority in an oppressed and discriminating society. However, advocates for the use of culturally relevant pedagogy believe that students do receive, analyze, and interpret information based on their cultural socialization (Allen & Boykin, 1992; Au & Jordan, 1981). Further, using culturally relevant pedagogy can enable students to pursue academic excellence and not abandon their cultural integrity, and it uses a framework that is consistent with the manner in which students of color communicate, learn, and conceive knowledge (Howard, 2001). But there should be a distinction between using culturally relevant pedagogy and using popular culture, such as hip-hop, to promote student development.

ADDRESSING ARGUMENTS FOR USING POPULAR CULTURE

Research of culturally relevant teaching practices reveals two major arguments for the use of these practices in the classroom. However, these arguments do not require these culturally relevant teaching practices to include the use of hip-hop, or popular culture. Further, these practices, sans hip-hop or popular culture, can also help students embrace their cultural identity and can be done in a manner that is more aligned with how students of color communicate and learn, as stated by Tyrone C. Howard (2001).

Argument 1

Argument 1: Culturally relevant pedagogy allows for the foundation of positive relationships to be built between teachers and students, and allows students of color to tell their side of the story. In support of culturally relevant pedagogy, Howard (2001) states that student voices can reveal the great challenges and deep pain that young people feel when faced with cold, unfeeling school climates. Additionally, students are often given the least opportunity to talk, and they have important lessons to teach educators and can provide important insights in the teaching and learning process (Nieto, 1994). To account for the lack of student voice, Howard conducted a qualitative study that examined students' perceptions and interpretations of instructional practices used by four elementary school teachers, identified as culturally responsive teachers for African American students. His findings showed that having teachers who care about students, who structure classrooms in a manner that valued home and community, and who are able to make learning fun and exciting was a foundation for student achievement and engagement.

Positive relationships can be built, and students of color can tell their side of the story, outside of the use of hip-hop. Teachers and other school staff with a working knowledge of cultural differences, or cultural competence, can actually promote the academic and social well-being of students of color. Cultural competence is being aware of one's own personal beliefs and biases, and having the awareness, knowledge, and skills needed to work with diverse populations. Teachers should have cultural competence when working with students, and school policies can help facilitate this by having workshops in which school staff openly explore their own values, biases, preconceived notions, and stereotypes. Finally, cultural competence also means that one recognizes that students of color may have different negative social experiences that may hinder academic development, such as living in communities populated by poverty and violence, so communicating with students and families allows for opportunities to provide the resources necessary for student achievement.

Argument 2

Argument 2: Culturally relevant pedagogy encourages active participation and engagement in learning by allowing teaching styles to be exciting and inviting, which leads to opportunities for students to grasp concepts that were strange and/ or uninteresting to them. Au and Jordan (1981) conducted a case study of the Kamehameha Early Education Program to examine how teachers, psychologist, linguists, and anthropologists teach Hawaiian children to read. Their findings demonstrated that reading lessons were successful due to the use of linguistic patterns found in native Hawaiian culture, and the use of culturally congruent practices. To have these culturally congruent practices, does Hawthorne's *The Scarlett Letter* need to be compared with 2Pac's "Keep Ya Head Up," using the same linguistic patterns, for students to think critically about social issues as recommended by David E. Kirkland (2008)? Why not simply ask,

> If Hester Prynne were living today in 2010 in your community or neighborhood, what would life be like for her? How would people treat her? How would the people in your neighborhood receive her? What if she were Black, Latino, or Asian? Support your answer with real-life anecdotes.

Just doing this allows for active participation and engagement in the learning process and for student voices to be heard. This process takes the traditional form of learning considered acceptable by society, albeit dictated by White, middle-class norms *(The Scarlett Letter)*, and allows for students to relate it to something they know (their own life) and to be able to analyze and interpret information based on their cultural socialization.

Linguistics, or communication styles, can play an active role in student achievement. Linguistically and culturally diverse students face many disadvantages in school due to language barriers (Portman, 2009). Many school personnel may believe that only those whose first language is not English face a language barrier in schools, but African Americans can also face this barrier. For example, while European Americans may be accustomed to more impersonal, emotionally restrained communication styles, the loud, intense, and confrontations styles of African Americans could be regarded as rude and inappropriate in the school setting (Day-Vines & Day-Hairston, 2005). Teachers must be aware of how they feel and respond to those who use communication styles that are different from their own, and not let these styles inform how they work with students and families. However, this does not mean speaking in slang, or using African American Vernacular English, is necessary to meet the needs of students with different linguistic or communication styles.

Although incorporating elements of different cultures in learning is warranted and necessary in today's schools, incorporating pop culture, or hip-hop, is a different strategy altogether. There are other ways to incorporate elements of different cultures into the learning environments that allow for students to transcend their cultural socialization and pursue academic excellence, which hip-hop cannot do. For example, if the English class is having a unit on Shakespeare, then include a unit on August Wilson, the two-time Pulitzer Award–winning playwright who told the story of Black America through a cycle of 10 plays that covered each decade of the 20th century. If implementing a unit on Nathaniel Hawthorne, then include a unit on Ralph Ellison's *Invisible Man*. How can students not relate to a book about African Americans who are caught between what White society expects of them and what Black society expects of them? Ernest Gaines's *A Lesson Before Dying*—about an African American male who gets charged with a crime he did not commit—could also be a good culture-specific unit to teach in classrooms, especially as Black men are often accused of crimes they did not commit.

CONCLUSION

It is necessary to summarize Ladson-Billings's (1995b) depictions of good teaching using culturally relevant pedagogy, which does not mention hip-hop or popular culture at all. Good teaching, using culturally relevant pedagogy, includes strongly identifying with the teaching profession; giving back to the community and encouraging students to do the same; having a fundamental belief that all students can succeed, and working hard to help make that happen; having a fluid and equitable relationship with students by having students act as teachers and teachers act as active learners in the class; attending community functions and using community services; having a passion about teaching demonstrated through enthusiasm and vitality about what is being taught and learned; and being open to critical analysis of the curriculum. Is hip-hop, or other popular culture, needed for this to occur?

RESPONSE TO POINT ESSAY

Latish Reed, Natalie A. Tran, and Christopher N. Thomas, the authors of the point essay, make valid points for infusing hip-hop into educational settings. However, the authors feel that hip-hop does not necessarily promote negative stereotypical images of youth, particularly those from a lower socioeconomic status. I disagree with this statement. Social learning theory tells us we learn from what we see and what we hear. When it comes to stereotypes, which pervades the school system, many White and middle-class teachers (including middle-class African American teachers) tend to learn about their minority students from mass media, the number one place where people in majority statuses receive messages about minority groups. This can take place in many forms: television, print, radio, Internet. The message we receive is that Blacks are more prone to violence, misogyny, and crime. To further add insult to this by saying African American children can better learn by infusing hip-hop because this gives them a voice only serves to perpetuate those stereotypes. If we truly want to promote access and equity for all students, we need to start combating the negative images that permeate all cultures and ethnic groups. Yes, culturally relevant pedagogy is needed, but there are more positive ways to do this than the use of hip-hop.

FURTHER READINGS AND RESOURCES

Alder, N. (2000). Part III: Creating multicultural classrooms: Teaching diverse students. *Multicultural Perspectives, 2,* 28–31.

Allen, B. A., & Boykin, A. W. (1992). African American children and the educational process: Alleviating cultural discontinuity through prescriptive pedagogy. *School Psychology Review, 21,* 586–596.

Au, K., & Jordan, C. (1981). Teaching reading to Hawaiian children: Finding a culturally appropriate solution. In H. Trueba, G. Guthrie, & K. Au (Eds.), *Culture and the bilingual classroom: Studies in classroom ethnography* (pp. 139–152). Rowley, MA: Newbury.

Chang, J. (2003). Stakes is high. *Nation, 276,* 1–21.

Day-Vines, N., & Day-Hairston, B. (2005). Culturally congruent strategies for addressing the behavioral needs of urban, African American male adolescents. *Professional School Counseling, 8,* 236–243.

Durden, T. (2008). Do your homework! Investigating the role of culturally relevant pedagogy in comprehensive school reform models serving diverse student populations. *Urban Review, 40,* 403–419.

Freire, P. (1971). *Pedagogy of the oppressed.* New York: Herder & Herder.

Gay, G. (2000). *Culturally responsive teaching.* New York: Teachers College Press.

hooks, b. (1994). *Outlaw culture: Resistant representation.* New York: Routledge.

Howard, T. C. (2001). Telling their side of the story: African-American students' perceptions of culturally relevant teaching. *The Urban Review, 33,* 131–149.

Howard, T. C. (2003). Culturally relevant pedagogy: Ingredients for critical teacher reflection. *Theory Into Practice, 42,* 194–202.

Jocson, K. M. (2006). "Bob Dylan and hip-hop": Intersecting literacy practices in youth poetry communities. *Written Communication, 23*(3), 231–259.

Kirkland, D. E. (2008). "You must learn": Promoting hip-hop education. *Youth Media Reporter, 3,* 42–46.

Kitwana, B. (2002). *The hip hop generation: Young Blacks and the crisis in African American culture.* New York: Basic Civitas Books.

Ladson-Billings, G. (1994). *The dreamkeepers: Successful teachers of African American children.* San Francisco: Jossey-Bass.

Ladson-Billings, G. (1995a). Toward a theory of culturally relevant pedagogy. *American Educational Research Journal, 32*(3), 465–491.

Ladson-Billings, G. (1995b). But that's just good teaching! The case for culturally relevant pedagogy. *Theory Into Practice, 34,* 159–165.

Mahiri, J., & Conner, E. (2003). Black youth violence has a bad rap. *Journal of Social Issues, 59*(1), 121–140.

Nieto, S. (1994). Lessons from students on creating a chance to dream. *Harvard Educational Review, 64,* 392–426.

Portman, T. A. A. (2009). Faces of the future: School counselors as cultural mediators. *Journal of Counseling & Development, 87,* 21–35.

Stovall, D. (2006). We can relate: Hip-hop culture, critical pedagogy, and the secondary classroom. *Urban Education, 41,* 585–602.

Taylor, C. S., & Taylor, V. (2004). Hip-hop and youth culture: Contemplations of an emerging cultural phenomenon. *Reclaiming Children and Youth, 12*(4), 251–253.

Weinstein, S. (2007). A love for the thing: The pleasures of rap as a literate practice. *Journal of Adolescent & Adult Literacy, 50*(4), 270–281.

9

Should all forms of ability grouping be eliminated in schools?

POINT: Tiffany R. Wheeler, *Transylvania University*
COUNTERPOINT: Deborah A. Harmon,
Eastern Michigan University

OVERVIEW

While ability grouping and tracking are long-standing educational practices, they often generate debate and consternation among administrators, teachers, and parents. *Tracking,* the formal practice of separating students into hierarchical groups based on their demonstrated academic performance in relevant subject areas, has been in use in public education in the United States since its early years. Indeed, the very concept of grade levels is a form of tracking, especially when schools require students to demonstrate certain academic competencies before promoting them to the next level.

Similar to tracking, *ability grouping* focuses on placing students into smaller, more manageable clusters that allow educators to concentrate on addressing their common interests and academic needs. In contrast to tracking, ability grouping functions as a less formal process. Whereas tracking often involves formalized school policies adopted across school districts, specific schools or teachers may employ ability grouping in more fluid ways as part of an effort to work on certain skills with their students. An example of ability grouping is the use of reading groups in elementary school classrooms.

Within the United States, many assume that tracking and ability grouping are basically the same. In practice, the impact of tracking is much more permanent than that imposed by ability grouping. Likewise, tracking often uses standardized exams or some other testing methods to determine students' academic levels and determine where to place them within the tracking structure. On the other hand, ability grouping may draw on a range of factors including in-class performance, academic potential, curricular interests, and teacher observations. Peer tutoring can also serve as a form of ability grouping by having academically high-performing students provide instructional support for their less academically prepared classmates or those in lower grade levels.

Outside of the United States, other countries use one, both, or a combination of tracking and ability grouping to make some or all of their academic placement decisions. For example, students in Austria and Germany enter a relatively rigid tracking system from age 10 focused on standardized testing. Well known for its tracking system, students in Germany find that many doors either open or closed to them based on their performance on standardized exams. German students who test well remain on track for better educational and professional opportunities. These students then receive priority appropriations of schools' resources by experiencing student to teacher ratios of 11.89 to 1 in the general (upper) track compared to 21.25 to 1 for students tracked to study and work in vocational areas. Similarly, high-performing Austrian students enjoy student to teacher ratios of 9.05 to 1 compared to 14.51 to 1 for their lower performing contemporaries. Although the nation does not start tracking students until age 15, academically high-achieving students in France experience student-to-teacher ratios of 6.75 to 1, while the lower performing students face ratios of 14.67 to 1 (Brunello & Checchi, 2007). In the educational context, tracking may jeopardize the academic development of students placed in the lower tracks in their countries since they are less likely to receive direct attention from their classroom instructors. Related to issues of employment preparation and life opportunities, tracking in these countries can also lead to or prevent individuals from accessing specific careers as adults.

Compared to the international applications of tracking and ability grouping, the use of these approaches in the United States is not as restrictive. Students who complete their basic education in any track or academic classification in American schools still have the opportunity to matriculate college, major in any area that they choose, and have a chance to pursue any career that they find appealing and are qualified to enter. Other positive aspects attributed to tracking and ability grouping in the United States include students being grouped with peers of similar intellectual capacities, greater attention to gifted and talented students, and opportunities to offer variations to the curricula.

Proponents of ability grouping support these policies because they provide the context for students of similar academic levels to work and receive academic attention within the same cluster. For gifted and talented students, these ability groups allow teachers to focus on giving them expanded and advanced lessons. Likewise, average and lower performing students also gain access to small group settings in which they can receive attention related to their academic needs. In each of these groups, teachers also have the opportunity to make alterations to the curricula to meet the skill levels of each group.

Even so, opposition to ability grouping and tracking policies suggests that not all of the outcomes associated with these policies are positive. Opponents note that one unwelcome by-product attributed to these policies is that they negatively influence the self-esteem of students. While students in gifted programs enjoy greater attention and higher status due to their placement in a high-ability group, students in the average and lower tracks may feel undervalued and lose confidence in themselves because of their group assignments. At the same time, the fact that each group receives different curricula may also inhibit the development of students in lower groups. Although these students will have an opportunity to master the curriculum used in their individual groups, this may prevent them from, rather than help them in, catching or keeping up with higher performing students since they will not have access to the same skill development opportunities.

Beyond the academic implications, ability grouping and tracking may also impact school desegregation efforts. Across ability groups, racial minority and lower income students tend to experience greater representation in the remedial and average performing tracks. On the other hand, fewer of these students end up placed in the higher performing groups. This helps to inhibit desegregation efforts by effectively reserving gifted and talented programs for White students. This amounts to resegregation, creating a situation where students attend mostly racially segregated classes within racially diverse schools and school districts.

Providing further investigation of the outcomes associated with ability grouping, the two debates in this section offer further insights into how these policies affect schools. Both essayists are in agreement that tracking should be eliminated but disagree on the benefits of ability grouping. Tiffany R. Wheeler (Transylvania University) states that research has consistently shown that the negative aspects of ability grouping far outweigh any potential benefits and advocates for its elimination. She feels that ability grouping is not in the best interests of students and calls for educators to design equitable instruction for all students. Deborah A. Harmon (Eastern Michigan University), on the other hand, argues that ability grouping, when done properly and for the right reasons, can be beneficial. She advocates for the use of flexible grouping that allows for differentiated curriculum and instruction and enables teachers to teach to the various needs of their students.

Saran Donahoo
Southern Illinois University Carbondale

POINT: Tiffany R. Wheeler
Transylvania University

I n most schools in the United States, and in some international settings, the processes of ability grouping and academic tracking have been pervasive. *Ability grouping* is defined as "the assignment of students to groups for instruction based on their academic ability or achievement" (Gamoran & Hallinan, 1995, p. 113). Ability grouping is more prevalent at elementary schools, usually in the areas of reading and mathematics. Within-class ability grouping occurs when teachers divide up students in a class into smaller instructional groups that are "relatively homogeneous with respect to ability" (p. 113). Similarly, academic tracking is more common in middle and high school and usually involves between-class ability grouping, where students in various grade levels are divided into classes based on perceived abilities. These classes often include categories such as "college preparatory," "vocational," and "general" (Wheelock, 1994). Even within these broad categories, there are levels of courses that influence the class "track" in which students are placed. For example, college preparatory courses might be leveled into advanced, honors, standard, and basic classes (Wheelock, 1994). While ability grouping and academic tracking have been popular and persistent with many supporters, this essay argues that ability grouping and tracking are harmful instructional practices that hinder the academic achievement of students from a variety of social backgrounds. Ability grouping, in particular, can lead to inequitable instructional experiences, unfairly influence teacher expectations, reproduce societal inequalities based on race and socioeconomic status, and negatively affect students' self-esteem and motivation, particularly if they are placed in lower ability groups.

HISTORY OF ABILITY GROUPING AND TRACKING

To understand how ability grouping and tracking became such widespread practices, it is important to briefly examine the history of these practices in American schools. From the turn of the 20th century to around 1930, approximately 18 million immigrants entered the United States, and they mainly came from various parts of Europe (Broussard & Joseph, 1998). Additionally, freed Africans were beginning to seek educational opportunities during this time. Before these demographic changes occurred, public schools, especially high schools, were overwhelmingly White, Protestant, middle class, and male

(Broussard & Joseph, 1998; Donelan, Neal, & Jones, 1994). From 1880 until 1918, the school population increased from approximately 200,000 to more than 1.5 million (Broussard & Joseph, 1998). To accommodate the growing diverse population of students in American schools, educators began instructional grouping schemes that reflected the ideology of social Darwinism, which posits that socially advanced classes are biologically superior to other classes. Ability grouping supported the notion of social Darwinism, as educators sorted and grouped students according to beliefs that some students have more innate abilities than others. Many educators believed that immigrant children, many of whom did not speak English fluently, were intellectually less capable, and schools became responsible for "Americanizing" them and helping them to "fit in," by focusing on teaching them English and preparing them for the job market (Donelan et al., 1994; Wheelock, 1994).

Debates about the role of public education and society in the early 20th century influenced the role of grouping and tracking in schools. Progressive educators who were part of an organization known as the Committee of Ten argued that, in a democracy, all students should have "a broad and general education regardless of the adult roles they were likely to assume in society" (Wheelock, 1994, p. 5). Members of the Committee of Ten believed that schools were not able to predict how students would use their education and should adopt intellectually stimulating programs for all of its students, which would include subjects such as geometry, algebra, and foreign language study. However, opponents of these ideas argued that immigrant children and other students from diverse backgrounds would not be able to handle rigorous academic programs because of their perceived low intellectual abilities. The rise of intelligence testing during this time period also seemed to "confirm" that immigrant students were intellectually inferior, and many educators believed that the school curriculum needed to provide more of a vocational and practical focus for immigrant children, since they were destined to become industrial workers. Thus, educators felt justified in establishing grouping schemes and separate academic tracks based on students "predicted" futures, as they believed that "some students were better equipped than others to benefit from access to certain knowledge" (p. 6).

THE CASE AGAINST ABILITY GROUPING

Debates about ability grouping and tracking have continued to dominate educational discussions for decades. Proponents of ability grouping argue that these practices are advantageous in a variety of ways. George Ansalone (2010) cites the research of A. H. Turney, which indicates that ability grouping can help facilitate instruction by individualizing instruction, empower instructors to modify teaching techniques according to class level, eliminate the probability that advanced students will experience boredom due to the participation of slower students, and encourage slower students to participate because they will not be intimidated by their more capable peers. As well, some supporters of ability grouping assert that students who have a low IQ will develop a more positive self-concept when they are grouped homogeneously with others of similar ability. Some educators also argue that ability grouping limits the academic diversity in a group and makes students easier to teach and manage (Ansalone, 2010; Broussard & Joseph, 1998).

However, opponents of ability grouping argue that these practices have detrimental effects on students' educational experiences. Critics note that ability grouping promotes inequitable opportunities for student learning in different tracks. For example, Jeannie Oakes (1985) found that in her seminal study of the tracking process in 25 secondary schools, students in higher track classes had markedly different access to knowledge and learning experiences than students in lower track classes. In high-track English classes, Oakes notes that students were exposed to content that might be classified as "high-status" knowledge because it generally reflected required knowledge that students would need if they were going on to college. Students in these classes studied classic and modern works of literature, analyzed literary elements of works in various genres, and were taught the conventions of writing in a variety of forms. In average English classes, the students engaged in learning some of the high-status knowledge, although not as in depth as the high-track classes. In contrast, Oakes found that students in low-track English classes rarely engaged in the study of this type of high-status knowledge and skills. Typically, students in these classes did not read high quality literature, and the literature they did read were often short novels written at a low level of difficulty. The low-track English classes tended to focus on teaching basic literacy skills through means of workbooks and reading kits. Oakes also found that "the writing of simple, short narrative paragraphs and the acquisition of standard English usage and functional literacy skills (filling out forms, applying for jobs) were also frequently mentioned as course content in low track classes" (p. 76). Although Oakes's research focused on tracking, its findings apply to ability grouping as well.

Additionally, Oakes (1985) found that math classes followed a similar pattern of differences. High-status math knowledge such as concepts about numeration systems, mathematical models, probability, and statistics were addressed in higher track classes, and, as in the average English classes, a "diluted" version of the high-status mathematical concepts was taught in average math classes. However, the low-track math classes focused on basic computational skills and arithmetic facts such as multiplication tables. Many low-track math classes addressed consumer math skills, which would be useful to students at any level, but these skills were taught to the exclusion of higher level mathematical ideas or concepts. The curricular content addressed in the different tracks is important to note because the types of content learned had an impact on students' abilities to move among the tracks. Students placed in lower track classes would have difficulty moving to an average or higher track because they would not have acquired the knowledge necessary to progress successfully in these classes. Thus, Oakes argues that students were "denied the opportunity to learn material that would be essential for mobility among track levels" (p. 78).

Consequently, critics of ability grouping argue that the different learning opportunities created among academic tracks also influence teachers' expectations of students who are grouped or tracked into particular classes. Consistently, studies have shown that teachers tend to hold higher expectations for students in higher ability groups and have lower expectations for students in lower ability groups (Ansalone, 2010; Broussard & Joseph, 1998; Oakes, 1985). Oakes observed that teachers of high-track classes engaged their students in activities that "demanded critical thinking, problem solving, drawing conclusions, making generalizations, or evaluating or synthesizing knowledge" (p. 76). Yet, students in low-track classes often focused on simple memory tasks or comprehension. In some rare cases, students in low-track classes were required to apply their knowledge to new situations, but these kinds of learning tasks occurred far less frequently than activities that involved basic skills and memorization. Opponents of ability grouping warn that teachers tend to label students based on their group or class placement, leading to the assumption that students' abilities are static and immutable. Moreover, many teachers prefer to teach upper level groups because they perceive the students to be more capable than those in average or lower ability groups, and some teachers define their status as teachers according to their teaching assignment (Ansalone, 2010). However, Anne Wheelock (1994) asserts that people experience cognitive growth at all ages, and that the "depth and extent of their development depends a great deal more on the academic challenges offered than on native ability" (p. 10).

Another key criticism of ability grouping is that it reproduces societal inequalities based on race, ethnicity, and socioeconomic status. Critics note that ability grouping serves to maintain the status quo in American society by gearing White, middle-class students to higher track classes and placing poor students and students of color into lower track classes. Jomills Henry Braddock, II and Robert E. Slavin (1995) report that African American students and Hispanic students are greatly overrepresented in low-ability groups in elementary schools. As a result, many teachers tend to have lower expectations of students of color and poor students because of their disproportionate placement in the lower tracks of most schools in the United States (Braddock & Slavin, 1995; Donelan et al., 1994; Wheelock, 1998–1999). For example, Oakes (1985) found that seventh-grade Latino students with high test scores were half as likely as White students to be placed in accelerated classes. In the tenth grade, Whites were more than twice as likely to be in the higher classes, and Asians were more than 4 times as likely to be placed in college preparatory math classes as Latino students with similar test scores (Oakes, 1985, cited in Wheelock, 1998–1999). When teachers were asked to explain their rationale for placing students in this way, they asserted that the home conditions in the students' lives would not help them to meet the challenges of the higher level classes (Wheelock, 1998–1999). Thus, the teachers' low expectations and stereotypes of students of color led to their unfair placement of students into classes that limited their learning opportunities and denied them access to knowledge that would prepare them for college and beyond. Similarly, Richarde W. Donelan, Gerald A. Neal, and Deneese L. Jones (1994) lament that ability grouping contributes to diminishing the life chances of African American youth because these practices have served to "lock disproportionate numbers of African American students into dead-end educational agendas" (p. 382).

Not only do many teachers harbor low expectations of students who are placed in lower ability groups, but students often begin to internalize these low expectations themselves, which negatively undermines their self-esteem. As previously mentioned, supporters of ability grouping assert that those students who are perceived to be "less capable" will have lower self-esteem if they are placed in groups or classes with high-achieving students. However, many researchers refute this claim and argue that students tend to have a lower self-concept when they are placed in lower ability groups (Ansalone, 2010; Braddock & Slavin, 1995; Donelan et al., 1994; Oakes, 1985; Wheelock, 1994). Students develop a sense of their abilities by the groups in which they are placed. Ansalone (2010) argues that tracks can "create a self-fulfilling prophesy of behavior in students and play an important role in defining the type of person that they believe themselves to be" (p. 12). An excerpt from Thomas J. Cottle's study (as cited in Braddock & Slavin, 1995) of an 11-year-old African American boy named Ollie Taylor, who had recently been assigned to the low academic group in his school in Boston, illustrates how ability grouping can influence a student's self-concept:

The only thing that matters in my life is school, and there they think I'm dumb and always will be. I'm starting to think that they're right. Hell, I know they put all the black kids together in one group if they can, but that doesn't make any difference either. I'm still dumb. Even if I look around and know that I'm the smartest in my group, all that means is that I'm the smartest of the dumbest. (p. 7)

This excerpt highlights so many of the problems with ability grouping. It is obvious that Ollie has received the message that he is less capable, or "dumb," because he was placed in the lower track, and that race plays a role in assigning students to tracks. Ollie also feels that even if he is a high achiever in the low-ability group, it doesn't matter because he is still perceived as "dumb." Consequently, critics of ability grouping warn that students like Ollie who are placed in lower ability groups are more likely to believe that they have no control of their academic fate and may be at a higher risk for delinquency problems and dropping out of school.

ALTERNATIVES TO ABILITY GROUPING

This essay has discussed some of the harmful effects of ability grouping on students, particularly for students who are placed in lower ability groups. Supporters of ability grouping argue that these practices are necessary to increase student achievement and that students learn better in a homogeneous group; however, most research studies do not support this assumption. In general, research has shown that there are no clear-cut benefits or positive effects from ability grouping (Ansalone, 2010; Braddock & Slavin, 1995; Oakes, 1985). Opponents of ability grouping suggest that alternative approaches to instruction need to be implemented to maximize learning experiences for students of all ability levels. Cooperative learning is often proposed as an alternative to ability grouping (Braddock & Slavin, 1995; Donelan et al., 1994). Cooperative learning methods that incorporate two major elements, group goals and individual accountability, have been found to have positive effects at all grade levels (Braddock & Slavin, 1995). Additionally, teachers should provide a rich curriculum and prepare stimulating instructional experiences for all children to engage them in learning (Donelan et al., 1994; Wheelock, 1998–1999). Active learning strategies that incorporate constructivist principles, higher level thinking, efficient use of technology, and problem solving are beneficial for students of all backgrounds (Braddock & Slavin, 1995; Donelan et al., 1994). Also, teachers need to revise their expectations about students who are perceived as less capable, particularly poor students and students of color, and work diligently to use instructional approaches to increase their academic achievement and engagement.

RESPONSE TO COUNTERPOINT ESSAY

In the counterpoint essay, Deborah Harmon rightfully acknowledges that students need to be grouped and regrouped according to frequent teacher assessments, since learning is a dynamic, not a static process. She also suggests that alternatives to fixed ability grouping include grouping by readiness, grouping by preferred learning style, and grouping by culturally preferred learning styles. While, as Harmon notes, grouping students according to their needs is not necessarily a bad idea, teachers need to think critically about the grouping structures that she suggests. For example, some teachers might have preconceived notions about which students are academically ready to move on to the next concept and may end up grouping students based on students' perceived abilities after all. Also, although it is very important to incorporate a variety of learning styles and culturally congruent concepts into instruction, teachers have to be careful not to essentialize and assume that all students of a particular cultural or ethnic group have the same learning styles and preferences. Additionally, grouping schemes that only focus on preferred learning styles or particular multiple intelligences might limit students from interacting from others who have different skills and abilities that could benefit their learning.

CONCLUSION

Although ability grouping has been a staple in academic grouping in many schools, particularly in the United States, research has consistently shown that the negative aspects of these practices far outweigh any potential benefits. As American schools become increasingly diverse, educators need to critically examine their instructional approaches and grouping structures to make sure that they are providing an optimal learning environment for students from a variety of racial, ethnic, and socioeconomic backgrounds. Ability grouping is not in the best interest of students, especially those who are placed in lower ability groups, and can set them up for educational failure and diminished life chances. It is time for educators to reject popular notions about the benefits of ability grouping and make a concerted effort to design challenging and equitable instruction for all students.

COUNTERPOINT: Deborah A. Harmon
Eastern Michigan University

Ability grouping and tracking of students have a long history of controversy in elementary and secondary education. While the terms *ability grouping* and *tracking* are often used interchangeably, they are not synonymous. It is critical to make this distinction, considering that ability grouping can have multiple outcomes while the impact of tracking has proven to be deleterious to students. Additionally, the common assumption that ability grouping and tracking are synonymous unfairly casts ability grouping into a negative light. Ability grouping is an instructional strategy that occurs in both tracked and untracked schools. *Ability grouping* refers to the practice of creating small groups of students within a classroom based on measured ability and performance determined by achievement tests or various assessments. For example, in reading, students may be grouped according to their levels and performances on assessments. Students normally remain in their assigned groups for designated time periods. *Tracking* is the placement of students in programs and schools based on overall achievement that is often defined as high, average, or low. Placement is generally determined by student's grades, achievement tests scores, counselor recommendations, parent requests, or arbitrary criteria established by teachers or counselors. Students take the courses identified for their program and are not able to take courses from other tracks, even if they have an interest or demonstrated ability. Ability grouping, when used correctly and for the right reasons, can be beneficial to students. To clearly make the distinction between ability grouping and tracking, and to emphasize the need to differentiate between these practices, each will be discussed in the sections that follow.

ABILITY GROUPING

Students arrive in classrooms with various levels of knowledge, skill sets, and experiences presenting a formidable challenge for teachers. Teachers are expected to teach reading and writing skills to students whose skills range from well below grade level to well above grade level. A common practice teachers use to address the various knowledge and skill levels students present in class is to use ability grouping, particularly in language arts, reading, and math. In theory, ability grouping increases student achievement by reducing the disparity in student ability levels, and increases the likelihood that teachers can provide targeted instruction that is neither too easy nor too hard for most students. The assumption is that ability grouping allows teachers to provide a challenge for high achievers and to provide more individual attention and detailed instruction for low achievers. In addition, high achievers are challenged by their peers, and low achievers don't have to compete with their more advanced peers.

Types of Ability Grouping

The use of ability grouping occurs more often in elementary schools than secondary schools and takes various forms such as (a) ability grouping by class assignment, (b) within-class grouping, and (c) between-class grouping using the Joplin Plan. Ability-grouped class assignment involves placing students in one self-contained classroom on the basis of their ability or achievement test scores. They remain together for all of their instruction. Gifted and talented self-contained classrooms, English language learners (ELL) classrooms, and even special education classrooms are examples of ability-grouped class assignments. Within-class grouping assigns students to heterogeneous classes and then regroups students according to their achievement level for one or more subjects. For example, students from homeroom classes are sorted into groups for reading and math based on their knowledge and skill level. One of the most widely used between-class groupings is the Joplin Plan. Students are assigned to heterogeneous classes for most of the day but are regrouped across grade levels for specific subject areas with different teachers. For example, a reading class at the fourth-grade level might be composed of a group of high-achieving third graders, a group of average-achieving fourth graders, and a group of low-achieving fifth graders with the same teacher. This type of grouping allows students to be with students who have similar knowledge, understanding, and skills.

TRACKING

Tracking refers to a practice that is used in secondary education where students are assigned to classes or a series of classes or programs based on their abilities. Students take the courses selected for their particular track and are not allowed to take classes from other tracks. The belief is that tracking makes it easier for teachers to provide an appropriate classroom experience that would meet the various levels and needs of their students. Tracking would reduce the range of students within the classroom allowing teachers to move through the curriculum more efficiently.

Examining the history of the American education system, one can see how tracking grew out of the move toward compulsory schooling and development of comprehensive high schools. One purpose of elementary and secondary education was to socialize or Americanize new immigrant children into society as well as prepare current American students for higher education. Teachers were forced to develop a differentiated curriculum to meet the needs of these two groups of students. Students entering high school were assigned to one of the two programs, giving birth to the practice of tracking. Over time, the two tracks evolved into a general education track, an academic track, and a vocational track. Schools had the responsibility of determining which students would be assigned to the different tracks and would usually make their decisions using criteria based on academic performance, race, culture, socioeconomic status, and gender. During the 1960s and 1970s, elementary and secondary education was greatly influenced by the civil rights movement, and tracking received a lot of attention and was considered to be a way of segregating students by class and race. This led to the transformation of tracking within secondary schools and the creation of courses in different subjects being differentiated into basic, regular, honors, and advanced courses. Regular, honors, and advanced courses are equivalent to the former academic track, while the basic and lower level courses make up the general and vocational tracks. More recently, schools experienced the introduction of magnet programs such as science and technology academies, the International Baccalaureate Program, Cyber High School, and early college experience programs. These programs have been added to the academic track, while project-based high school programs and cyber-school programs have been added to the general and vocational tracks. While most of these programs are presented as options to all students, selection or placement of students into these programs is reported to be determined by academic criteria such as grades, standardized test scores, recommendations from teachers and counselors, as well as the students' prior track assignment.

Tracking affects every aspect of the educational experience. The curriculum, instruction, social interactions, learning opportunities, and access to further education are all affected by the practice of tracking students. According to Jeannie Oakes (1985, 1992), students who are tracked do not receive the same quality of education. The most profound impact is on students who are assigned to the lower tracks. The stigma attached to lower track membership conveys a lower social status and contributes to the development of low self-esteem in students. Students who are assigned to lower tracks move through the curriculum at a slower pace and often score lower on standardized tests than those students who are placed in regular education tracks. For those who occupy the lower tracks, there are fewer learning opportunities for college preparation than for those in higher tracks. Tracking perpetuates unequal access to college. Students in the higher tracks receive high social status. The classes that are offered are taught by more experienced teachers who offer an engaging curriculum with interesting materials. Students in higher tracks learn more content and move through the curriculum quicker than students in lower tracks. There are many opportunities for learning, and students have access to college.

While tracking is reported to be based on specific academic criterion, the fact that African American students, Latino students, and students from low-income communities are overrepresented in the lower tracks and underrepresented in the higher tracks suggests that additional nonacademic criteria related to class and race are being used to determine track assignment. Oakes studied the impact of tracking for several years and states that tracking serves as a device for sorting students by class and race. Even in integrated schools, students are resegregated through tracking, and it is looked on as de facto segregation. According to Oakes (1985, 1992), tracking plays a crucial role, as it is a primary contributor to systemic inequality and has created a structure whereby individuals come to accept their social status as natural. She states that the practice of tracking is demoralizing for children of color and for poor children. The research on tracking clearly indicates that it is an ineffective practice that is also inequitable. The lack of evidence on the effectiveness of tracking and the insurmountable proof of the harm it has on student's academic esteem, self-concept, self-efficacy, and achievement led to the condemnation of tracking in the 1980s and 1990s by such groups as the National Governors Association, the Carnegie Council for Adolescent Development, College Board, and the National Council of Teachers of English. Tracking in schools is considered to be a violation of students' civil rights and has been struck down by courts.

ELIMINATION OF ABILITY GROUPING

Critics have expressed concerns about ability grouping for approximately the past 50 years. The concerns focus on social and economic equity, including issues related to the experiences of students, the social stratification of the classroom, and the teacher. Questions about equity bring attention to the methods of determining group assignment. Placement in ability groups is based on students' performance on an achievement or aptitude test at the beginning of the school year. Teachers assess students to determine their level of knowledge at that time and make decisions based on these results or what they think students are capable of doing. There are great concerns about the appropriateness of tests used for placement and possible test bias, privileging some populations of students and putting others at a disadvantage. Since the placement of students is usually for a marking period or full year, it limits the degree to which they can move into different groups.

Oakes (1985, 1992) and Robert E. Slavin (1995) have both investigated the impact of ability grouping practices on students' self-concept, self-esteem, and self-efficacy. Concerns related to students included the labeling of students, academic pressure, and the development of a negative academic self-concept. They find that ability grouping leads to the practice of labeling students according to their group membership, forcing them to deal with the stigma associated with such labels. Students in high-ability groups report feeling pressured to perform and demonstrate an unwillingness to seek help when needed. Students in low-ability groups often come to believe they cannot and will not achieve, leading to a negative academic self-concept and disengagement in learning.

Teachers' expectations can be affected by ability grouping with those teaching high-ability classes having higher expectations for their students and raising the standards and goals once they have achieved them. Teachers in low-ability classes tend to have lower expectations for students and set lower standards and goals. They do not readjust their goals once their students have achieved them, as they feel students have accomplished enough and cannot achieve at a higher level.

Elfrieda H. Hiebert (1983, 1987) has investigated the differences in instruction and teacher interaction with students in various ability groups to see if the quality of instruction is lower in low-ability groups than in average and high-ability groups. Teachers selected for high-ability classes tend to be more experienced than those teaching low ability classes. High-ability classes engage in higher level, critical, and creative thinking. Less-experienced teachers are found in low-ability classes. Low-ability classes engage in lower levels of thinking with very little problem solving and repetitive drills. In fact, teachers often complain about low achievers being deprived of the stimulation provided by high-achieving students with ability grouping.

Slavin (1995) has examined the impact of various types of grouping on student achievement. Research on the impact of ability grouping on student achievement suggests that between-class grouping and flexible within-class grouping created significant gains in achievement for able learners. For average and struggling learners, this was not the case. Carol L. Tieso (2003), who studied the impact of ability grouping on gifted and talented students, found that they benefited substantially. In fact, gifted students gained almost a full year or more when they were grouped with other gifted students and were provided an accelerated curriculum. As a result, Slavin has great concerns over the creation of academic elitism within the classroom. Issues of equality are raised when students in high ability groups obtain more knowledge than average or low ability groups and subsequently gain access to more opportunities.

Slavin's (1995) and John Hollifield's (1987) research suggests that ability grouping in and of itself is generally not very effective in increasing the academic performance of students. Additionally, it has not proven to be more effective than grouping students in heterogeneous groups. Even students with mild and moderate disabilities appear to perform at higher rates when placed in heterogeneous groups. With the exception of able and gifted and talented students, who do achieve at higher rates when grouped with other gifted and talented students, ability-grouped class assignment does not appear to enhance student achievement.

Proponents of ability grouping suggest that the grouping of students allows teachers to provide students with similar knowledge and skills the instruction and challenge they need to progress more effectively through the curriculum. Yet, even within ability groups, students have differing degrees of knowledge, understanding, and experiences, requiring teachers to adjust their curriculum and instruction to meet students' various learning needs. For example, regrouping students for reading and mathematics proves to be effective if the level and pace of instruction is adjusted to the needs of the students.

With ability grouping, students are placed according to their performances at the beginning of the year and may remain in that group throughout the year. The assumption is that students within a given group will progress uniformly. According to research on ability grouping, placement in ability groups should be flexible and not permanent. Student learning is not static but is instead a dynamic process, and students should be given the opportunity to move according to their educational needs. Frequent reassessment of students' knowledge, skills, and understanding is necessary to provide flexibility for reassigning students to groups based on their current progress and achievement.

There are circumstances where it is appropriate to regroup students—for example, when specific concepts and skills that are being taught require regrouping due to disparities in students' previous knowledge and understanding. Grouping should be based on multiple criteria and not solely on IQ tests or overall achievement levels. Criteria for placement in groups can include readiness, preferred ways of learning, or culturally preferred learning styles.

Grouping by Readiness: Grouping based on the concept of readiness provides teachers a different lens to evaluate their students' performance and behavior. Ability grouping involves evaluating students' performance and making a judgment about what students are "able" to learn.

Grouping by Preferred Learning Styles: Grouping based on preferred learning styles allows students who have common interests and ways of learning to work together.

Grouping by Culturally Preferred Learning Styles: Culturally preferred learning styles refers to cultural-specific ways of learning. These include such things as a preference for oral communication, expressive individualism, creativity, communalism, social learning, movement, and verve.

To summarize, it is not that the idea of grouping students based on their needs is a bad idea. It becomes a problem when issues of equity are pervasive throughout the whole process, including the way students are assessed and evaluated. Further, assignments to ability groups, teacher expectations of students, disparities in the quality of instruction and curriculum, and lack of opportunities for students to move from one group to another can have a negative impact on students. Ability grouping creates a social stratification within the classroom that can have a deleterious impact on students and teachers. With ability grouping, teachers are forced to ascertain what they think individual students are capable of learning based on their performance at that particular time. Teachers base their expectations of students according to their assigned ability group. Teachers then teach according to their beliefs about the student's ability. Flexible grouping—grouping students according to their readiness to learn and understanding of the new concept being presented—is highly effective. With flexible grouping, students are put into groups based on whether they need more time and experience with previously taught concepts and content or whether they are ready to learn the new concept being taught or whether they already know the concept being presented and need more of a challenge. Flexible grouping also involves frequently assessing students to determine in which group to place students and allows for students to move easily from one group to another. According to Carol Tomlinson and Kristina Doubet (2005), flexible grouping is the basis for differentiating curriculum and instruction that enables teachers to teach to the different levels of knowledge and skills students bring to the classroom.

RESPONSE TO POINT ESSAY

As reflected in Tiffany R. Wheeler's essay, when ability grouping is used synonymously with tracking, it is difficult to see the merit within the practice. Tracking puts into place a finite structure and pathway for students based on criteria that do not always give an accurate portrayal of what students can master and achieve, is often guided by deficit thinking, and produces inequities related to access to and excellence in education. Ability grouping is an instructional practice inclusive of multiple grouping strategies, some of which address the realities that students bring a variety of skills and knowledge into the classroom that make it difficult to teach a common lesson.

Wheeler warns that teachers have to be careful not to assume all culturally or ethnically diverse students have the same preferred ways of learning for fear of marginalizing groups of students. Currently, teachers are trained to teach in ways that fit White, middle-class students and are told these are best practices—which has marginalized culturally diverse students. With the additional knowledge and understanding about the learning needs and preferences of culturally diverse students, teachers will be better prepared to provide a more culturally responsive learning environment for all students. In fact, teaching that incorporates the use of flexible groupings, combining culturally preferred learning, readiness, multiple intelligences, and students' interests, provides multiple opportunities for all students to work cooperatively with peers with whom they might not have had the opportunity to interact before. Equitable education will occur when teachers are knowledgeable about all of their students' learning needs and preferences and are able to teach students in ways that give all students access to knowledge by teaching them in ways that afford all students the ability to learn.

FURTHER READINGS AND RESOURCES

Ansalone, G. (2010). Tracking: Educational differentiation or defective strategy. *Educational Research Quarterly, 34*(2), 3–17.

Braddock, J. H., II, & Slavin, R. E. (1995). Why ability grouping must end: Achieving excellence and equity in American education. In H. Pool & J. A. Page (Eds.), *Beyond tracking: Finding success in inclusive school* (pp. 7–19). Bloomington, IN: Phi Delta Kappa.

Broussard, C. A., & Joseph, A. L. (1998). Tracking: A form of educational neglect? *Social Work in Education, 20*(2), 110–120.

Brunello, G., & Checchi, D. (2007, October). Does school tracking affect equality of opportunity? New international evidence. *Economic Policy, 52*(22), 781–861.

Donelan, R. W., Neal, G. A., & Jones, D. L. (1994). The promise of *Brown* and the reality of academic grouping: The tracks of my tears. *The Journal of Negro Education, 63*(3), 376–387.

Gamoran, A., & Hallinan, M. T. (1995). Tracking students for instruction: Consequences and implications for school restructuring. In M. T. Hallinan (Ed.), *Restructuring schools: Promising practices and policies* (pp. 113–131). New York: Plenum.

Hiebert, E. H. (1983). An examination of ability grouping for reading instruction. *Reading Research Quarterly, 18,* 231–255.

Hiebert, E. H. (1987). The context of instruction and student learning: An examination of Slavin's assumptions. *Review of Educational Research, 57,* 337–340.

Hollifield, J. (1987). *Ability grouping in elementary schools.* ERIC Clearinghouse on Elementary and Early Childhood Education, Urbana, IL (ED290542). Retrieved September 1, 2010, from http://www.ericdigests.org/pre-927/grouping.htm

Oakes, J. (1985). *Keeping track: How schools structure inequality.* New Haven, CT: Yale University Press.

Oakes, J. (1992). Detracking schools: Early lessons from the field. *Phi Delta Kappan, 73,* 448–454.

Rubin, B. C. (2006). Tracking and detracking: Debates, evidence, and best practices for a heterogeneous world. *Theory Into Practice, 45*(1), 4–14.

Slavin, R. (1995). Detracking and its detractors: Flawed evidence, flawed values. *Phi Delta Kappan, 77,* 220–221.

Tieso, C. L. (2003). Ability grouping is not just tracking. *Roeper Review, 26*(1), 29–36.

Tomlinson, C., & Doubet, K. (2005). Reach them to teach them. *Educational Leadership, 62*(7), 8–15.

Wheelock, A. (1994). *Alternatives to tracking and ability grouping.* Arlington, VA: American Association of School Administrators.

Wheelock, A. (1998–1999, Winter). Keeping schools on track. *Rethinking Schools, 13*(2) [online]. Retrieved from http://www.rethinkingschools.org/restrict.asp?path=archive/13_02/tracksi.shtml

Do current funding structures and districting criteria of public education marginalize ethnic and racial minority students?

POINT: Robert C. Knoeppel, *Clemson University*
COUNTERPOINT: Enid Beverley Jones, *Professor Emeritus*

OVERVIEW

The debate in this chapter is concerned with the issue of whether current funding structures and districting criteria of public education disenfranchise ethnic and racial minority students. In all states, except Hawaii, which has only one school district, local school boards are delegated the responsibility of managing public schools with different financial abilities to support education. Financial ability to support education varies from district to district, and within individual school districts, there are funding disparities between neighborhood schools. However, more racial minority students tend to live in low-income neighborhoods, which receive less funding for their schools than schools in wealthier neighborhoods.

Public school funding is very complex, as is shown in many essays in the *School Finance* volume in this series. Given that public education is a state responsibility, a school district's financial support is based on funding from local and state entities. Further, the source of local and state funds varies widely by state. For example, some states fund up to 75% of the cost of public education with 25% coming from local funds, and any combination in between. The source of local and state funds also varies widely. Some states generate education funds from sales or income taxes while others obtain funds from property taxes. In many states, education is funded through a combination of taxes. Basically, local funds are drawn mainly from property taxes and local sales taxes if permitted by the state (Thompson, Wood, & Crampton, 2008).

There are state formulas for providing funds for local schools (Odden & Picus, 2008). First, states may use an equalizing formula by providing funds based on the school district's enrollment, property wealth, tax rate, and students' level of schooling: elementary, middle, or high school. Second, states will provide each school district a basic support level regardless of the district's wealth per student and the district's property tax rate—again, except for Hawaii, with only one school district. But there are several states that provide each local school district a single funding rate per teacher per class without regard for property value per pupil but will grant school districts permission to collect addition funds via local property taxes. School districts must get approval from their respective states on how to collect local school funds and how these funds should be spent regardless of the source of the funds.

The federal government provides about 6% of local school budgets based on needs for special programs such as special education, meals for poor children, and Tile I compensatory education programs for disadvantaged students in qualifying schools, under its No Child Left Behind program. The federal government also supports bilingual education and Native American education. These programs address special needs but do not address the unequal education among the states based on local and state support. Racial bias is often associated with these programs because they tend to marginalize minority students by sorting these students into segregated or remedial classes (Oakes, 2005). There is a high correlation between the overrepresentation of minority students and these programs, such as special education, remedial courses, and Title I programs.

Parents have challenged the unequal funding of public education in federal and state courts over the past 40 years (Odden & Picus, 2008). These legal challenges have produced court decisions mandating an adequate education for all students but not an equal education for all. Results have not been positive for the many lawsuits filed against unequal funding of state schools, and this situation is unlikely to change (Guthrie, Springer, Rolle, & Houck, 2007). Legal challenges have not resulted in increased revenues for schools servicing disadvantaged children. Further, state finance systems for supporting education are not aligned with the academic outcome goals set by the states.

The U.S. Supreme Court in *San Antonio v. Rodriguez* (1973), a dispute from Texas involving equity in state funding, held that unequal funding across school districts did not violate the Equal Protection clause of the Fourteenth Amendment to the U.S. Constitution. Thereafter, school equity cases were processed through state courts, where plaintiffs complained about inequality involving facilities, teachers' salaries, pupil–teacher ratios, funds for students with special needs, students in small and poor districts, municipal overburden in districts with more poor children, and lower per-pupil expenditures for education. All of these state cases involved school districts with large low-income populations; however, the courts only supported an adequate education for all, not an equal or excellent education for all children.

In this chapter, Robert C. Knoeppel of Clemson University argues in the point essay that current school district–funding criteria, generally, does not marginalize racial and ethnic minority students, and Professor Emeritus Enid Beverly Jones takes the opposite position. Both authors made excellent points about the complex systems of school funding and the many legal challenges in the courts without great results to change the funding system to better aid minority students in poor schools.

In the point essay, Knoeppel contends that the failure to change current finance distribution mechanisms has prolonged a system whereby many children have not been given adequate resources. Knoeppel states that funding systems that do not recognize student need are inadequate while observing that no state system currently includes an adjustment for race. He concludes that education finance systems must be reformed to align resources with outcome goals and must include a calculation of individual student need that includes race.

Jones, in the counterpoint essay, emphasizes that education finance systems can be modified to serve all populations equitably, adequately, and efficiently, but state legislators and administrators are not taking the necessary steps to do so. Even so, noting that with the resources available today in an age of highly developed technology, Jones concludes that education can be provided on a level playing field.

In reading this chapter, you may want to think about two questions. First, what is the best means for achieving funding equity between schools in poor and wealthy neighborhoods? Second, can technology be a sufficient equalizer even when resources are not allocated according to need?

Frank Brown
University of North Carolina at Chapel Hill

POINT: Robert C. Knoeppel
Clemson University

D o state systems of education finance marginalize students from minority populations? By examining the means by which states fund public education, accountability policy, the lack of changes to systems of education finance, and the bias that has resulted from the use of weightings and categorical funding, I believe that one could answer this question in the affirmative. In an exhaustive review of the state finance policy, Deborah A. Verstegen, Teresa S. Jordan, and Paul Amador (2009) found that the vast majority of state finance systems (45) make use of a foundation program and are based on antiquated notions of equity. These programs ensure an equitable amount of funding for all students. Some states include weighted per-pupil expenditures or compensation for specific student groups: English language learners (ELL), impoverished students, and exceptional students. These weightings are largely disparate and rarely based on research, while compensation programs may not pay the full cost. Recently, researchers have called for changes to the means by which schools are funded (National Working Group on Funding Student Learning, 2008). They note the disconnect between finance policy and state and federal mandates for equitable learner outcomes, the lack of decision-making authority at the local level, and the inability of principals to apply the principles of strategic management to align resources with intended learner outcomes and suggest a distribution model that links funding to children.

The failure to change finance distribution models has not only prolonged a system wherein many children have not been provided adequate resources; it has also solidified deficit thinking that has resulted from the current systems. State school finance systems are complicated models. Funding for education comes from three sources: federal, state, and local. Each state makes use of some type of program to distribute funds, typically a foundation, with additional sources of categorical funding available. Categorical funding is provided for specific purposes such as free and reduced lunch, special education, and ELL. The purpose of these funds is to increase the resources available to students in specific populations in an attempt to provide greater equality of opportunity. Federal funding for public education is exclusively categorical aid. Rather than looking at the total cost of educating all students based on individual need, the way that we describe cost places students in different groups. Bias is associated with those groups and that bias can further marginalize students and families. No state currently has categorical funding associated with race; however, when one considers that there is a high correlation of race with incidence of poverty and that students from ethnic minorities are over-represented in special education, it is easy to see how these children are the victims of lower expectations.

STATE EDUCATION FUNDING

Despite the fact that all 50 state constitutions contain a clause that specifies that the state must establish and fund a system of education, the governance of public schools in the United States has historically rested at the local level, with funding being raised through local property taxes. Early in the 20th century, states began to implement new funding models that included funding from both the state and local levels in an attempt both to increase funding for public education and to more equally distribute revenues to schools. As noted previously, the predominant funding mechanism used by the states is a foundation program. Basically, a foundation program includes a cost to educate the students and either a required local tax effort or a required local contribution that is a percentage of the base cost. State funding makes up the difference between the cost of the educational program and local funds. With some exceptions, such as in Maine and Tennessee, the dollar amount associated with educating children is a political decision wherein legislators estimate the total amount of revenues available for public education and divide that number by the projected enrollment in the state's public schools. As such, there is no empirical research that is used to discern the actual cost of educating students, and a disconnect is said to exist between allocated funds and the actual cost of funding the system of public education. Over time, states began to make use of weighted per-pupil expenditures and cost reimbursements to provide additional funds for children who qualify for programs such as ELL, special education, free and reduced lunch, or compensatory education. In addition, cost reimbursements or per-pupil weightings are also used based on district characteristics such as size or location.

THE CURRENT CONTEXT OF EDUCATION

Currently, all states employ accountability standards that specify levels of proficiency for students. James E. Ryan (2008) notes that the intersection of standards and testing with school finance litigation has dominated the world of education law and policy. This intersection of standards and school finance is seen in the literature in the evolution of the concepts of equity and adequacy.

While often introduced as two separate concepts, our understanding of the term *adequacy* is in large measure the result of an iterative process engaged in by both the judiciary and researches to define and distill our understanding of the term *equity*. Equity can be defined in myriad ways. Helen F. Ladd (2008) stated that equity could be thought of in terms of inputs and outputs. When measuring equity by the more traditional focus on inputs, an equitable finance system would be measured by what Robert Berne and Leanna Steifel (1984) identify as *horizontal equity*. Under such a system, all students would have access to a similar amount, or "package" or resources (Ladd, 2008).

The definition of equity in terms of outputs would, according to Ladd (2008), require that schools be provided sufficient resources to achieve similar outcomes. Because schools are differentially situated, this may require that some schools require more or different resources than others. Differential treatment of unequals is termed *vertical equity* by Berne and Steifel (1984). This concept is especially relevant in the current policy context of schooling that requires equitable outcomes for all children. John E. Roemer (1998) argues that educational achievement should not be permitted to differ due to factors outside of the child's control. As such, policymakers must provide additional resources to students or districts to assist these students to reach equity standards.

Some have argued that vertical equity in its ideal may be characterized as adequacy (King, Swanson, & Sweetland, 2003); however, Ladd (2008) argues that adequacy is not just about differential treatment, but rather sufficiency of resources. The focus is not only on funding but also on what dollars buy and whether that allows all children to reach proficiency goals. As such, the focus of research in educational finance has moved away from traditional notions of equity and is now specifically identifying the relationships between resources and the different phases of the schooling process. These studies inform the estimation of the cost of adequacy as well as the weights assigned to specific groups of children in state funding formulas.

MARGINALIZATION AS A RESULT OF FUNDING INADEQUACY

To date, a challenge to the system of public finance has been heard in nearly each state. Largely, these class action suits were fueled by spending differences resulting from the historical reliance on local wealth or property taxes, with legal arguments changing from one of equity to one of adequacy over time. In most cases, plaintiffs sought equalization and augmentation of funding for public education (Superfine, 2009). The result of these suits is seen largely through an influx of additional funding, although doubt remains as to how one defines an adequate education, measures the cost of an adequate education, and properly distributes funding to ensure an adequate education for all children (Ryan, 2008).

In the counterpoint essay, my colleague Enid Beverley Jones offers an exhaustive review of school finance litigation across the states. For scholars of school finance, this review is most helpful. She concludes that the focus of the challenges to school finance systems is flawed. These challenges have centered on issues such as disparate funding, underfunding of special needs, facilities, teacher salary, and class size. I agree that each of these issues is of concern and also agree that intradistrict funding differences are of concern. However, I believe that the ultimate problem with school finance mechanisms is the fact that they do not address individual needs. My colleague correctly argues that little has changed in school finance distribution models as a result of these legal challenges. I would argue that we must change the focus of analysis. Rather than examining finance at the state or district level, the level of analysis must be at the student level. Funding must flow to individual classrooms. While there are certainly issues about obtaining data at the classroom level, this is the proper level of analysis to truly discern resource allocation. When conducting an examination at this level, a researcher is better able to discern the relationship between resources and student achievement and to draw conclusions as to how those resources were used to address student need.

In their examination of the impact of school finance litigation, Matthew G. Springer, Keke Liu, and James W. Guthrie (2009) found significantly decreased within-state revenue disparities in states where the finance system was overturned based on an equity challenge. Further, they found significantly less within-state revenue disparities in states where the finance system was overturned based on adequacy challenges as compared to states where the state finance system was upheld. However, these decreases in horizontal equity were not as great as those found in states with an equity challenge. Lastly, the researchers found that adequacy challenges did not result in increased revenues for disadvantaged children. Terming this phenomenon the "right kind of inequity," the authors found no evidence to support findings that would suggest that resource allocation patterns have changed to meet the needs of children in underrepresented populations.

It is the refusal to change the systems of public education that has led to the marginalization of children in underrepresented populations. Both Beatrice S. Fennimore (2005) and Jeff Howard (2000) argue that the unwillingness of schools to change educational practices to aid students from underrepresented populations in achieving mandated levels of proficiency has disillusioned those populations for whom the policy was designed to help most. Their writings are in reference to hoped-for changes to the process of teaching and learning that were supposed to result from the standards movement. The same reasoning can be applied to education finance. Countless studies have been conducted to learn more about how schools make a difference in student achievement, how resources are distributed to schools, and what processes are particularly helpful in helping children from different populations to meet proficiency goals. Despite that research, schools that are most in need, that are populated by the highest concentrations of minority students, and that are situated in communities in areas of rural and urban poverty are staffed by the least qualified educators, do not include rigorous curricula, are plagued by unacceptable rates of failure, and are housed in crumbling buildings. Clearly, the system is not serving those who are most in need, and despite calls for change in the judiciary and in the extant literature, state legislatures have not made meaningful changes in the means by which they distribute education funding to school districts. This failure to change has a direct impact on minority populations and calls in to question whether or not states are committed to providing equality of educational opportunity.

MARGINALIZATION AS A RESULT OF WEIGHTING BIAS

Over the course of the last 30 years, tremendous progress has been made in efforts to understand the relationship between resources and student achievement. It is now widely accepted in school finance literature that schools and resources do matter in student achievement. Scholars have shifted their focus to improving their understanding of exactly what resources are needed in different settings and with different populations. Recently, Joseph Murphy (2010) summarized the literature on closing achievement gaps and improving educational opportunity for all children. His work cites research that suggests that improving educational outcomes for children who have historically been underserved requires a multifocal approach that both improves the economic and social factors faced by these students and changes educational practices in schools. According to Murphy (2010), the research does not point to one specific course of action. Rather, the solution to the problem is found though the use of an intensive, sustained effort to accelerate student achievement so that gaps may be eliminated. This requires an influx of additional resources.

One way that researchers have attempted to provide additional resources to students from underrepresented populations is through weighted per-pupil expenditures. Earlier, I argued that these weights are not based on the research, which is clearly problematic. The problem is exacerbated by the way that these policies are interpreted. Studies of the relationship between resources and student achievement are conducted in the aggregate. These studies typically make use of state, district, or school level data. Nearly all of these studies included some independent variable that is entered into the model as a covariate. These included measures of poverty, participation in special education, ELL, ethnicity, or gender. Typically, each of these characteristics was found to be a significant predictor of student achievement.

Gloria M. Rodriguez (2004) notes that one difficulty that schools serving a high percentage of disadvantaged students face is the bias that has resulted from research that found a statistical relationship between various background characteristics and patterns of student achievement. She argues that practitioners have misinterpreted the results from these correlational studies as causal. As such, these studies have contributed to deficit thinking, or the practice of explaining school failure or low academic performance on cultural, racial, class, or gender related characteristics of students. To truly provide an adequate level of education, education practice must focus on an individual examination of all students to discern the difference between actual and desired performance. According to Rodriguez, a better way to conceptualize adequacy is to consider school responsiveness to student need. Ladd (2008) concurs and argues that we must conceptualize both educational processes and finance distribution models that address individual student need. In addition, she argues that true equity will be improved only if funding systems provide additional resources to populations that have historically been underserved.

THE FUTURE OF EDUCATION FINANCE

This brief review of state education finance has highlighted two flaws in the current systems used by states that have marginalized students from underrepresented populations, especially minorities. First, state education finance systems are not aligned with the outcome goals of education that are stipulated in state and federal education policy. Despite the fact that each state constitution includes the requirement that states provide and fund systems of education, and that plaintiffs have increasingly been successful in mounting challenges to the system of education finance in the respective states on adequacy grounds, the means by which states distribute funding to school districts has remained relatively unchanged, with little evidence that underrepresented populations have received additional or adequate funds. Second, attempts to provide additional funding for different groups of students in the form of weighted per-pupil expenditures have led to misinterpretations of the research and bias in the educational process. These processes examine student groups in the aggregate and fail to recognize individual need. More work is needed in attempts to understand the educational process at the classroom level and to more accurately estimate costs for individual students.

No state system of education currently includes an adjustment for race, nor have cost function studies included estimates of the cost of educating students from different races. In an attempt to fill this gap in the knowledge base, Ryan Yeung (2010) made use of a cost function to estimate the additional costs associated with educating minority students in California. He found that race was in fact a cost factor in California's schools. Yeung further found that districts must spend more money when the percentage of African American students increased in school districts. The finding in this study was statistically significant, although the actual amount of spending was not large. Yeung estimates that the additional cost of educating African American students was 25 cents. The interesting result of the study was that race was found to be independent of socioeconomic status. One may conclude from this study that current funding that does not recognize student need is inadequate. To fulfill the promises of standards-based education reform to change the process by which we educate all children, the system of education finance must be reformed so that resources are aligned with outcome goals. An adequate system of education funding must include a calculation of individual student need, and that includes race.

COUNTERPOINT: Enid Beverley Jones
Professor Emeritus

T he subject of education is constantly mentioned in the mass media, in journals dedicated to the study of concept and philosophy of education, in every household, and in every major political campaign speech. This is because one can go through life without using all of the social services such as hospitals, fire stations, and child welfare services, but it is very unlikely that one will go through life without accessing the education system, a system that is less modernized than other sectors of the society in terms of funding, operations, and training for change in the industry of education. Of note is the fact that despite no true gain in achievement levels of all students and of poor and minority students in particular, there has been no major change in using property as the basis for funding since Congress passed the Land Ordinance of 1785 in an effort to consolidate schools and make education compulsory (VanZandt, n.d.).

Over time, the governance of education systems changed, and as state legislatures became more didactic in the education arena, state aid for education became the norm due to precepts of the Tenth Amendment and federal support being limited to what is morally possible under the General Welfare Clause of the U.S. Constitution. Since the majority of education funding comes from state and local sources, we must examine states' funding systems to answer the question posed in this chapter.

Each funding formula used by the state can be adapted to provide for the neediest of students in the schools if resources are distributed according to need and used more efficiently than is the situation today. The current ability to determine the needs of each student by using the technology being applied so effectively in the business sector allows for the satisfaction of education requirements for each child in the system. Hence, the point has to be made that while education finance systems can be modified not once, but continuously to serve all populations equitably, adequately, and efficiently, the state legislators and administrators are not taking the necessary steps to do so. This is evidenced in the sameness of the complaints brought to the courts in education finance cases from the 1970s to 2010.

SCHOOL FUNDING

Traditionally, there has been one basic method used by the states to fund public education and contribute to nonpublic education for services needed in certain geographical and subject areas. State legislatures have enacted mandates, laws, regulations, and policies to meet students' needs based on the location of the student in the state, that is, based on the school district. Where the school district line coincides with neighborhood lines, there has been, and will be, rich and poor neighborhoods and rich and poor schools. State legislatures have, over time, embraced a basic minimum foundation program to achieve equity in funding. Foundation programs, and all the variations that have been developed, simply allow funding formulas that pour more funds into districts that cannot generate sufficient funds from their efforts than in those districts that can. The cutoff or break-even point, as it were, for state funding to begin is predetermined by a sum of money defined as the minimum needed to educate a student to a standard established by the very group who set the standard.

A clear response to the question of state legislatures' measure of success, or lack thereof, in achieving educational goals through funding can be found in the history of education finance cases, the complaints brought before the courts, and the rulings in these cases. The dubious results or changes emanating from the rulings are not always obvious, so a passing reference to some results may throw light on the outcomes.

Using information garnered on each state from the U.S. Department of Education (2010) and National Education Access Network (2010), it is possible to show a pattern of nonchange, as it were, emerging for the students in each state from 1971 to the present. As is well documented, the first major case is *Serrano v. Priest.* In 1971, the California supreme court ruled education a fundamental constitutional right under the state constitution, in what is generally regarded as the first of the modern-era education finance litigation decisions. This case held that a property tax–based funding structure was unconstitutional because of the disparities in per-pupil spending that it created.

In May 2010, a lawsuit with essentially the same complaint was filed in the superior court in the state of California: *Robles-Wong et al. v. State of California.* The complaint alleges that the current education finance system is unconstitutional and that California be required to have a system that provides equal opportunity for all students.

The events in California are symptomatic of issues raised in every other state by poorer, and in many instances minority-populated, school districts when the resource allocation and outcomes are compared to those of wealthier districts in the state. It is no accident then that approximately 40 states have experienced education finance cases similar to this one in California. Deborah Verstegen (1998) has written about the three waves of litigation that have occurred in the state courts on equity and adequacy since 1971. Lauren Nicole Gillespie (2010) argues that education reform needs a fourth wave of litigation that pursues a federal adequacy litigation strategy. However, it is also possible to see this phenomenon on the basis of changes that could have occurred with movement to the information age in the United States where advanced technologies could be used during the 21st century to remove physical and geographical differences between districts, thus removing the very basis for these cases.

If education finance cases in the courts were viewed in terms of before and after the year 2000, the same integral complaint would be evidenced, thus suggesting that once states have achieved fiscal neutrality as decided by the first case rulings, no true attempt had been made to provide for all students. This is partly because of inefficient use funds, partly because of the major source of funds for public schools (property taxes), and partly because of the vagaries of the economy that have been manifest since 2008. Fissures and cracks in the funding systems have become chasms now that all sources of funds (state, local, and federal) are unable to provide sustainable monies using the current rigid method of providing services to students in the recession. It is time for change, true reform, in the distribution of services regardless of available funding.

COURTS' ATTEMPTS AT LEVELING THE FIELD

Several state courts have attempted to legislate equity and adequacy of funding education; however, the mere fact that the same complaints and scenarios are being played in the 21st century as in the 20th century suggests that the desired outcome for poor and, in many instances, minority-populated districts and minority students is not being achieved. Further, it could mean that litigation may not be the way of reform since there will always be rich and poor school districts.

Examples of the events in states representing the four regions of the country attesting to the inadequacy of policy responses are numerous.

Western Region

In the western region in 1976 in *Olsen v. State*, the Oregon supreme court recognized the disparities and the lack of resources that led to reduced educational opportunity for students in lower wealth, lower spending districts. The court found that the school finance system did not violate either the equal protection or education clauses of the Oregon constitution. Then in 2008, the Court of Appeals decided the case of *Pendleton School District v. State of Oregon*. The court declared that the legislature had not funded the public school system at the constitutionally required level.

In 1975, the Idaho supreme court, in *Thompson v. Engelking*, rejected a claim that the state school finance system violated equal protection principles under state and federal law. Nearly 2 decades later, the same court in *Idaho Schools for Equal Educational Opportunity v. Evans* (1993) found that an adequacy claim under the state constitution's education clause should go forward to trial. In 2005, the Idaho supreme court affirmed the district court's conclusion that the funding system simply did not meet the legislature's duty under the constitution.

In 1977, suit was brought against the Colorado state board of education, claiming that disparities in school funding deprived students of equal educational opportunities in violation of the state and federal constitutions. This decision was reversed in *Lujan v. Colorado State Board of Education* in 1982. Then in *Lobato v. State* (2009), the Colorado supreme court held that the plaintiffs may challenge the state's public school financing system as violating the Colorado constitutional mandate.

Southern Region

In the southern region, in Texas, plaintiffs in *Rodriguez v. San Antonio Independent School District* (1971) unsuccessfully asked the federal courts to declare the state's school funding system unconstitutional under the U.S. Constitution due to gross disparities in funding among districts. On appeal, the U.S. Supreme Court held that the Texas system does not violate the Equal Protection Clause of the Fourteenth Amendment. In *Neeley v. West Orange-Cove Consolidated Independent School District* (2005), plaintiffs maintained that public school systems cannot achieve a general diffusion of knowledge as required by the Texas constitution because the system was underfunded.

In Florida in 1995, plaintiffs filed an adequacy case, *Coalition for Adequacy and Fairness in School Funding v. Chiles*, to challenge the state's system of funding its public schools. Two recent lawsuits later alleged that the state had failed to provide an adequate education in accordance with these enhanced requirements. In 2008, in *Citizens for Strong Schools, Inc. v. Florida State Board of Education*, the court issued a decision based on the precepts that a high quality education is to be provided for all students in the state.

In 1989, the state supreme court in *Rose v. Council for Better Education* issued a ruling declaring Kentucky's entire system of common schools unconstitutional, that is, not just the education finance program. In 2003, Kentucky education stakeholders expressed concerns that the state's education finance system does not provide adequate funding for a quality education, alleging that that the state's funding system had fallen back into inadequacy (National Education Access Network, 2010).

Midwest

In the Midwest in 1979, in *Ohio Board of Education of Cincinnati v. Walter*, the court upheld the state's then-current funding system on the basis that all districts had the fiscal resources necessary to meet state minimum standards. Despite subsequent funding increases, the court found the funding system unconstitutional in 2000, in *DeRolph v. State*, where the plaintiffs were hailed to be victors as the majority of the court concluded that, despite complete revisions to Ohio's school funding statutory scheme by the general assembly, the requirements of the Clause for Education of all children in the Ohio constitution had not been met.

In 1994, in the equity case *Bezdicheck v. State*, brought by school districts against the state, a South Dakota circuit court declared the state's education finance system constitutional, despite acknowledged funding disparities. In

2006, a lawsuit claiming that the state's education finance system failed to provide sufficient resources for the state's students as required by the South Dakota constitution reversed the holding of the trial court.

In 1990, plaintiff taxpayers and students filed suit contending that Nebraska's statutory scheme for financing public schools denied them equal and adequate educational opportunity and uniform and proportionate taxation, in violation of the state constitution. In 2007, the Nebraska supreme court ruled that educational adequacy is nonjusticiable in *Coalition for Educational Equity and Adequacy v. Heineman.*

Northeast

In the Massachusetts education finance case *McDuffy v. Secretary* (1993), students claimed that their own less affluent school districts were unable to provide them with an adequate education. At about the same time that the court issued its *McDuffy* decision, the legislature passed the Education Reform Act of 1993, which established a foundation budget for each school district to be phased in more than 7 years. Subsequently, in *Hancock v. Commissioner of Education* (2005), the court denied the plaintiffs' motion for further relief.

In New York in 1978, a group of property-poor school districts, joined by the five large urban New York districts, filed *Levittown v. Nyquist* to challenge the state's education finance system. The court held that the state constitution guarantees students the right to the opportunity for a "sound basic education." This right was at the center of the *Campaign for Fiscal Equity (CFE) Inc. v. State* complaint filed in 1993, which asserted that New York state was failing in its constitutional obligations. In 2006, the court held that the state failed to appropriately fund the CFE mandate.

Judicial reform in education finance in New Jersey began more than 3 decades ago. In 1973, the New Jersey supreme court found, in *Robinson v. Cahill,* that the state's school funding statute was unconstitutional. Issuing its 20th decision in the 2-decade-old *Abbott v. Burke* litigation, the supreme court ruled in 2009 that the state's new education funding system, the School Funding Reform Act of 2008, meets the constitutional requirement.

Six states have a different kind of judicial history in education finance: Delaware, Indiana, Mississippi, Nevada, Hawaii, and Utah. Delaware's case, *Gebhart v. Belton,* was consolidated into *Brown v. Board of Education* (1954). In 2008, however, *Bonner v. Daniels* was filed based on an earlier case that was withdrawn in 1987. In Utah, Mississippi, Hawaii, and Nevada, no such case has been filed.

CONCLUSION

While the plaintiff's complaints in these cases were centered on common themes such as facilities, teachers' salaries, pupil–teacher ratios, insufficient funds for students with special needs or students in small and rural schools, issues of municipal and metropolitan overburden, and differences in per-pupil expenditure, the disparities cited were mainly between rich and poor districts within the state. However, a more troubling phenomenon is the disparity within the districts, which is cited as early as 1978 in New York in *Levittown v. Nyquist* and repeated in North Carolina in 1997. When a state has adjusted its funding formula to establish equity between districts, little is done to ensure the same equity within the districts, although needs between neighborhoods can be as varied as those between districts. Further, it seems irrelevant in this age of highly developed technology to discuss disparities due to funding. Limited resources could be made a nonissue by providing universal access for all students through the Internet (computers and other ancillary equipment). Education can be provided on a level playing field.

FURTHER READINGS AND RESOURCES

Berne, R., & Steifel, L. (1984). *The measurement of equity in school finance: Conceptual, methodological, and empirical dimensions.* Baltimore: Johns Hopkins University Press.

Fennimore, B. S. (2005). Brown and the failure of civic responsibility. *Teachers College Record, 107*(9), 1905–1932.

Gillespie, L. N. (2010). *The fourth wave of education finance litigation: Pursuing a federal right to an adequate education.* Retrieved September 24, 2010, from http://www .lawschool.cornell.edu/research/cornell-law-review/upload/Gillespie-note-final.pdf

Guthrie, J. W., Springer, M. G., Rolle, R. A., & Houck, E. A. (2007). *Modern education finance and policy.* Boston: Pearson/Allyn & Bacon.

Howard, J. (2000). Still at risk: The causes and costs of failure to educate poor and minority children for the twenty-first century. In D. T. Gordon (Ed.), *A nation reformed? American education 20 years after* A Nation at Risk (pp. 81–97). Cambridge, MA: Harvard University Press.

Hunter, R. C., & Brown, F. (2003). *Challenges of urban education and efficacy of school reform.* Oxford, UK: Elsevier Science.

King, R., Swanson, A., & Sweetland, S. (2003). *School finance: Achieving high standards with equity and efficiency* (3rd ed.). Boston: Pearson Education.

Ladd, H. F. (2008). Reflections on equity, adequacy, and weighted student funding. *Education Finance and Policy, 3*(4), 402–423.

Murphy, J. (2010). *The educator's handbook for understanding and closing achievement gaps.* Thousand Oaks, CA: Corwin.

National Education Access Network. (2010). *California.* Retrieved from http://www .schoolfunding.info/states/ca

National Working Group on Funding Student Learning. (2008). *Funding student learning: How to align education resources with student learning.* Center on Reinventing Public Education, University of Washington Bothell. Retrieved December 20, 2010, from http://www.crpe.org/cs/crpe/download/csr_files/pub_sfrp_wrkgrp_oct08.pdf

Oakes, J. (2005). *Keeping track: How schools structure inequality* (2nd ed.). New Haven, CT: Yale University Press.

Odden, A. R., & Picus, L. O. (2008). *School finance: A policy perspective* (4th ed.). Boston: McGraw-Hill.

Rodriguez, G. M. (2004). Vertical equity in school finance and the potential for increasing school responsiveness to student and staff needs. *Peabody Journal of Education, 79*(3), 7–30.

Roemer, J. E. (1998). *Equality of opportunity.* Cambridge, MA: Harvard University Press.

Ryan, J. E. (2008). Standards, testing, and school finance. *Texas Law Review, 86,* 1223–1262.

Springer, M. G., Liu, K., & Guthrie, J. W. (2009). The impact of school finance litigation on resource distribution: A comparison of court-mandated equity and adequacy reforms. *Education Economics, 17*(4), 421–444.

Superfine, B. M. (2009). Deciding who decides questions at the intersection of school finance reform litigation and standards-based accountability policies. *Educational Policy, 23*(3), 480–514.

Thompson, D., Wood, C., & Crampton, F. E. (2008). *Money and schools* (4th ed.). Larchmont, NY: Eye on Education.

U.S. Department of Education, Institute of Education Sciences. (2010). *Litigation.* Retrieved from http://nces.ed.gov/edfin/litigation.asp

VanZandt, K. (n.d.). *The Land Ordinance of 1785 and the Northwest Ordinance of 1787.* Retrieved from http://www.nd.edu/~rbarger/www7/ord17857.html

Verstegen, D. A. (1998). Judicial analysis during the new wave of school finance litigation. *Journal of Education Finance, 24*(1), 51–68.

Verstegen, D. A., Jordan, T. S., & Amador, P. (2009). *A quick glance at school finance: A 50 state survey of school finance policies.* Retrieved October 20, 2011, from http:// nced.info/schoolfinance/a-50-state-survey-of-school-finance-policies-2007

Yeung, R. (2010). *The cost of race: Evidence from California.* Paper presented at the annual conference of the American Education Research Association, Denver, CO.

Court Cases and Statutes

Abbott v. Burke, 971 A. 2d 989 (N.J., 2009).

Bezdicheck v. State, CIV 91–209 (S.D., 1994).

Board of Education of Cincinnati v. Walter, 390 N.E.2d 813 (Ohio, 1979).

Bonner v. Daniels, 885 N.E.2d 673 (Ind. Ct. App., 2008).

Brown v. Board of Education, 347 U.S. 483 (1954).

Campaign for Fiscal Equity, Inc. v. State, 86 N.Y. 2d 307 (1995).

Citizens for Strong Schools, Inc. v. Florida State Board of Education, Case No. O9-CA-4534 (Fla., 2008).

Coalition for Adequacy and Fairness in School Funding v. Chiles, 919 So.2d 392 (Fla., 2006).

Coalition for Educational Equity and Adequacy v. Heineman, 731 N.W.2d 164 (Neb., 2007).

DeRolph v. State, 728 N.E.2d 993 (Ohio, 2000).

Hancock v. Commissioner of Education, 443 Mass. 428, 822 N.E.2d 1134 (Mass., 2005).

Idaho Schools for Equal Educational Opportunity v. Evans, 123 Idaho 573, 850 P.2d 724 (Idaho, 1993).

Levittown v. Nyquist, 408 N.Y.S.2d 606 (N.Y., 1978).

Lobato v. State, 218 P. 3d 358 (Col., 2009).

Lujan v. Colorado State Board of Education, 649 P.2d 1005 (Col., 1982).

McDuffy v. Secretary, 615 N.E.2d 516 (Mass., 1993).

Neeley v. West Orange-Cove Consolidated Independent School District, 176 S.W.3d 746 (Tex., 2005).

Olsen v. State, 554 P.2d 139 (Ore., 1976).

Pendleton School District v. State of Oregon, 185 P3d 471 (Or. App., 2008).

Robinson v. Cahill, 303 A.2d 273 (N.J., 1973).

Robles-Wong et al. v. State of California (2010), http://www.fixschoolfinance.org.

Rodriguez et al. v. San Antonio Independent School District, 337 F. Supp. 280 (W.D. Texas, 1971), *reversed* 411 U.S. 1 (1973).

Roosevelt Elementary School District No. 66 v. Bishop, 877 P.2d 806 (Ariz., 1994).

Rose v. Council for Better Education, 790 S.W. 2d 186 (Ky., 1989).

San Antonio Independent School District v. Rodriguez, 411 U.S. 1 (1973).

Seattle School District No. 1 of King County v. State, 585 P.2d 71 (Wash., 1978).

Serrano v. Priest, 487 P.2d 1241 (Cal., 1971).

Thompson v. Engelking, 537 P.2d 635 (Idaho, 1975).

11

Are English-only models the most appropriate means for teaching English to English language learners?

POINT: Linwood J. Randolph, Jr., *Chapel Hill-Carrboro (North Carolina) City Schools*
Xue Lan Rong, *University of North Carolina at Chapel Hill*
COUNTERPOINT: Patrice Preston-Grimes and Wendy W. Amato, *University of Virginia*

OVERVIEW

Since its inception, one goal of public education in the United States has been to help immigrant children and their families acclimate to the social and cultural structures operating in this country. In the late 19th century, educators and policymakers placed greater emphasis on the assimilating function of public schools as part of their efforts in dealing with increased immigration from China, Japan, and previously underrepresented areas of Europe. To fulfill this function, public education helped students learn to speak and read English. Although continued immigration into the United States requires public schools to maintain these services, it remains unclear which approach provides the best and most effective way of helping students learn both English and the other academic skills taught at their respective grade levels.

Over the years, educators have experimented with various methods for helping non-native English-speaking students acquire and improve their verbal and written English skills. Models for helping non-native speakers learn English include the English as a second language (ESL) model, the transitional bilingual model, the dual immersion model, and the English-only model.

The ESL model focuses on non-native speakers. This model recognizes the native language that these students bring with them to school and provides staff, materials, and other educational assistance in that language to help students keep up with their other academic areas and develop valuable social skills as they learn to speak and read English. Schools find it easier to implement this model when all or most of their non-native English-speaking students share a common linguistic and cultural background. For example, schools that serve large numbers of students who come from Spanish-speaking households have an easier time implementing the ESL model than schools that serve students with several different native languages. Schools using this model follow different implementation strategies such as breakout sessions for individuals or groups of non-native English-speaking students, shifting these students to a self-contained classroom dedicated specifically to ESL instruction throughout the day, or requiring these students to participate in ESL-focused instructional activities during activity periods such as physical education.

Compared to the ESL model, the transitional bilingual model works at moving students to learn English in a more direct manner by offering instruction in both English and their native tongue. This model provides instruction in both languages in the hopes that consistent English instruction will help students to learn the language and that receiving some academic instruction in their native language will help students to progress academically in other areas. Unlike the ESL model, the transitional bilingual model familiarizes students with English instruction on a regular basis as a way of working toward the eventual elimination of any instruction in their language of origin. Similar to the ESL model, the transitional bilingual model requires schools to employ instructional staff that specifically speak the native tongues of their English language learners (ELL) and may also involve the acquisition and production of materials in both languages.

While the ESL and transitional bilingual models concentrate on ELL students, the dual immersion model provides language instruction to both native and non-native English speakers. Under the dual immersion model, teachers offer instruction in both English and another language in an effort to help all of these students become bilingual. Using this model, ELL students continue to develop their full academic skills and knowledge, while learning English. Recognizing the need to prepare students to live and function in a global society, the dual immersion model expands the education offered to native English speakers by starting them on the path of learning a second language. The amount of English instruction that students receive in dual immersion model programs varies according to the structures used by schools and their instructors. Similar to the other two models, the use of the dual immersion model requires schools to employ teachers and aides trained to provide instruction in both English and a common second language, supply materials that communicate language and other academic content in both languages, and restructure various elements of the school day to allow time for students to receive instruction in all academic areas throughout the school day.

In each of the three previous models, ELL students receive instruction and access to materials in their native language during some part of the school day in an attempt to design a system to meet them where they are while also transitioning them into fluent English speakers. In contrast, English-only models ask schools to abandon these efforts and concentrate solely on teaching ELL students in the same ways that schools serve native English speakers.

From a management standpoint, English-only models appeal to school financial officers and other officials because they are cost-effective to implement. While the other models require schools to produce or acquire materials in languages other than English, English-only models do not. Likewise, English-only models also spare schools the expense of hiring teachers and other instructional support staff specifically to serve the needs of ELL students. At the same time, offering instruction in English only makes it easier for schools to implement other curricular programs such as special education, Response to Intervention (RtI), and afterschool programs to address No Child Left Behind (NCLB)–related performance deficiencies.

Despite the fiscal appeal of English-only models, these programs suffer from certain limitations. Among them, these programs do not address the larger academic issues that ELL students face as they work to acclimate to the culture of the U.S. education system. Linguistically isolated from their teachers, it is difficult to provide instruction to these students or ascertain the impact of these efforts. Finally, English-only models generally function as the antitheses to the stated purpose of NCLB, RtI, and other academic improvement policies by ignoring specific needs of this segment of the school population.

The authors of both essays in this chapter acknowledge that there is more than one way to effectively teach English to ELL students. In the point essay, Linwood J. Randolph, Jr. (Chapel Hill-Carrboro [North Carolina] City Schools) and Xue Lan Rong (University of North Carolina at Chapel Hill) state that the ultimate goal of English-only models, according to proponents, is English monolingualism, rather than heritage language maintenance or true bilingualism. After reviewing the research on the question and examining non-English-only programs, Randolph and Rong conclude that there is no one-size-fits-all program for learning English. They argue that an appropriate approach is to identify the components that will work in a specific situation as determined by local factors. The counterpoint essay authors, Patrice Preston-Grimes and Wendy W. Amato (University of Virginia), agree that as with all high quality education, the particular needs of individual learners must be considered central to the decisions that teachers make in educational goals and instruction. Even so, they feel that ELL students need more than English-only instruction. In their opinion, there is a need for a degree of inclusion of heritage languages in ELL instruction.

Saran Donahoo
Southern Illinois University Carbondale

POINT: Linwood J. Randolph, Jr.
Chapel Hill-Carrboro (North Carolina) City Schools

Xue Lan Rong
University of North Carolina at Chapel Hill

The education of English language learners (ELLs) in the United States is a highly complex subject that has been a topic of discussion in the realm of educational research for centuries. The debate for bilingual education or teaching English only has become increasingly heated in recent years, resulting in the passing of Proposition 227 in California in 1998 and of the Official English law in 31 states by 2010.

A historical examination reveals that the language policy-making and adapting process in the United States has been highly politicized. At the heart of the issue lie sensitive ideals that relate to how people perceive race, culture, identity, immigration, and patriotism, as well as the impacts of xenophobia and ethnocentrism. From pedagogical and practical perspectives, educators, researchers, and politicians have discussed and debated the best ways to facilitate the process of students' English learning and at the same time they continue to argue about the roles heritage languages may play in that process (e.g., enhancing or interrupting the process). We would like to make our position clear regarding this debate: Acquiring fluency in both academic and social English is crucial for ELLs' schooling; however, maintaining their heritage languages is also necessary for these students' cognitive development, healthy self-concept, and smooth socialization in family, community, and the larger society. Moreover, children who possess the competence to speak two or more languages and who grow up with dual or multicultural frameworks will have an edge in the global economy over monocultural and monolingual children. However, we acknowledge that what we have advocated is neither the reality nor the outlook in the near future in the United States. The methodologies used in U.S. public schools to facilitate ELLs' English language are largely based on philosophies and pedagogies of teaching English only. This essay will address two reasons for which schools and educators are proponents of these programs: (1) the political opposition and (2) the pedagogical and other oppositions to bilingual education.

TEACHING ENGLISH ONLY

Legally, schools must provide some type of language support for students who are not fluent in English, as defined by *Lau v. Nichols* (1974). *Plyler v. Doe* (1982) further requires that public schools offer those same services to undocumented immigrants. Most school systems respond to the academic needs of language minority students by incorporating English as a second language (ESL) instruction into their curricular models. Such programs are considered "English only" since their ultimate goal is to develop English monolingualism rather than bilingualism or multilingualism in the students' native or heritage languages. The most common type of English-only programs are pull-out programs in which ELLs, or limited English proficient students, take special English classes in addition to other required courses. Variations of this model may include "sheltered" instruction where the students are taught ESL and subject area content in the same self-contained class. Early-exit transitional bilingual programs also fall into the category of English only since support in the minority language is quickly tapered off as the student develops proficiency in English. Such programs stand in contrast to true bilingual programs, which provide support for bilingualism as well as academic content in the minority language.

The contemporary English-only approach employed by most U.S. school systems continues to benefit from public and legal support, including the No Child Left Behind Act—one of the most important pieces of educational legislation in recent history. With the focus on learning English "as quickly as possible," schools invest much of their resources toward the endeavor of developing fluency solely in English. Even if the minority language is used during instruction, its use is limited to the extent necessary to promote fluency in English.

POLITICAL OPPOSITION TO BILINGUAL EDUCATION

As evidenced by the history of heritage language education in the United States, sociolinguists and researchers often find themselves at odds with policies, philosophies, and educational practices that promote monolingualism and turn a critical eye to bilingual education. This divide between research and practice has much to do with the dynamics of language and power and how the understanding of those concepts by majority and minority cultures alike has evolved over time.

Contemporary political and popular support of English-only instructional practices is engrained in our nation's ideas of patriotism and identity. By 1918, the sense of patriotism ignited by World War I prompted over 30 states to develop laws that required instruction in English (Castro Feinberg, 2002). Such a move marked a critical turn in public opinion toward bilingual education and language education as a whole. Ironically, a nation once rooted in the tradition of immigrant and indigenous languages had now made a concerted effort to promote English alone as the language of patriotism and national identity. Not only was there a sentiment among the majority population that minority language education was "un-American," but minority language speakers themselves also began to buy into the hegemonic notion (albeit by coercion) that speaking a minority language was not an accepted practice. Remnants of such perspectives still exist among certain minority language populations (Arias & Casanova, 1993).

With the civil rights movement, several key court cases, and subsequent federal regulations in the 1960s, 1970s, and early 1980s, bilingual education began to gain credibility as a way of supporting the academic achievement of language minority students. In the 1980s, however, the political landscape shifted when several key leaders began to speak out against bilingual education, thus giving way to the current English-only movement. In 1981, President Ronald Reagan declared that bilingualism was ultimately wrong and a disservice to citizens because it focused on native language maintenance rather than the instruction of the English language that citizens needed to be competitive members of the workforce (Castro Feinberg, 2002). In the same year, the state of Virginia became the first state to enact English-only legislation in the 1980s. In the mid-1980s, William J. Bennett (Reagan's secretary of education) spoke out against the Bilingual Education Act of 1968. Calling it "a failed path . . . a bankrupt course," he claimed that "too many children have failed to become fluent in English" and that the Hispanic dropout rate had remained "tragically as high now as it was twenty years ago" (Crawford, 1995, p. 83). He went on to claim that "a sense of cultural pride cannot come at the price of proficiency in English, our common language." With such powerful words coming from a high-profile political leader, the English-only movement was able to gain considerable momentum and public support. Several grassroots political organizations sprouted with goals ranging from doing away with bilingual education to establishing English as the nation's official language. The word *bilingual* even became less prevalent in official government business. For example, the Federal Office of Bilingual Education and Minority Languages Affairs transformed to the Office of English Language Acquisition, Language Enhancement, and Academic Achievement for Limited-English-Proficient Students. Similarly, the National Clearinghouse for Bilingual Education became the National

Clearinghouse for English Language Acquisition and Language Instruction Educational Programs (Crawford, 2002).

Armed with government backing, this new push disassociated much of the negative connotations that had accompanied the English-only perspective in the 1960s and 1970s. No longer was English only seen as a discriminatory practice; rather, it was championed as a method to quickly increase student achievement (especially among Latino students) and to promote English as a unifier for all American students. In light of the perceived failure of bilingual education, English only had now become the patriotic and academically sound solution. Fueled by that philosophy, during the 1990s, some states began to adopt legislation that limited bilingual education. In California, the passing of Proposition 227 (which requires schools to offer only 1 year of ESL instruction) drastically reduced the enrollment in bilingual programs. Other states began to follow suit, implementing laws that restricted the amount of public resources that could be spent on heritage language maintenance efforts. The philosophy that continues to drive such legislation today is the perspective that it is not the school's duty to instruct children in their native or heritage languages; instead, school systems should be more concerned with the students' academic performance and competency in English. If native language maintenance, then, is not seen as having a role in helping a student achieve the ultimate goal of learning English, it becomes a challenging task to garner political and public support for bilingual education programs.

In the contemporary public arena, bilingual education often gets intertwined with issues relating to immigration. This is not surprising, since immigrants (including undocumented residents) are the beneficiaries of ESL education. Given that connection, it often becomes difficult to separate one's political stance on immigration (especially illegal immigration) from one's views on bilingual education. Topics relating to immigration are currently at the forefront of political debate, from arguments over the constitutionality of Arizona's deportation enforcement practices to the recent congressional vote on the Development, Relief and Education for Alien Minors Act. Certainly, all candidates hoping to hold a public office in today's political climate are expected to articulate their stance on immigration as part of their political platform. Just recently, Alabama gubernatorial candidate Tim James famously criticized the fact that Alabama offers its driver's license test in multiple languages, stating, "This is Alabama. We speak English. If you want to live here, learn it." Other leaders of various political parties have voiced comments that (at varying degrees) support the notion that immigrants should adapt to the cultural practices of the majority, even at the expense of losing their own cultural heritage. It seems that when immigrants do not assimilate to the cultural norms established by the majority, a certain element of the defining notion of what it means to be "American" becomes threatened. Bilingual education in essence is a rebellion to the idea that there is a unifying language that defines American culture, a realization with which the majority culture may find difficult to come to terms.

For majority and minority cultures alike, there is an undeniable, almost indestructible link among language, culture, and heritage. English-only instruction at its core is a move by the majority culture to maintain the identity of what is known as "American" culture and heritage. Throughout history, our country has struggled with issues regarding what defines us as a nation, both at the cultural and linguistic levels. This cultural struggle manifests itself in such political debates as whether the national anthem should be sung in Spanish, whether a mosque or Islamic community center should be constructed near Ground Zero in New York City, and whether the nation should establish an official language. As long as the United States continues to grapple with these issues, the debate of English only versus bilingual education will continue to be at the forefront of politically charged discourse.

PEDAGOGICAL AND OTHER OPPOSITIONS

There are several consensuses among educators who work with ELLs. These include the belief that learning English is crucial for immigrant students' academic success in U.S. schools and is a basic step to enable new immigrants to participate in the larger community, get an education, find a job, obtain access to health care or social services, and apply for citizenship. These consensuses also include developing an awareness of the special needs of immigrant and refugee children. Many transitional bilingual education programs hire and train the parents of ELLs as paraprofessionals or classroom aids, and this therefore has promoted parental understanding of U.S. schools and encouraged parental involvement in school activities, including family literacy, as a by-product. Nonetheless, educators who believe in English-only teaching have spelled out their oppositions to bilingual education, including their doubts on ESL pull-out programs and early-exit bilingual transitional programs, though these programs are widely viewed as a part of English-only teaching.

There is also consensus in a more pragmatic way: In the area where a variety of languages are spoken by ELLs, people may agree that ESL programs focusing on English only can accommodate students from different language backgrounds in the same class, and teachers do not need to be proficient in the home language(s) of their students. This section will problematize the practical integration of bilingual education and other non-English-only programs by examining program evaluation, student and parental rights, and other concerns.

First, based on the review of research literature, some educators and scholars (e.g., Porter, 1998; Rossell, 1996) did not find that bilingual programs were better than the English-only teaching programs. As put by Rosalie Pedalino Porter, bilingual education was a classic example of an experiment begun with the best of humanitarian intentions but ultimately demonstrated to be wrongheaded. Porter and others have claimed that there was no evidence to show bilingual programs' long-term advantages to students and that students who were taught in English and native languages (including in transitional programs) did not show higher academic achievement and lower school dropout rates. Furthermore, there is no evidence indicating that students in bilingual programs have higher self-esteem or lower stress levels in school.

However, these conclusions might owe more to the confusion surrounding program labels. For example, pull-out or early-exit transitional bilingual programs are actually English-only teaching programs, not ideal bilingual programs. The major concerns about appropriate comparison of the results across students in different programs lie on the design of the evaluation program, since it is very difficult to control the preexisting differences, including the variation among the schools, students, communities, teacher quality and credentials, the program implementation, and so on. As pointed out by James Crawford (2002), the designs of the evaluation, regardless of the outcomes, can be criticized methodologically.

Second, many educators view some ELLs' participation in bilingual programs as (a) involuntary (including students not having been correctly notified of their options, being there without parents' consent, and having difficulties in transferring between the programs); (b) segregated from the mainstream English speakers (many students, most likely ESL students from Asia, Africa, and Europe, were in pull-out transitional bilingual programs but were not taught in their native languages); and (c) stagnated/locked in the bilingual programs for a lengthy period of time (3 or more years) without achieving English proficiency. Critics of bilingual education programs have also argued that oftentimes such programs are expanded beyond their original objectives—to develop ELLs to full English proficiency—into developing students' full abilities in their native languages. Furthermore, according to poll data, a majority of the ELL students' parents felt teaching the heritage language, history, and culture is the family's duty, not that of the school.

There are also other concerns opposing bilingual programs, including the perceived high cost of the program in an era of draining federal, state, and local budgets in education and a scarcity of truly bilingual and fully certified teachers. In addition, bilingual education programs have been highly controversial in the legislature and public arena, with heated pedagogical and political debates since their very beginning. Furthermore, creating bilingual programs is becoming more complicated for U.S. schools. Not only has the percentage of immigrants from non-English-speaking countries been increasing rapidly, but so has the variety of the languages ELL children speak. More than 400 languages (i.e., nearly every language in the world) were reported to be spoken in U.S. schools in 2000, and more than 70 languages were spoken by at least 10,000 of the students in the United States. Furthermore, foreign-born children from Africa reported speaking more than 50 different languages, and about 70 different languages were spoken in 2000 by immigrant children who identified themselves as Asians.

Bilingual programs are typically seen as most easily implemented in districts with a large number of students with the same language background, such as Latinos; however, such a generalization fails to consider several variables. For example, although most Hispanic children in the United States do indeed speak Spanish, some speak Portuguese, and others use tongues indigenous to regional areas of Latin America. When taking into consideration the language variation within ethnic and nationality groups, the tasks in designing language programs and in training and recruiting teachers and counselors in language services become challenging as well. This is especially the case since true bilingual programs are often more difficult to implement: A successful bilingual program entails the recruitment and hiring of bilingual teachers who are also certified in various content areas; however, there have been severe shortages in fully credentialed bilingual teachers in every state.

There has been no consistent research since the 1980s suggesting that heritage language education is in any way detrimental to heritage language learners or their counterparts, or that bilingual education cripples a student's capacity to learn English. Instead, educational research over the past several decades suggests that language programs supporting bilingualism and multilingualism are, in fact, more conducive to the individual's cultural, social, and academic well-being. However, some researchers caution that the evaluation of language education programs has been politicized by advocacy groups who selectively promote research findings to support their positions (e.g., August & Hakuta, 1997). They suggest that rather than choosing a one-size-fits-all program (bilingual or not), the key issue should be to identify the components, backed by solid research findings, that will work in a specific community.

RESPONSE TO COUNTERPOINT ESSAY

Although we agree with the major points the authors of the counterpoint essay have made, such as the rationales and strategies for working with ELLs, the difference in our arguments lies in the classification of the programs into the English-only category. In our essay, we explored a wide range of the programs that are in this category, since the ultimate goal for these programs is to support students' learning of English, not to help them maintain their heritage languages, and especially not to facilitate students' development of age-appropriate literacy in their heritage languages. Considering the practical constraints of current budget deficits and the push for accountability, we view some of the programs in the English-only category as viable programs along with the many other viable programs. However, selection of the program should be best determined by local factors, such as the sociodemographic characteristics of the students, the size of the ELL population, the variety of the heritage languages, and the pool of truly bilingual and fully certified teachers.

COUNTERPOINT: Patrice Preston-Grimes and Wendy W. Amato
University of Virginia

There is no question that English proficiency benefits the immigrant and refugee populations in the United States. For a country without a declared national language, the United States has social and civic structures in which English is the primary language of access to official services, political power, resources, and employment. The U.S. Supreme Court's 1974 ruling in *Lau v. Nichols* upheld the right of limited-English-proficient students to receive equal treatment in their schooling, including, but not limited to, English language instruction.

Debate continues today, however, about what type of English language instruction is most effective. Factors that educators must consider include the cost and scale of maintaining language programs in public schools, the number of children being served, and the demands for accountability. A preferred method to instruct an English language learner (ELL) should consider what is known about second language acquisition, classroom instruction, and selecting a program. To suggest that English-only classes should be the model for teaching English proficiency is to deny the importance of these areas and to reject significant research in the field. Methods other than English-only instruction can share the end goal of students gaining English language proficiency and content knowledge.

SECOND LANGUAGE ACQUISITION

Successful second language acquisition (SLA) uses the learner's background knowledge of a first language to develop proficiency in a new language. Empirical research supports the critical role of interaction in the language learning process. The old view of a language learner suggested that knowledge was transferred from a knower to a learner—like making a deposit to an account. More and more, people recognize that language is acquired through use. Today's view considers that language learners arrive at knowledge through different social activities in specific environments.

ELLs have many opportunities in schools to develop social language through their interaction with other children. Critics argue that the resulting social language proficiency comes at the expense of children developing more formal, classroom language skills. However, in SLA, there is a distinct difference between developing interpersonal and academic language skills, because ability in one area does not necessarily mean talent in the other. Teachers can hear an ELL's casual social English and then incorrectly assume that the student's formal academic English would be at the same level of fluency. Since it is generally accepted that social interaction increases social language skills and academic interaction increases academic language skills, it follows that more frequent social interaction would strengthen a student's social language skills.

A person's culture also influences his or her language learning. Cultural beliefs and experiences can help a learner to understand the spoken and unspoken language cues that accompany spoken English. For example, the rate of speech or accent, pauses between words, length of utterances, facial expressions, eye contact, and gestures are some of the ways in which ELLs interpret the meaning of words in a given situation. Each of these cues can vary depending on cultural norms and cultural context. Consider, for example, the meaning of a raised hand. On a city street corner, it may hail a taxi. From a student in a classroom, the raised hand may indicate a request for permission to speak; in the same classroom, a raised hand by a teacher may be a request for silence. Likewise, pursed lips may accompany a Latino's statement indicating (like pointing a finger) a choice or a French person's expression of disagreement (like head shaking). Cultural understanding allows those cues to enhance language acquisition. Teachers are most effective with ELLs when they acknowledge, understand, and respect the culture that students bring to the classroom.

A single English-only response to instruction also contradicts what we know about language acquisition because of the tremendous individual differences (IDs) that exist, not only between cultures but also between speakers. Some IDs are motivation, aptitude, personality characteristics, duration of instruction, and the quality and quantity of language input. Each ID can influence the instructional needs and the academic success of an ELL. They also explain why two ELL students in the same class may acquire English proficiency at different rates. Other considerations include the learner's particular location, socioeconomic or sociolinguistic status, and family expectations. Each factor influences an ELL's connection with other language speakers within the school community and the ways in which they may use academic resources. The number of significant variables identified in working with ELLs makes the field challenging. However, an English-only, one-size-fits-all approach to language learning dismisses the different teaching opportunities that make learning effective and disregards the particular needs of ELL students.

As a result, it is shortsighted to suggest that English use in the classroom should be all or nothing. There are many varieties of ELL programs that incorporate English use in different ways, with English-only classes at one end of a continuum and heritage language instruction at the other end. Split-day programs, course-specific English-only instruction, on-site translators, sheltered instruction, and transition programs are variations between these two extremes. Not one of these options will work in all contexts. Nonetheless, knowledge of SLA and student characteristics indicates sheltered instruction and transition programs as most effective for ELLs. These programs prepare ELLs to gain a functional level of language competence, academic skills, and content knowledge while they develop English competency. Language gains can be immediate or transitional, like a dimmer on a light switch that allows variation in illumination in a room.

SLA research has also established that language systems are interactive. Features of any one language can feed on the knowledge and understanding of another. As a result, greater learning can occur when prior language knowledge is used to develop English competency. Although some mainstream SLA studies characterize language learners as computer-like processors, other SLA research suggests that understanding the role of general background knowledge in language learning can aid ELL instruction.

Teachers are recognizing the importance of SLA in their classroom instruction as well. As students progress in school, they are expected to gain content and background knowledge. Secondary school teachers, for example, often require students to demonstrate critical thinking and content knowledge at a higher level than in middle school because the previous year's language and academic learning support new knowledge acquisition. In the same way, a student's first language—especially when there is proficiency and literacy—can support second language learning.

INSTRUCTION

It is an overgeneralization that English-only classes are best for all students, because no two teachers are alike and no two schools provide the same context for learning. A more accurate prescription for instruction considers various program types (e.g., elementary, secondary, open classroom, instruction support structure), categories of instruction, content areas, teacher training, and student characteristics.

Legislation and policy decisions also influence the ways in which language instruction takes place, with judgments not always made at the classroom or local levels. California's Proposition 227 in 2008, Arizona's Proposition 103 in 2006, and Massachusetts's Question 2 (Mass. Gen. Laws, ch. 71A) in 2002, for example, require English-only instruction and use standardized test scores to measure success. Likewise, No Child Left Behind legislation has also shined a spotlight on ELLs because literacy proficiency is based frequently on students' standardized test scores. Many teachers now emphasize test-taking skills and strategies to measure language progress rather than authentic language acquisition. This presents problems for ELL students because some standardized tests are not designed specifically to measure language proficiency. The tests also fail to take into account the social and cultural influences that can affect student test performance on any given day.

From an administrative point of view, it is easier and less expensive to offer English-only instruction than to adjust instruction to meet individual needs of students. In many cases, English-only teachers do not have to meet specific qualifications, may not be required to complete professional development, and can operate with more flexible course schedules than those who teach ELL or a similar method. These factors may make English-only classes convenient to offer, but do not account for the failure to address the course content needs of the fastest growing group of students enrolled in schools today. English-only classes imply that language acquisition is the sole goal of instruction.

Successful teachers who work with ELLs consider a variety of instructional goals and use skills beyond those required for traditional content instruction.

They also take into account their students' learning profiles, readiness, interests, and culture to help students acquire both language proficiency and content knowledge. In reality, only a handful of U.S. teachers who work with ELLs have special training to differentiate for language learning. Few teachers are multilingual and have SLA knowledge to support their planning, instruction, and assessment. The English-only approach then becomes a submersion strategy instead of immersion, with students sinking instead of swimming in the classroom.

Competent teachers also consider the cultural and social differences that students bring to language learning. Students can vary in motivation, aptitude, and personality; age of language acquisition; and the quality and quantity of language input. Each difference influences the instructional needs and the academic success of an ELL. Other considerations are the learner's physical environment, immediate needs, sociolinguistic status, and family expectations. Each of these differences is a language factor that can influence the ways in which students learn to speak English. The overall result is that any single instructional method may produce a range of student outcomes simply because the student "ingredient" can vary in any setting.

As in any educational discussion, real-world influences on language learning cannot be ignored or dismissed. English-speaking students, for example, who study a foreign language in school often find themselves in classrooms where the use of English is strongly discouraged because mastering the foreign language is a course goal. However, students who have the knowledge and experience of using their first language can fill vocabulary gaps with first language words to structure sentences according to known first language grammar rules. In this way, the first language knowledge helps anchor the acquisition of the second language. Yet, ELLs are often expected to learn English devoid of any prior knowledge or experiences associated with their heritage tongue. By design, much of the foreign language instruction in U.S. schools often supports using one's main language to acquire another. Why would someone expect ELL students not to benefit from the same learning experience?

After all, the tremendous variance between students, teachers, instruction, and schools makes comparison of language acquisition programs complex. There are few "apples to apples" opportunities to contrast programs because of the difficulties in creating experimental settings that replicate real classroom instructional conditions. Real-life classes are not determined by random assignment. Consequently, none of these variances or limitations contradicts what is known about SLA and effective teaching.

DECISION MAKING AND LANGUAGE PROGRAM SELECTION

Education reflects the values of the society in which it takes place. Therefore, educators must examine the implicit bias shaping the devaluing of one language and culture of one group for another group. For example, when U.S. educators perceive math and science competence as the tools for global success, schools tend to emphasize math and science teaching and learning, often to the reduction of teaching the arts and humanities. Although English proficiency enables access to services and opportunities in the United States (and often abroad), there is another dynamic at play—cultural power and privilege. Immigrants and refugees are overrepresented in the underachieving academic segments of U.S. society. To exclusively promote English immersion instruction, at the expense of children losing their native language, deprives everyone—especially ELLs and native English speakers—of intellectual and cultural growth and of the opportunity to learn about cultures through language.

In the end, low language proficiency of ELL students also must not be translated to mean that they have weak cognitive skills. Teachers must set high expectations for language proficiency and content knowledge acquisition because content knowledge and language knowledge are not measures of each other. An ELL student may be able to express an idea only in his or her heritage language. When teachers reject students' expressions in their native language, ELLs may interpret that rejection personally, that is, as a criticism of one's self-image and identity. This can further impede English acquisition, especially in classroom settings.

RECOMMENDATIONS FOR ELL INSTRUCTION

There are no quick fixes or blanket recommendations for academic content teaching regarding ELL instruction. Recommendations for planning, instruction, and assessment must consider the learning context. Educators must understand the students' background knowledge and skill sets, and use a broad spectrum of empirical research and SLA knowledge. Ongoing reevaluation and appropriate curricular adjustments will add to the success of ELLs in academic content courses.

English-only classes are not the only solution to enable ELLs to acquire proficiency. Educators and policymakers should consider what is known about SLA, effective teaching, and the students' learning needs. Sheltered instruction and transition programs, for example, have proven to meet many ELL needs. Other options include supporting content area teachers' understanding of well-developed, accessible instructional methods that address language, culture, and ELL instruction. A "backwards design" approach (starting with identifying learning objectives, developing assessments, and then planning instruction), for example, asks teachers to detect content and language objectives for students and then create instruction that would support reaching those objectives. In the feedback and follow-up stages, teachers should emphasize progress, indicate avenues for improvement, and foster self-directed learning.

In summary, ELL students need more than English-only instruction, given the knowledge of how students learn second languages and the variation in quality instruction that exists in today's schools. Teacher–student interactions, existing cultural contexts, and the social and academic language present, combined with the wide range of instructional options, indicate a need for a degree of inclusion of heritage languages in ELL instruction. As with all high quality education, the particular needs of the individual learner must be considered central to the decisions that teachers make in educational goals and instruction.

RESPONSE TO POINT ESSAY

Our response to the points raised by Linwood J. Randolph, Jr. and Xue Lan Rong falls into three categories: assumptions about what constitutes English-only classes, misunderstanding of "should" in the topic discussion, and failure to address the essential issue of language acquisition. Prefaced by acknowledging the areas on which we agree, each of the three categories is briefly addressed in this response.

We agree that English language proficiency is essential for successful navigation of American society. We also agree that while the question of English language instruction is politically charged and controversial, English is nonetheless the gateway language into employment, social services, legal protection, healthcare, daily activities, and education. We agree that English language proficiency affords access to American culture and heritage and that it is a valid educational goal.

What Are English-Only Classes?

As the title indicates, English-only classes are those classes in which English is the only language allowed. If English-only classes are allowed to be defined as classes in which the goal is to learn English, then the substance of this discussion is eliminated; we have already established that we agree about the goal of learning English. The heart of the question is one of instructional practice—should English alone be the language of instruction for learning English? As soon as this question is modified, support is offered to the counterpoint, that English only should not be the model for enabling ELLs to acquire English proficiency.

English-only classes are not polar opposites of bilingual instruction. Again, we return to the shared acknowledgement that English proficiency is the end goal. To compare English only to bilingual instruction in which the end goal is proficiency in more than one language is to skew the goal that we both accept as valid.

Should?

There is a wide variety of English language instruction for ELLs in American schools. In support of their point essay, Randolph and Rong describe a range of programs from immersion to pull-out to sheltered instruction. While the information about various programs reveals the complexity of responding to the need for English language instruction, it fails to prove which model should be used. The question is not asking which model will generate the most political support. The question is not asking what it means to be "American" (although that becomes an interesting angle here as one must ask why we do not insist on learning a language of the people indigenous to this continent). The question certainly does not ask for ESL support to be translated into support for illegal immigration. Our response asks for the focus to be appropriately redirected to the question of English proficiency for ELLs.

Language Acquisition

In our third category of response, we return to the essential element of the question at hand—acquiring English proficiency. There is a tremendous body of knowledge about language acquisition. Empirical studies indicate that prior language and literacy knowledge support additional language acquisition. Linguistic knowledge is transferable. Imagine, for example, teaching the word *book* in an English-only context. Taking a great deal of time, the teacher may point to books, repeat the word, draw a picture, model using a book, and label books throughout the classroom. There is potential for the language student to understand alternative meanings—such as cover, paper, page, the color of a book, the verb *read*—or assume that the reference is to the content of the book rather than the book itself. How much more clear would it be for the teacher to use a student's background knowledge and offer a quick translation such as *libro* or *livre* or کتاب or 책 or *Buch* and then be able to move on to—and have time for—higher proficiency concepts like literacy, oral traditions, genres, or research? If we seek proficiency, do we not owe it to our students to move them beyond identification level instruction and use all the information that is available about how humans learn language?

Finally, it is not accurate to conclude that movement away from the term *bilingual* in official government business reflects disapproval of the concept. In reality, those very changes indicate recognition of the fact that a growing number of people speak more than two languages. Randolph and Rong themselves said it best when they concluded that "educational research over the past several decades suggests that language programs supporting bilingualism and multilingualism are, in fact, more conducive to the individual's cultural, social, and academic well-being."

FURTHER READINGS AND RESOURCES

Arias, M. B., & Casanova, U. (1993). *Bilingual education: Politics, practice, and research.* Chicago: University of Chicago Press.

August, D., & Hakuta, K. (Eds.). (1997). *Improving schooling for language minority children: A research agenda.* Washington, DC: National Academy Press.

Castro Feinberg, R. (2002). *Bilingual education: A reference handbook.* Santa Barbara, CA: ABC-CLIO.

Crawford, J. (1995). *Bilingual education: History, politics, theory, and practice* (3rd ed.). Los Angeles: Bilingual Educational Services.

Crawford, J. (2002). Obituary: The Bilingual Education Act 1968–2002. *Rethinking Schools Online, 16*(4). Retrieved from http://www.rethinkingschools.org/special_reports/bilingual/Bil164.shtml

Hinkel, E. (Ed.). (2005). *Handbook of research in second language teaching and learning.* Mahwah, NJ: Lawrence Erlbaum.

Krashen, S. D. (1981). *Second language acquisition and second language learning.* New York: Pergamon.

Lantolf, J. P. (2006). Sociocultural theory and L2: State of the art. *Studies in Second Language Acquisition, 28,* 67–109.

Porter, R. P. (1998, May). The case against bilingual education. *The Atlantic Monthly.* Retrieved from http://www.theatlantic.com/past/docs/issues/98may/biling.htm

Rossell, C. (1996). Is bilingual education an effective educational tool? In J. Amselle (Ed.), *The failure of bilingual education* (pp. 18–28). Washington, DC: Center for Equal Opportunity.

COURT CASES AND STATUTES

Lau v. Nichols, 414 U.S. 563 (1974).

No Child Left Behind Act, 20 U.S.C. §§ 6301–7941 (2006).

Plyler v. Doe, 457 U.S. 202 (1982).

12

Should gender be applied as a diversity criterion in educational programming and placement?

POINT: Wayne D. Lewis, *University of Kentucky*
COUNTERPOINT: Cosette M. Grant, *Pennsylvania State University Greater Allegheny*

OVERVIEW

Over the years, much attention has been devoted in the United States to giving true meaning to our nation's creed, as espoused in documents created by the Founding Fathers of this great and diverse country. This quest for equality has brought to center stage the historic and systematic discrimination against selected racial, ethnic, sexual-orientation, and gender groups, who have been denied full participation in such areas as safety under the law, employment, politics, and education. Gender discrimination is great in the United States and as mentioned has been associated with most sectors of American life. It continues to be one of the most insidious forms of discrimination and has been difficult to fully address. There are many examples of sex discrimination in the United States, and only a few are selected for this work for our consideration.

One area of discrimination against women is violence, which is supported by our legal system. In the United States, a woman is raped every 6 minutes, and one is beaten or battered every 15 seconds. Violence against women is rooted in historic English law and the Judeo-Christian ethic in the United States, which has been used to deny women equal rights. Violence against women feeds off basic discrimination and reinforces it when women are abused by rape and are viewed as the "spoils of war," are terrorized by violence in their homes, and face unequal power relations that exists in our society between men and women. Violence against women has been compounded by discrimination on race, ethnicity, sexual identity, social status, class, and age. These multiple forms of discrimination have restricted women's choices, increased their vulnerability to violence, and made it even harder for them to obtain justice.

Another example of discrimination against women was that prior to World War II, women were not permitted to serve officially in the U.S. military. In the United Kingdom, on June 28, 1939, the Women's Auxiliary Air Force (WAAF) unit was formed, and women were permitted to serve in noncombat units in that country. Noncombat service for women in the U.S. military did not begin until World War II, and since December 1941, approximately 350,000 women have served. Various branches of military service established units for women, including the Army's WACS, Navy's WAVES, Air Force Service Pilots, and Coast Guard's SPARS, which were all formed in 1942. Noncombat service for women in the U.S. military was fully approved when President Franklin Delano Roosevelt signed Public Law 773 on November 23, 1942. These persons worked as typists, clerks, mail sorters, and nurses. Today, approximately 20% of all uniformed military personnel are female.

After World War II, male and female workers did not receive equal wages, and women continued to receive less money for comparable work. This prompted passages of the Equal Pay Act of 1963, which made it illegal to pay men and women differently for similar work. In spite of this legislation, women in the United States continued to receive unequal pay. Lilly Ledbetter, a corporate administrator, discovered she was paid less by her employer than men who were performing similar work in her company. Because of this condition, she elected to file litigation against her employer in *Ledbetter v. Goodyear Tire & Rubber Company* (2007), which was decided against her by the U.S. Supreme Court. The Court not only ruled against her but also made it harder for women to sue their employees for sex discrimination. To counteract the effect of the high Court's decision, the 111th U.S. Congress passed the Lilly Ledbetter Fair Pay Act of 2009, which signed into law on January 29, 2009, by President Barack Obama. The bill amended the Civil Rights Act of 1964, which challenged the 180-day statute of limitations on filing an equal-pay discrimination imposed by the Supreme Court, by resetting it so that each new paycheck represents a discriminatory act and can be litigated against an employer.

One of the most important examples of discrimination against women was voter discrimination, which required federal legislation to give women the right to fully participate in the governmental sector, as they were not permitted to cast their votes in national, state, and local elections. Finally, legislation was passed by the 66th Congress, which approved the Nineteenth Amendment to the United States Constitution. For a constitutional amendment to become law, it is necessary for it to be ratified by a majority of the states. On August 26, 1920, Kentucky became the 24th state to ratify the amendment, which gave women the right to vote in political elections in the United States.

In addition to using the rule of law to perpetuate violence against woman, prohibiting them from officially serving in the military, not providing equal pay for equal work, and denying them the right to vote, women have been discriminated against in K–12 and higher education. This discrimination in education has taken several forms, including denying them admission into selected colleges and universities, particularly as it related to certain curricula, such as engineering, medicine, and law. In these areas, males were given preferential treatment over females regarding their admissions in these fields. Discrimination in education has also taken the form of denying women or young ladies placement in advanced academic courses in science and mathematics subjects in K–12 schools. And it has also denied female students the same opportunities as male students to participate in interscholastic athletics. To correct the later discrimination, legislation was required to begin the process of establishing equality, and that has allowed female students and women to fully participate in K–12 and higher education athletic programs. Title IX, Education Amendment of 1972, prohibits discrimination against persons based on their sex in all aspects of education, including athletics.

Our experience with sex discrimination in the United States indicates that legal action and federal legislation are essential to ensure the rights of minorities and women are protected. Over many years, these groups have been discriminated against, and in every case, it was necessary to seek legal remedies to ensure their rights were satisfactory adjudicated. The issue of whether gender should be applied as a diversity criterion in educational programming and placement in public education is discussed and debated by the authors of the essays in this chapter on this very important subject. Wayne D. Lewis (University of Kentucky) takes the position that since we are not there yet, this is not the time to dismantle the policies that paved the way for the progress that has been made. Cosette M. Grant (Pennsylvania State University Greater Allegheny), in the counterpoint essay, argues that gender-based criterion in education as a means to diversify classrooms meets the needs of some students but not all, and that using objective, performance-based evaluation criteria instead of a gender-based criterion is more beneficial.

Richard C. Hunter
University of Illinois at Urbana-Champaign and
Bahrain Teachers College, University of Bahrain,
Kingdom of Bahrain

POINT: Wayne D. Lewis
University of Kentucky

In reference to U.S. educational institutions' fulfillment of the aims of Title IX of the Education Amendments Act of 1972, R. Vivian Acosta and Linda Jean Carpenter (2009) asked, "Are we there yet?" They concluded that while we have made progress toward the elimination of gender discrimination in educational institutions, much more remains to be done. Acosta and Carpenter likened the course of fighting gender discrimination in education to "an aggravating trip that seems to take forever to arrive at its destination" (p. 22). This essay seconds their contention that indeed we are not there yet and further argues that because we have so much further to go before reaching the destination of gender equity in education, gender *must* continue to be applied as a diversity criterion in educational programming and placement.

Opponents of this position argue that because of the progress institutions have made over the last 3 decades, policies that apply gender as a diversity criterion in educational programming should be dismantled. They assert, and truthfully so, that women now account for the majority of college students in the United States and have ascended to leadership positions across the P–20 education spectrum. However, they mistakenly claim that gender bias in the United States no longer exists, except against men who face reverse-discrimination at the hands of feminists. Those adherents fail to recognize several truths. First, while gender bias today is less problematic than in previous decades, "its influence is no less virulent" than it has ever been (Sadker, 2000, p. 80). Second, the progress that we have made toward achieving gender equity has only been made possible by the very policies and processes that they seek to dismantle. And third, they fail to see that while educational institutions in the United States have made significant advances toward achieving the goal of gender equity in education, much more remains to be done for that goal to be fully realized. Without policies that use gender as a diversity criterion, not only will that progress come to a screeching halt, but we also face the very real possibility of losing much of the ground that we have covered over the last several decades.

TITLE IX OF THE EDUCATIONAL AMENDMENTS OF 1972

Title IX of the Education Amendments of 1972 is widely considered the most influential piece of legislation toward achieving the goal of gender equity in educational programming in the United States. While it is most widely known for its impact on collegiate athletics, the law requires gender equity in all educational programs receiving federal funding, prohibiting educational institutions from deliberately or unintentionally engaging in conduct or implementing policies that treat students or employees differently on the basis of gender (Pieronek, 2007; Suggs, 2002). The idea of a law granting equal opportunities for women was not universally popular in 1972; as such, the strategic political decision was made to slip the measure into a larger civil rights bill to protect it from being derailed (Suggs, 2002).

Title IX's regulations for collegiate athletics have been the subject of considerable controversy over the years. The law's regulations require colleges to use a "three-part test" to determine how many women a college ought to have participating in athletics. The test gives colleges the following three options for showing that they have complied with Title IX requirements: (1) women's participation on sports teams could be proportional to female undergraduate enrollment; (2) the institution could show that they have a "history and continuing practice of expanding opportunities for women"; or (3) it could offer evidence that is "fully and effectively accommodating the interests and abilities" of its female students.

In 2005, during the George W. Bush presidential administration, Title IX was amended to allow colleges and universities receiving federal funding to assess women's interest in sports using an electronic survey to comply with the gender equity law. The Bush administration's changes resulted in institutions attributing low survey response rates to women's low interest in sports, and either mistakenly or deceptively reporting that they were accommodating women's athletic interests and abilities. Critics of the policy change charged that it "enabled schools to avoid providing gender equity in sports programs" (Jones, 2010, p. 8). Subsequently, the U.S. Department of Education under the Obama administration has highlighted the inadequacy of using survey results alone, and overturned the policy. Now, institutions may no longer use only surveys to gauge female students' interests in sports or characterize low survey response rates as female students' lack of interest in athletics. Schools and colleges must provide stronger evidence that they are offering equal opportunities for athletic participation (Jones, 2010; Sander, 2010). The reversal of the Bush administration's policy has been seen as a significant victory for gender equity advocates.

HOW MUCH FURTHER DO WE HAVE TO GO?

As a result of Title IX, a considerable amount of ground has been covered on the course to achieving gender equity in education, particularly with respect to the participation of women and girls in athletics. At the time of Title IX's enactment, very few colleges hosted varsity sports for women, with just shy of 30,000 women competing in college varsity and recreational programs compared with 170,000 men (Suggs, 2002). As a result of the policy, both men and women now enjoy an increased number of athletic opportunities in schools and colleges; more than 9,000 women's intercollegiate teams compete annually; nearly 15,000 women are employed in intercollegiate athletics as athletic directors, assistant or associate directors, coaches, trainers, or sports information directors; and one of every five athletic directors is female. However, even in athletics, progress toward equity should not be confused with the achievement of equity. Indices of arrival at the point of gender equity in athletics would include things like antidiscrimination requirements seen as the normal way of conducting business as opposed to things to be circumvented or feared; the value of the athletic experience determined by the experience of athletes and not by the size of the fan base; and coaches' salaries relating to the actual job that they do and not the gender of the athletes that they coach. We are not there yet (Acosta & Carpenter, 2009).

Outside of athletics, Title IX has had a modest impact on gender equity in education. It has been instrumental in opening the doors to medical and law schools for women, but it has had less impact on increasing the representation of women in the STEM fields in education—science, technology, engineering, and mathematics. Researchers have used the term *pipeline* to describe how students enter science education programs and progress to careers in STEM fields. The "leaky pipeline" has been identified as a major problem, with women exiting the pipeline at somewhat predicable points. In 2004, only one in five students earning baccalaureate degrees in engineering, engineering technology, physics, and computer science was female ("Engineering lags," 2006). In 2007, women accounted for fewer than 1 in 5 faculty members in computer science, mathematics, engineering, and the physical sciences, and only 1 in 10 faculty members in engineering were women (Pieronek, 2007).

The U.S. Department of Education has identified several cases where institutions are out of compliance with Title IX requirements, but because federal granting agencies routinely fail to verify compliance, these violations go unchecked and unremedied. The Government Accountability Office has concluded that relatively few Title IX complaints have been filed with the federal agencies that grant most STEM research funding to higher education institutions because faculty and students are unaware that they have the right to do so (Pieronek, 2007).

It is also apparent that in primary and secondary schools, many educators and educational leaders do not have the knowledge, skills, or dispositions to make meaningful strides toward achieving gender equity; however, it is not completely their fault. Educator and educational leadership preparation programs fail to appropriately equip educators and leaders with the tools to do so. While some programs give lip service to valuing diversity, "systematically modifying and implementing courses related to diversity" has consistently been a challenge for preparation programs (Bruner, 2008, p. 497). Issues of sexism and gender discrimination are often discounted in preparation programs with the excuse that social justice and diversity are "soft" issues that are only about emotion and controversy; thus, they are relegated to the fringe of programs, if they are addressed at all.

According to Catherine Marshall and Larry Parker (2010), "Rarely do teachers or administrators have courses or in-depth professional development that would include reading Title IX requirements." Further,

> Licensure requirements for teachers and administrators do nothing to demand their being ready to think and act creatively and assertively to stop the activities within and beyond their classrooms and corridors from perpetuating gender inequities and the damages of sex-role stereotyping. (p. 235)

The result is that female students suffer silently through gender bias and discrimination in their classrooms on a daily basis. David Sadker (2000) talks of a "syntax of sexism" so elusive in schools that "most teachers and students [are] completely unaware of its influence" (p. 80). Research shows that both male and female teachers unconsciously focus more on males during instruction, providing them with more frequent and precise attention. Sadker contends, "Teacher education and staff development programs do little to prepare teachers to see the subtle, unintentional, but damaging gender bias that characterizes classrooms" (p. 80).

This must change. Policies and their enforcement must reflect the importance of achieving gender equity and eradicating gender discrimination in U.S. schools and higher education institutions. Leadership preparation programs must be revamped to prepare educational leaders who can identify and root out sexism and gender discrimination in their schools, and evaluation standards for educational leaders must be revised to hold them accountable for doing so. As George Theoharis (2007) asserts, "Leadership that is not focused on and successful at creating more just and equitable schools for marginalized students is indeed not good leadership." Good leadership, he contends, is "leadership centered on enacting social justice, and leadership that creates equitable schools" (p. 253).

CONCLUSION

Title IX and state-level policies and regulations outlawing gender discrimination have started us down the path to achieving gender equity in educational programming. Women now make up the majority of college and university students; females' participation in athletics has grown exponentially since the 1970s; and female enrollment in math and science courses increased significantly during the 1990s, with girls now more likely than boys to take biology and chemistry courses (Sadker, 2000). But much more remains to be done. Colleges and universities still look for ways to maneuver around Title IX requirements in athletic and academic programs instead of seeking ways to institutionalize equity. Females continue to be disproportionately underrepresented in the STEM fields in education. Gender bias remains a reality in P–12 and higher education classrooms. And women remain disproportionately underrepresented in administration in both P–12 schools and higher education institutions.

This is not the time to dismantle the policies that have paved the way for the progress that we have experienced. Instead, we should expand the reach of those policies and strengthen their enforcement mechanisms. "Seemingly neutral, fair, administrative action and even pro-equity policies are not sufficient to address the inequalities that lie deep within social structures" (Marshall & Parker, 2010, p. 234). Dismantling policies that address sexism and gender discrimination head-on would be irresponsible and detrimental to our progress toward achieving gender equity in education.

RESPONSE TO COUNTERPOINT ESSAY

Educational institutions across the P–20 spectrum have indeed made strides toward the goal of achieving gender equity. The evidences of their successes lie in increases in college and graduate school graduation rates of females, increases in the number of female faculty members serving at institutions of higher education, and improvement in the athletic opportunities available to female students in high schools and institutions of higher education. While these numbers are cause for celebration, these indicators of improvement must not be confused with markers of attainment. Much work remains to be done. Females continue to be underrepresented in the highest echelons of leadership and administration in local school districts, state education agencies, and higher education institutions; females continue to be underrepresented as graduates of university programs in the STEM fields; and while significantly more females hold faculty positions at higher education institutions, they continue to be underrepresented in the STEM fields and overrepresented in the ranks of nontenure track faculty members. So yes, significant progress has been made, but much more work remains to be done. Policies and practices that apply gender as a diversity criterion in educational programming and placement have been instrumental in reaching past milestones, and they must continue to be a part of any effort to reach toward the goal of attaining gender equity in education.

COUNTERPOINT: Cosette M. Grant
Pennsylvania State University Greater Allegheny

Imposing a gender-based criterion to increase or improve diversity in educational programming and placement in K–12 public schools would seriously threaten the ability to meet the normal developmental needs of young children in a classroom. The belief of some educators, parents, and teachers is that schools should ban preferences based on gender in public sector education. Rather, using objective, performance-based evaluation criteria instead of gender-based criterion is more beneficial. Indeed, research on gender-based integrated education in general, not to mention the controversy of using gender to place students in different educational programs in public schools, within schools, and between schools, has been inconclusive. However, research suggests that what counts as progress or improvement—for example, gender inclusion as a means to mainstream education, thus enhancing equity in educational programming and placement—contains uncertainties and contradictions. To this end, do we assume that the mainstream education is to be extended and enhanced to accommodate or include the diversity of learners? Or do we assume that there is something exponential or different about special education compared to mainstream or general education? Is any reference to anything supplemental or different a form of discrimination? Or does dialogue about inclusive education just perpetuate divisiveness by making special provision to address special educational needs? This dichotomy further alludes to the ongoing tension and debate on whether or not to enforce a gender-based criterion to diversify educational programming and placement. This also further supports the notion that there is no clear overall and coherent set of principles or values that can justify policy and practices at all levels in education. Because of these tensions and the dilemmas they give rise to, there is no ideological clarity in education in general.

Furthermore, institutions have made progress over the last 3 decades that ensure education equity for all children. Therefore, enforced policies that apply gender as a diversity criterion in educational programming and placement should be dismantled.

INCLUSIVE EDUCATION AND EDUCATIONAL PROGRAMMING

Opponents of the aforementioned position argue for inclusive education that applies a diversity criterion in educational programming and placement as a means of achieving gender equity in education. It is also argued that there is a strong educational, as well as social and moral, foreground for educating children with special educational needs (SEN), for example, with their peers, which aims to increase the level and quality of inclusion within mainstream schools. This entails inclusion as a process by which schools, educational leaders, and stakeholders develop policies and practices through training initiatives, strategies, and support mechanisms so that nearly all children with SEN can be successfully included in mainstream education. However, many questions have been raised, and continue to be raised, about the efficacy and effectiveness of this policy, about just how far it is actually resulting in more inclusive approaches to education, and whether it contributes to the needs of all children being safeguarded and adequately identified, addressed, and met (Warnock, 2005). Further, Mary Warnock argues, "Even if inclusion is an ideal for society, it may not always be an ideal for school" (p. 43). An equal opportunity for children with SEN is not necessarily best secured by those children having the same educational provision as their peers.

IMPEDIMENTS TO INCLUSIVE EDUCATIONAL PROGRAMMING AND PLACEMENT

Although some argue for the benefits of integrated schools, not everyone agrees that diversity in the classroom is beneficial. Inclusive education has been subject to heavy criticism (Barton, 1998) for suggesting that some children are being harmed by the application of inclusive principles. Some educators argue that this idea is simply incorrect. Accordingly, full inclusion isn't always the best way to meet student needs. Full inclusion does not consider that children with disabilities are individuals with differing needs, some benefitting from inclusion, while others not, who are more likely to be harmed than helped when they are placed in regular classroom settings. Teachers are not necessarily equipped with the training to accommodate unique and special needs (Huestis, 1994).

Opponents of inclusion argue that total integration of all students with special needs into regular education classrooms violates existing legal mandates. They further claim that the functional needs of many exceptional children—such as the basic communication and living skills that children with severe cognitive impairment need, and the self-management and social skills that children with serious emotional or behavioral problems need—cannot be addressed adequately in full-time regular academic classes (Braaten, Kauffman,

Braaten, Polsgrove, & Nelson, 1988). Such students require at least some individualized instruction in a controlled environment, which can be provided only by a teacher who has received extensive specialized training. The degree of mainstreaming into regular classes should depend on the carefully assessed individual needs of each exceptional student, and a continuum of special education placements and services must be maintained (Fuchs & Fuchs, 1994). Aligned with similar thinking, further adding to the debate on the issue of gender-based criterion in educational programming and placement, protesters of inclusive education give many reasons as to why it is not profitable. One common complaint that warrants mention is made primarily by parents of excelled students—that when children that are slow learners are placed into a regular classroom, they bring down the level of learning of the other students. Another concern of many protesters of inclusion is that students with disabilities have social difficulties. They believe disabled students who are integrated into the regular classroom will become outcasts in that setting. Besides, the problem with inclusion, it is argued, is being stalled because educational institutions are not fit to include all children because of the barriers of "lack of knowledge, lack of will, lack of vision, lack of resources and lack of morality" (Clough & Garner, 2003, p. 87)

LIMITATIONS OF GENDER-BASED CRITERION IN EDUCATIONAL PROGRAMMING AND PLACEMENT

Some argue that there are limitations to a gender-based criterion imposed in educational programming and placement. A more productive and rational approach may be to consider the ethics in placement for each student identified as educationally challenged. That said, there has been much concern of a widening gender gap with regard to educational achievement and attainment in public education that has become a national issue in the past decade. Male students, as a group, are lagging behind female students on a number of important indicators of school success. U.S. statistics show that boys are achieving at lower levels across most school subjects as a group than are girls; they earn lower grades and exhibit higher school dropout rates. Boys are much more frequently diagnosed with attention deficit hyperactivity disorder and are also much more frequently placed in special education programs. More males than females are referred to alternative schools, usually for disciplinary reasons, because of not being able to make it in a mainstream school program.

In addition to achievement data, there are attitudinal and motivational data indicating that boys as a group do not seem to think school is as important in their lives as do girls. In response to this trend, there have been efforts to address this issue through gender inclusion programs to accommodate the unique learning needs of male students. In particular, there have been cases where classes were organized on the basis of general perceived ability, or ability in a particular subject. Both are problematic. In this case, boys' education is a priority over that of girls. Arguments against inclusion proffer that this process has disadvantaged a number of girls in particular school settings.

Clearly, the goal of all educators is to provide each and every student with the appropriate education that he or she deserves. However, providing each child with an appropriate education does not mean every child should be forced to learn in a way that does not conform to his or her strengths. There are varying and differing views as to which way of educating students with learning disadvantages is best. In the contemporary debates about boys' education, it is repeatedly argued that improving boys' outcomes should not come at the expense of girls. However, in this case where gender reform seeks to improve the educational outcomes of boys, it was at the expense of girls' interests. There are specific cases in which a school engaged in the proactive tactics of mobilizing discourses about "poor boys" to justify and market the school's gender equity initiative designed to improve the educational outcomes for boys. There is a case in point whereby a school was developed in response to the market and parental pressures in relation to boys' education (Warnock, 2005). This strategy led to girls who were achieving least in comparison with other girls, but often higher than a substantial numbers of boys, being placed in lower performing classes than their academic achievements, compared with boys. This was done to address problems being encountered with lower level boys-only classes. It was claimed that boys-only classes are difficult for teachers to manage and are unlikely to be productive for the students. It was further argued that the presence of girls in these classes would have a mediating effect on boys' behavior and academic achievement. Thus, the girls who were selected to be in this class were placed in a set lower than boys who had achieved comparable results.

Additionally, there was a second strategy intended to address the gender imbalance in top-level English classes—more girls than boys in the school achieved higher test results and more girls than boys qualified for the top-level class—by placing equal numbers of boys and girls in the top level. The result was that some girls were displaced from the top-level English class to one of mixed ability. This was in response to addressing concerns about boys' lower performance relative to girls in English. There was a sense that this move would somehow impact positively on boys' self-esteem and lead to better participation and achievement in English. The use of gender-based criteria in both instances demonstrates inequitable practices in that the process was not based on concepts of merit, the usual justification for selection in these classes, but on a need to improve boys' academic outcomes through striking an artificial gender balance.

Moreover, while all children have the right to a good education and the opportunity to fulfill their potential, this inclusion process has failed to meet the needs of some but not all students. This remains an ongoing challenge to forced gender inclusion in education.

FURTHER ARGUMENTS TO ANTI–GENDER DIVERSITY CRITERION

It is more than 30 years since the enactment of the special education legislation that established the current framework of special provision in educational programming and placement to diversify schools. Among other elements, this legislation introduced the legal concept of special educational needs and formalized an inclusive principle of educating all children in the mainstream. Though this legislation reflected current practice, it also moved provision toward a greater emphasis on the educational needs of children with difficulties and disabilities. Because of No Child Left Behind, all subgroups are expected to make gains. Thus, Title IX and state-level policies and regulations outlawing discrimination have started us down the path to achieving gender equity, for example, in educational programming; however, those advances should not be made at the expense of prioritizing one subgroups' educational need over another. In the point essay of this chapter, Wayne D. Lewis agues in favor of the application of gender as a diversity criterion in educational programming and placement, showing how progress has been made toward achieving gender equity through such policies and processes. While there is agreement that policies and their enforcement must reflect the importance of achieving gender equity and eradicating gender discrimination in U.S. schools and higher education institutions, the trend, for example, has been to favor the needs of boys who have been underachieving and force them into higher performing classroom settings dominated by girls. This is not gender equity. It becomes inequity because girl students will no longer receive the variety, types, or intensity of services that they deserve in higher performing settings. Rather, teachers under inclusion are made to divide their time, expertise, and in-classroom instruction among lower performing boys versus higher performing girls in a classroom setting.

It is important that the issue of male underachievement and attainment in public education be addressed in schools and communities. An increased awareness of the issue as a societal and systemic problem is a critical first step. However, forced placements based on a need to improve boys' academic outcomes, thus striking an artificial gender balance, is unfair to girls who are achieving.

Lewis further argues in the point essay that now is not the time to dismantle the policies that have paved the way for the progress that has been experienced through gender-based criteria and that, instead, we should expand the reach of those policies and strengthen their enforcement mechanisms. Also highlighted was current research demonstrating that in the P–20 spectrum, female enrollment in math and science courses has increased significantly over the last decade, with girls now more likely than boys to take biology and chemistry courses; more females are participating in sports since the 1970s; women represent the majority of college and university student enrollment in the United States; females' participation in athletics has been on a rise since the 1970s; and women have ascended to leadership positions across the P–20 education spectrum (Sadker, 2000). Given this transforming progress of women and girls thriving in nontraditional disciplines and roles, typically dominated by men and boys, there is no need for policies or their expansion that enforce gender as a diversity criterion in educational programming and placement.

CONCLUSION

School success is important for all students, and the educational achievement of our young people affects all of us, including our structures and future generations to come. Also, gender is a significant variable in the education of our students today. In an era in which gender roles and attitudes have changed rapidly, it is vital that as educators we recognize the significance of gender in our lessons, our attitudes, and our efforts to help all students reach their potential and be the best they can be. However, despite the acclaimed significance of "inclusive education" to government policy, its progress is challenging (Department of Education and Skills, 2004). This is because it is a complex process, and its implementation gives rise to contradictions, inconsistencies, and tensions in professional practice. These arise because of policy and practice dilemmas resulting from issues of how to allocate programming equitably. As you can see from the aforementioned strategies, a gender-based criterion in education as a means to diversify classrooms—in particular, taking lower performing males and integrating them with higher achieving girls—meets the needs of some students but not all. Further, it prioritizes the needs of some over the needs of all. Concern about the expense of traditional lower performing boys in education, rather than concern about the needs and rights of exceptional female students, for example, violate the rights of these exceptional students to an appropriate education. Herein remains tension within the issue of whether inclusion can be facilitated by one curriculum that fits all children.

FURTHER READINGS AND RESOURCES

Acosta, R. V., & Carpenter, L. J. (2009). Are we there yet? *Academe, 95*(4), 22–24.

Barton, L. (1998). Markets, managerialism and inclusive education. In P. Clough (Ed.), *Managing inclusive education—from policy to experience.* London: Paul Chapman.

Braaten, S., Kauffman, J. M., Braaten, B., Polsgrove, L., & Nelson, C. M. (1988). The Regular Education Initiative: Patent medicine for behavioral disorders. *Exceptional Children, 55,* 21–27.

Bruner, D. Y. (2008). Aspiring and practicing leaders addressing issues of diversity and social justice. *Race, Ethnicity and Education, 11*(4), 483–500.

Clough, P., & Garner, G. (2003). Special educational needs and inclusive education: Origins and current issues. In S. Bartlett & D. Burton (Eds.), *Education studies: Essential issues* (pp. 72–93). London: Sage.

Department of Education and Skills. (2004). *Removing barriers to achievement: The government's strategy for SEN, executive summary.* London: Author.

Engineering lags in grad diversity: Still a paucity of women and minorities earning diplomas. (2006). *Industrial Engineer.* Retrieved July 30, 2010, from http://www.allbusiness.com/industrial-engineer

Fuchs, D., & Fuchs, L. S. (1994). Inclusive schools movement and the radicalization of special education reform. *Exceptional Children, 60,* 294–309.

Huestis, T. (Ed.). (1994). AFT continues dire warnings against full inclusion. *Special Education Report, 20*(2), 8.

Jones, J. (2010). Obama administration touts Title IX policy change. *Diverse Issues in Higher Education, 27*(7), 8.

Marshall, C., & Parker, L. (2010). Learning from leaders' social justice dilemmas. In C. Marshall & M. Oliva (Eds.), *Leadership for social justice* (2nd ed., pp. 219–241). Boston: Pearson Education.

Pieronek, C. (2007). Not just for sports. *ASEE Prism, 17*(4), 96.

Sadker, D. (2000). Gender equity: Still knocking at the classroom door. *Equity & Excellence in Education, 33*(1), 80–83.

Sander, L. (2010). Education department nixes Bush-era policy on Title IX compliance. *The Chronicle of Higher Education, 56*(3), A14.

Suggs, W. (2002). Title IX at 30. *The Chronicle of Higher Education, 48*(41), A39–A41.

Theoharis, G. (2007). Social justice educational leaders and resistance: Toward a theory of social justice leadership. *Educational Administration Quarterly, 43*(2), 221–258.

Warnock, M. (2005). *Special educational needs: A new look.* London: Philosophy Society of Great Britain.

COURT CASES AND STATUTES

Ledbetter v. Goodyear Tire & Rubber Company, 550 U.S. 618 (2007).

Title IX of the Education Amendments of 1972, 20 U.S.C. § 1681 (2008).

Is the full-service community school model for involving parents and community members from diverse backgrounds useful in furthering equitable educational opportunity among majority-minority school populations?

POINT: Dana Griffin, *University of North Carolina at Chapel Hill*
COUNTERPOINT: Natalie A. Tran and Miguel Zavala,
California State University, Fullerton

OVERVIEW

There is considerable dissatisfaction over the status of the public educational system in the United States, and many efforts to reform the system have been undertaken at each level of government: federal, state, and local. Still, public education is in need of improvement, and the nation continues to look for a silver bullet that, once implemented, will dramatically improve public education for the nation's poor and minority students, whose educational quality lags far behind that of most middle-class White students. One strategy that has been developed is for public schools to become full-service institutions. We are used to the idea of full-service institutions from industries, such as banking or automobile dealerships, but this idea has not gained much traction in the K–12 educational sector. There are several reasons why this has not occurred, primarily because our system of government in the United Sates follows a Federalist system, where there are multiple levels of government that are semiautonomous or even autonomous. I am referring primarily to local municipal government and public school districts, which have a great deal in common in that they are where the rubber meets the road. Unfortunately, these units of government do not always work together to solve social and health problems that affect public school students. In many cases, they do not even communicate with each other and certainly do not collaborate on ways that will permit them to address the many important public health and social issues that affect students in public schools, such as poverty and unemployment, which impact the quality of education that public schools provide to their students.

Why is there so much interest in full-service schools? There are several important reasons why this topic is receiving consideration at this time. First, there are serious public health issues and social service issues that directly impact how well public school students are doing in their studies. Research indicates that children do better in school when they are properly fed and are not suffering from serious medical issues, such as contagious medical diseases or malnutrition. Unfortunately, there are public school–age students in the United States today who are suffering from such health issues as malnutrition, were born underweight, or have parents who are addicted to drugs and alcohol. There are many heath issues, such as nutrition, sex education, and pregnancy prevention, that are negatively affecting student learning in public schools.

Also, there are other social issues that impact children who attend public schools, such as low income or poverty. Unfortunately, there are many children who are being raised by families who do not have enough economic resources to properly take care of their children. Many public school students are homeless and live from day to day without adequate shelter. Further, the issue of one-parent families is great when it comes to students from minority and low-income family backgrounds. There is also the issue of students whose parents are illegal aliens and for whom additional public health and social services are routinely required. Are these problems present in public school children in the

United States, given that we are the wealthiest country in the world? The answer is clearly yes.

One approach to greater communication and collaboration between municipal officials of public health and social services and public school officials is municipal takeovers of public school districts. The full-service school model is another, arguably more acceptable, alternative to school district takeovers. What is a full-service school? *Full-service schools* are generally public schools that not only provide educational services to their students, but may also provide public health, social services, and other related community services to the entire community where the school is situated. The public health and social services personnel who work in the school come from local municipal government and report to the appropriate city department head. The workers are housed in health clinics and social services offices, which are located on public school facilities. This model represents a different way of delivering services to public school students and to members of the community, who reside near the school building. Having health clinics in the school has many positive outcomes. For example, students can walk down the hall to take their athletic physical examinations and they can receive personal medical and dental treatment without leaving the school and missing time from classes.

In this chapter, two well-respected authors debate the pros and cons of the full-service community school model. In the point essay, Dana Griffin (University of North Carolina at Chapel Hill) advocates for the use establishment of such models but acknowledges that the high costs of setting up and running full-service schools can be an insurmountable impediment. Griffin suggests that partnerships with local churches can be a viable, and affordable, alternative. Citing the fact that at this time there is not any clear evidence that full-service community schools have a positive impact on the academic, social, and psychological well-being of students, Natalie A. Tran and Miguel Zavala (California State University, Fullerton) present the opposing point of view. Tran and Zavala argue that, given the lack of data showing that community-based approaches produce results in terms of equity and access for all students, the wisest action would be to be critical in evaluating their long-term impact. Further, these authors suggest that we should not be so quick to adopt reforms that come along just because we are dissatisfied with the current educational system.

Richard C. Hunter
University of Illinois at Urbana-Champaign and
Bahrain Teachers College, University of Bahrain,
Kingdom of Bahrain

POINT: Dana Griffin
University of North Carolina at Chapel Hill

A frican American children face frequent challenges from sociocultural factors such as racial discrimination and institutionalized racism and
oppression, and community factors such as poverty, violence, crime, and drugs
(Goldstein & Noguera, 2006). Additionally, African American children experience higher rates of suspension, expulsion from school, and special education
placement (Gregory, Skiba, & Noguera, 2010). Further, they are challenged by
such barriers as drug and alcohol abuse to engaging in risky sexual behaviors,
and they can suffer from mental health problems that result from stress and
violence they can encounter on a daily basis (Dryfoos, 2003). These challenges
often place African American children at risk for school failure. Indeed, the
academic achievement of many low-income students and students of color
often falls below that of middle- and upper-class Asian and White students. I
believe one way to overcome these challenges, and foster greater equitable educational opportunities among majority-minority school populations, is
through greater collaboration among families, schools, and communities,
which can be accomplished through the use of full-service community school
models.

FULL-SERVICE COMMUNITY SCHOOL MODELS

The term *full-service community schools* describes schools that are open longer
than traditional schools, offer a variety of health and social service programs
to families and children, have partnerships with communities and community
agencies, involve parents in meaningful and significant ways, and integrate
high quality teaching with activities offered in extended hours. In essence, full-
service community schools are the heart of the communities they serve
(Dryfoos, 2003). Full-service community school models are designed differently and can be adapted to meet the needs of the school and community.
Some services are offered on site, while others are offered through structured
collaboration with community agencies. As schools cannot handle the number
of services children need to be fully supported alone (Dryfoos, 2002), the overall objective of full-service community school models is to bring different
services into schools that give children and families access to the supports they
need (Dryfoos & Maguire, 2002). The goal of a full-service community school
model can be to improve student learning, improve school performance, or
have access to school-based health and mental health services among other

nontraditional services (Peebles-Wilkins, 2004). Advocates for full-service community school models believe that achievement scores for many will not improve unless schools work with parents and communities to help children overcome health, mental health, social, and economic barriers to learning.

While African American communities exhibited strong ties between the home, school, and community during school segregation, currently, African American families and communities are perceived to have low involvement and low expectations for African American children's educational achievement (Abdul-Adil & Farmer, 2006). However, full-service school models actually boast high parental involvement and school–family–community collaboration, which brings the parents, communities, and schools together to help bolster academic success for their children. For example, the Quitman Street Community School, located in the inner city of Newark, New Jersey, went from a low-performing school to a high-performing full-service community school through the implementation of a full-service community school model using the Children's Aid Society model. At this site, parental involvement is high, with many parents coming to the school daily as classroom and cafeteria aids, some as volunteers, others paid. Further, parents can take courses that are available during the day and early evening and receive GED preparation help (Dryfoos, 2002).

Having been implemented at over 100 sites across the nation, successful components of this model include a 7:30 am to 9:00 pm school day, where children can receive homework help and academic enrichment in the after-school program. Strong community partnerships are implemented by having parents and community stakeholders come in to run programs from 6:00 to 9:00 pm, including sports and other recreational activities and arts programs. This program also includes a school-based primary health clinic staffed with a full-time nurse practitioner, an aide, a social worker, a part-time dentist, a pediatrician, and a psychiatric consultant. Students and their families can receive free physical examinations, treatments for problems such as asthma, medications, and mental health counseling. By the school using this model, students are able to have access to new educational experiences such as having field trips to places normally unavailable to students—for example, museums, ball games, nature preserves, and amusement parks. Data from this program demonstrate that students have higher achievement, better behavior, and are more independent (Dryfoos, 2002).

IMPLEMENTATION ISSUES

So one must ask, if full-service community school models can offer the supports that low-income and African American children need to be successful, then why is this model not implemented in low-performing schools? It could be that implementing these models is time-consuming and takes a lot of coordination to develop. Although having a full-service model can be more effective in providing services that meet the various needs of students, the outset of collaboration is hard work and requires a number of meetings, patience, and understanding; it also requires a deep commitment, strong administrator support, open communication, and, most importantly, strong financial support (Dryfoos, 2002). However, it seems that once the models are implemented, positive changes begin to occur. For example, Wilma Peebles-Wilkins (2004) describes how Lucy Stone Elementary School, an inner-city school in Dorchester, Massachusetts, has been able to increase achievement with the implementation of a full-service community school model. The Lucy Stone Elementary School is one of four elementary schools in a full-service partnership with Boston Excels, an educational intervention operated by the Home for Little Wanderers. The school has 210 enrolled students: 81% Black, 13% Hispanic, 4% White, and 1% Asian. Successful components of this model include the use of a number of prevention services, such as structured out-of-school time, crisis intervention, therapy programs, family literacy programs, and parent outreach and leadership development. Further, programs in this school are conducted in both English and Spanish, and English classes are offered for parents through the family literacy program.

It is surprising that more schools do not adopt full-service community school models, especially as educational reform efforts have not been successful at closing achievement and opportunity gaps for students of color and those from low-income backgrounds. Further, the many policies that have been implemented to address the educational inequities that exist, such as No Child Left Behind, have continued to fail and allow systemic injustices to remain. We, as educators, must begin to admit that the current policies fail to address the complex needs of low-income students and students of color, and we must admit that majority-minority schools are not receiving the services they need to develop and enhance student achievement. Further, we must admit that responding to student needs by only focusing on improving schools does not guarantee the drastic changes necessary to enhance student educational outcomes (Noguera, 2003).

PARTNERSHIPS

As we all can agree that financial support can probably be one of the biggest barriers to implementing a full-service community school model, I would like to offer one cost-saving suggestion that could easily be implemented in the schools: *school–family–community* partnerships. School–family–community partnerships are defined as collaborative relationships in which school coun- selors, school personnel, students, families, community members, and other school stakeholders work jointly to implement school and community-based programs and activities that improve student outcomes and meet student needs (Bryan, 2005). Not only are collaborative partnerships the cornerstone of full-service community school models, but school–family–community part- nerships have also been important components of previous education reform initiatives, and the contributions of partnerships to students' academic, personal/ social, career, and college success have been highlighted in numerous studies. Some view school–family–community partnerships as methods to meet the diverse and numerous needs of students and/or their families (Bryan, 2005). Indeed, in current education reforms, such as the *Blueprint for Reform* (U.S. Department of Education, 2010), the authors consider partnerships between schools, families, community members, and organizations as vital to support- ing student success. Therefore, I assert one way to implement a cost-saving full-service community school model is to develop a school partnership with a community church.

As churches are important institutions in African American communities, partnering with churches can become the low-cost foundation to implement- ing a full-service community school model. Churches can be used to house after-school programs, and church members and retirees can provide tutoring services, and even social/emotional programs. For example, many churches have smaller groups and organizations that are pledged to community service. A school can begin to offer a full-service community school model by develop- ing an intensive partnership with a church. Church groups can then begin to center their community service on providing services for the school. One way would be having church members provide free tutoring to students every eve- ning from 6:00 to 7:00. Another way would be to offer computer training and education for parents looking to enter the workforce. Yet another way could be enlisting church members with medical backgrounds to offer nutrition and health classes for families. In essence, the full-school community model would entail having a school–church partnership.

Although a school–church partnership is a type of school–family–community partnership, in which the partnership is exclusively with a church community, it does not have to include a faith-based component. In other words, the partnership is based on receiving services as opposed to faith development. This would be an important piece of the partnership to ensure that those who are of different religions or faiths could also benefit from the services offered. Although not as exclusively discussed in the literature, church-based partnerships are not new. The U.S. Department of Education began urging school–church partnerships in 2001 during the George W. Bush administration (Unmuth, 2009). Using an Internet search engine to search school–church partnerships yields thousands of examples of effective school–church partnerships, including a Facebook page dedicated to connecting churches with schools in need. These websites, newspaper articles, and Facebook pages show that churches are playing an increasingly important role in facilitating full-service community school models. For example, church members are providing services in the realm of mental health services, day care, tutoring and mentoring, adult education, and health and nutrition, in additional to more traditional forms of aid such as providing school supplies and clothing to students and their families. Churches are also providing volunteers to help fix and maintain playground equipment and area parks and providing transportation to help parents attend school meetings and other school-based activities; church members are also working as teacher aides, all free of charge. In essence, a school–church partnership may not be the epitome of what a full-service community school model is supposed to be, but given the huge financial barrier of implementing full-service community school models, starting with a school–church partnership seems to be one that can be easily initiated and implemented by the schools.

CONCLUSION

Full-service community school models can be useful in furthering equitable educational opportunities among majority-minority school populations because these models bring needed resources into the schools to better address and support the student population. This in turn allows greater educational opportunities to majority-minority populations as the additional resources can help eliminate barriers to student academic success. Partnering with churches to help deliver needed resources can be a mutually beneficial arrangement for all parties involved—schools, students, families, and communities.

RESPONSE TO COUNTERPOINT

Natalie A. Tran and Miguel Zavala, the authors of the counterpoint essay, make some valid points regarding the use of full-service community school models to help meet the needs of marginalized student populations. The voices of marginalized populations do need to be included in the development of a full-service community model, and the model could exacerbate the gaps in educational opportunities if it is not implemented with care. It can also be agreed that correctly implementing the model is time intensive. The counterpoint authors do not appear to be against full-service community school models per se, but more against the implementation barriers of full-service community school models. However, the cautions the authors list are ones that need to be heeded when any type of school reform is being considered or implemented. But one of the great things about full-service community school models is that the models can be tailored to meet the needs of individual schools and thus take into consideration the school location, resources, and needs of the students, parents, and community. Because we know that individuals, families, and communities are different, this model is ideal because it can consider the "social, political, and economic repercussions" the model could have on historically marginalized youth, and develop goals to ensure that all children receive an education that prepares them to be competitive in today's market. A goal can be designed to ensure that kids leave school with the skills and knowledge they need to be competitive in a technologically advanced world, just as a goal can be designed to ensure that students are exposed to diverse perspectives inside and outside of their communities.

However, one thing I disagree with is the view expressed in the counterpoint essay on the lack of or limited resources available in marginalized communities. This view takes a deficit approach to looking at communities, and we need to begin to look at communities through a strength-based framework. Every community, and every individual in that community, has an asset or a strength that can be used to instill the necessary skills needed to help promote academic achievement. Viewing communities through a deficit approach continues to perpetuate the cycle of disenfranchisement and systemic oppression that continues to limit the academic success of low-income students and students of color. Full-service community school models take into account the assets of various communities and community members, and use their strengths to help further the academic success of their students.

COUNTERPOINT: Natalie A. Tran and Miguel Zavala

California State University, Fullerton

I n contemporary discussions of K–12 public schools, one controversial issue has been the ability of full-service community schools to provide equitable educational opportunities among majority and minority student groups, and whether alternative organizational approaches to schooling should be considered. On the one hand, there is strong evidence showing that traditional public schools are failing to meet the needs of marginalized student populations, mainly Native Americans, Blacks, Latinos, and a sector of Southeast Asian Americans. On the other hand, alternative organizational approaches to schooling such as full-service community schools require further examination. While there appears to be potential in organizational structures that bring together a series of support services to one locale, the issue is much more complex and requires an understanding of the social, cultural, and economic structures that are richly embedded within the education system. If the question of structural embeddings is not treated with care, organizational reforms such as full-service community schools could exacerbate the gaps in educational opportunity among majority and minority student populations, a major point of discussion in this section.

Proponents of the full-service community school model condemn public schools in their failure to educate historically marginalized students. They argue that students are often either "kicked out" or "pushed out" of traditional schools under negative circumstances as the result of academic disengagement, poor relationships with teachers and administrators, substance abuse, and social and personal problems (Baldridge, Lamont Hill, & Davis, 2011; Castaneda, 1997). Community-based education can provide better educational experiences for these students by using a holistic approach to educating youth and integrating social services and resources that are available in the community (Dryfoos, 2002, 2003). However, this approach overlooks logistical issues associated with the development and implementation of such a model and fails to consider the social, political, and economic repercussions the model could have on the historically marginalized youth.

Public schools in the United States have had a long and rich tradition beginning with racial segregation and discrimination that left a deep scar running through the veins of American history and persisting to live on through the cultural rebirth of the American experience (Spring, 2009). This wound, which began with a history of racism starting in the 17th century with slavery, continued to run deep into the 21st century. Even though the idea and application of racism was not novel in the many facets of life, it took nearly 3 decades for America to recognize its presence in the American education system. Not until the 1950s was the American public ready to face racism in one of its many manifestations—segregation of public schools. This confrontation led to the landmark case known as *Brown v. Board of Education* in 1954, aiming to end de jure segregation.

Today, schools are resegregated by race/ethnicity, language, poverty, and parental education resulting in overcrowded schools and underqualified teachers in classrooms attended by poor students of color (Orfield & Eaton, 1996; Tatum, 2007). This is the case for many schools in large urban areas where the demographic composition is largely made up of African American and Latino students who come from low socioeconomic backgrounds. Many of these students are placed in overcrowded classrooms taught by unqualified teachers. Students must be bused if their parents wish for their children to attend a better school outside of their residential area. Examining the current conditions of public schools in the United States, one may be inclined to argue that segregation of public schools in the United States has not changed very much since the *Brown* decision in 1954. However, a careful look at the public schools in the United States suggests that, for over the last 50 years, some progress has been made. All children in the United States are entitled to a free public education on a nondiscriminatory basis with respect to race and abilities.

More than ever, educating U.S. youth is critical to developing a highly skilled workforce that can be competitive in the global economy. Despite great efforts to increase the number of participants in the science, technology, engineering, and mathematics disciplines to preserve the future prosperity of the United States, current trends indicate that the social and economic conditions of the United States may be jeopardized as a result of globalization (National Academy of Sciences, 2007). A report on scientific literacy performance of 15-year-olds in 2009 indicates that while the average score of U.S. students is not significantly different from the average score of students from the other 32 participating countries, U.S. students trailed behind their peers in countries such as Finland, Japan, and Korea (Bybee & McCrae, 2009). This crisis raises concerns for educating the diverse student population, especially those who have been traditionally marginalized. How can we be sure that full-service community schools, though they provide much-needed social services to youth, have adequate resources to provide students with the sophisticated skills and knowledge they need to be competitive in this technologically advanced world? This becomes a greater challenge for youth living in communities with limited resources since resources available will most likely provide social support and much less for academic and economic support.

IMPLEMENTATION

First, several practical challenges can be anticipated with the development and diffusion of full-service community schools. Extensive leadership capacity is needed to bring various stakeholders who are representative of the community and who share common interests that would benefit youth in the community. The process of community development may not necessarily represent the community at large, thus leaving out voices of youth, parents, and other community stakeholders who may not have a social, political, and economic influence. This point cannot be underestimated: Given the history of social service delivery to marginalized groups, one has to question how "community" and nongovernmental agencies themselves benefit from the constitution of new organizational models such as full-service community schools.

In addition, there is an inherent organizational challenge to developing, implementing, and scaling up community-based schools. On the one hand, not all community-based organizations have experience working with schools or knowledge about the functional aspects of schools. On the other hand, not all schools willingly accept resources from the community and value community partnerships. Assuming that organizational alignment can be achieved, such school–community partnerships require adequate funding for sustainability. The full-service community–school model will include a wider range of health and social services that reflect the unique needs of youth in the school and community. These services will inevitably decrease the amount of fiscal and human resources available for other school programs such as instructional activities and extracurricular opportunities. Furthermore, in a time of scarce resources, educators and policymakers will need to know whether full-service community schools are effective in a short time period. Considering the issue of resources needed to fully implement full-service community schools, some district officials and local politicians have argued that school–family–community partnerships is fundamental to addressing the education and social needs of poor, urban students. However, and in line with our argument, we contend that this is simply a liberal idea that on the surface looks promising but in the long run obfuscates the real issue, which is lack of funding for public education altogether. Given the complexity of this work, developing effective partnerships will require several years and even a longer time frame to evaluate the various aspects that can be attributed to the success of such partnerships. Finally, to have an impact on policy, a comprehensive assessment plan must be put in place to evaluate the effectiveness of scaling up full-service community schools. As researchers and scholars commit to community–school building, we worry that advocates for full-service community schools are quick to decry this as a viable reform option. For example, mixed results are found for schools cited as exemplary full-service community schools, such as Lucy Stone Elementary in Dorchester, Massachusetts. While proponents argue for the potential benefits of a full-service community school model implemented at this site (Peebles-Wilkins, 2004), a report generated by the Massachusetts Department of Education (2003) for Lucy Stone Elementary shows that problems of student achievement, curricular development, and teaching prevail. These findings raise serious concerns about the effectiveness of such model. Further research and development are needed before such practice can be institutionalized in K–12 schools across the United States.

EXPOSURE TO DIVERSE PERSPECTIVES

Second, while the community-based approach to education may support youths' development of knowledge about their cultural background, cultural pride, self-esteem, civic engagement, and, to a certain extent, preparation for future employment, currently there is no clear evidence that full-service community schools have a positive impact on the academic, social, and psychological well-being of students who attend these schools (Castaneda, 1997). While knowledge about one's language, culture, and heritage is valuable, the current movement toward globalization suggests that it would be even more beneficial for all youth to have a diversified educational experience—a learning experience that builds on and reflects the different perspectives of various student groups. Yet community-based education programs are turning inward, focusing mainly on issues related to a given local community, and turning to their immediate surroundings for support and resources. Since these communities tend to have limited resources compared to more affluent communities, how will they help youth develop the skills they need to be competitive in mainstream society—a society that had once marginalized them for who they are, and will now penalize them for the skills that they lack?

Lack of exposure to diverse perspectives readily available in many public school settings is disadvantageous to youth development and the acquisition of knowledge made possible by daily interactions with peers from various racial, cultural, and linguistic backgrounds. In the long run, the lack of exposure to diverse perspectives will be detrimental to youth from disadvantaged communities. It will hinder students from being fully integrated into events outside of their community. While proponents of community-based education are right to argue that the traditional public schools are failing to educate all students, it does not follow that full-service community schools will provide superior educational experience for all youth who have been failed by traditional public schools. Furthermore, it is an exaggeration to claim that this alternative approach to education will provide an equitable educational opportunity among marginalized youth. In sum, although services can be brought to a particular school setting, creating diverse student bodies at each school campus can best generate exposure to diversity of perspectives and the resources that different populations bring. However, noting the history of racial and economic injustice outlined above, de facto segregation has severely limited the resources that historically marginalized groups receive and are able to generate, with the school being a main vehicle for the perpetuation of social inequality and disenfranchisement.

ACCESS TO RESOURCES

Third, and perhaps most important, it is unclear whether the educational opportunity and career paths reflected in alternative education programs foster the skills and knowledge required by high-paying jobs or low-skill wages. At a fundamental level, students should be given the opportunities to develop the intellectual and critical thinking skills they need to reassess their social and economic realities and the roles they play in society. To develop these skills, students need to make gains in their social and educational capital. Educational capital, coupled with cultural capital form the gateway to social mobility (Bourdieu, 1984). Thus, it is crucial that these students have an *equal opportunity* to access a range of educational experiences, including college preparatory curriculum—a critical component that full-service community schools must have.

While equitable educational opportunity among majority-minority school populations is not currently achieved, adoption of the community-based education model may further exacerbate the education gap. This becomes more apparent when comparing how individuals from more affluent communities might use resources in the full-service community school model. Youth in these communities will continue to benefit from alternative models as the greater amount of social, cultural, and political resources from the community is funneled to their school system, thus widening the opportunity and achievement gaps among majority-minority student populations. Acknowledging that social, cultural, and political factors shape the educational experience of youth in the United States, these alternative programs will fall short in their capacity to prepare productive citizens, train high-skilled workers, and mobilize the resources needed to uplift historically marginalized youth economically.

CONCLUSION

In this counterpoint essay, neither the resources in the community nor the holistic approach to education is being questioned. Nor is the concept that equitable educational experiences should be available for all students challenged. Rather, the contention is that full-service community-based education, in its current condition, may not be equipped to provide youth with educational experiences that will prepare them to become productive citizens and competitive workers in the current global economy. Public schools, since their inception, have sought to fulfill the democratic mission to educate students from various racial, cultural, linguistic, and social backgrounds. While it is true that certain groups of students benefit more from public schools than others, it does not necessarily mean that students from marginalized groups cannot profit from the existing educational system. Yet some readers may challenge this view and insist that public education should provide equitable educational opportunity for *all.* After all, many believe that the main function of public schools is to educate the masses for a better democratic society, thus reflecting the core values of the "American" people. To achieve this lofty goal, changes in educational practices and policies must be considered. However, community-based approaches to education have yet to produce results that would yield equity and access for all students. Therefore, it would be wise to be critical in evaluating their long-term impact and not be so quick to adopt any "reforms" that come along when dissatisfied with the current educational system. Acting on carelessness may reverse the social progress that has been made throughout history, as not all reforms are progressive movements (Apple, 2001). The overall service approach, to fix social problems through social services, oftentimes neglects the enduring impact of economic and historical structures. Service approaches often rely on clinical models of social change. While providing psychological and social services for youth is vital, how these services are aligned with the goal of preparing poor, urban youth jobs in an unstable market economy is quite a stretch.

FURTHER READINGS AND RESOURCES

Abdul-Adil, J. K., & Farmer, A. D., Jr. (2006). Inner-city African American parental involvement in elementary schools: Getting beyond urban legends of apathy. *School Psychology Quarterly, 21,* 1–12.

Apple, M. (2001). *Educating the "right" way.* New York: Routledge-Falmer.

Baldridge, B., Lamont Hill, M., & Davis, J. E. (2011). New possibilities: (Re)engaging Black male youth within community-based educational spaces. *Race, Ethnicity and Education, 14*(1), 121–136.

Bourdieu, P. (1984). *Distinction: A social critique of the judgement of taste.* Cambridge, MA: Harvard University Press.

Bryan, J. (2005). Fostering educational resilience and academic achievement in urban schools through school–family–community partnerships. *Professional School Counseling, 8,* 219–227.

Bybee, R. W., & McCrae, B. J. (Eds.). (2009). *PISA science 2006: Implications for science teachers and teaching.* Arlington, VA: National Science Teachers Association Press.

Castaneda, L. (1997). Alternative to failure: A community-based school program for Latino teens. *Education and Urban Society, 30*(1), 90–106.

Dryfoos, J. (2002). Full-service community schools: Creating new institutions. *Phi Delta Kappan, 83*(5), 393–399.

Dryfoos, J. (2003). A community school in action. *Reclaiming Children and Youth, 11*(4), 203–205.

Dryfoos, J., & Maguire, S. (2002). *Inside full-service community schools.* Thousand Oaks, CA: Corwin.

Goldstein, M. J., & Noguera, P. A. (2006). Designing for diversity: Incorporating cultural competence in prevention programs for urban youth. *New Directions for Youth Development, 111,* 29–40.

Gregory, A., Skiba, R. J., & Noguera, P. A. (2010). The achievement gap and the discipline gap: Two sides of the same coin? *Educational Researcher, 39,* 59–68.

Henderson, A. T., Mapp, K. L., Johnson, V. R., & Davies, D. (2007). *Beyond the bake sale: The essential guide to family-school partnerships.* New York: The New Press.

Massachusetts Department of Education. (2003). *School panel review report.* Retrieved April 2011 from http://www.doe.mass.edu/sda/review/school/2003/00350211report1.pdf

National Academy of Sciences, National Academy of Engineering, & Institute of Medicine. (2007). *Rising above the gathering storm: Energizing and employing America for a brighter economic future.* Washington, DC: National Academies Press.

Noguera, P. A. (2003). *City schools and the American dream: Reclaiming the promise of public Education.* New York: Teachers College Press.

Orfield, G., & Eaton, S. E. (1996). *Dismantling desegregation: The quiet reversal of Brown v. Board of Education.* New York: The New Press.

Peebles-Wilkins, W. (2004). The full-service community model. *Children & Schools, 26,* 131–133.

Spring, J. (2009). *Deculturalization and the struggle for equality: A brief history of the education of dominated cultures in the United States.* New York: McGraw-Hill.

Tatum, B D. (2007). *Can we talk about race? And other conversations in an era of school resegregation.* Boston: Beacon Press.

Unmuth, K. L. (2009, October). Dallas-Fort Worth area church–school partnerships give children a classroom lift. *The Dallas Morning News.* Retrieved October 9, 2011, from http://www.txcn.com/sharedcontent/dws/news/localnews/stories/1004dnmetchurchschool.43b63e9.html

U.S. Department of Education, Office of Planning, Evaluation and Policy Development. (2010). *ESEA Blueprint for Reform.* Retrieved January 2, 2011, from http://www2.ed.gov/policy/elsec/leg/blueprint/blueprint.pdf

Should pull-out instructional programs be retained under Title I's compensatory education provisions?

POINT: John A. Oliver and Miguel A. Guajardo, *Texas State University–San Marcos*

COUNTERPOINT: Latish Reed, *University of Wisconsin–Milwaukee*

OVERVIEW

Compensatory education became fashionable during the period of public school desegregation following the U.S. Supreme Court's landmark decision in *Brown v. Board of Education* (1954). It was viewed as an alternative to public school desegregation that was unpopular with the majority of White Americans who did not want their children to attend racially and culturally diverse schools. What is compensatory education? *Compensatory education* is representative of supplementary educational programs or services that are designed to help children at risk of failing in school and whose low achievement will prevent them from reaching their full potential. The children served by such programs are those who are considered 2 or more years below grade level in the areas of reading and mathematics. Many of these children have been born into families who are living in poverty and from whom they have not received proper nurturing in their early childhood years. Because of this, they are not equipped with the basic knowledge and skills to succeed in school. They enter school not knowing the alphabet and how to write their names. They also lack fundamental and basic literacy skills because they were not raised in an environment that offered them language and speech development, which is a basic foundation for schooling and is provided in more economically privileged households.

Numerous compensatory education programs have been created to help children who are at risk of not reaching their full potential, including Head Start, a federally funded compensatory education created by President Johnson's administration in 1965 as part of his famous War on Poverty. Head Start is currently administered by the Department of Health and Human Services and has served thousands of children throughout the country. This program, in addition to language development, provides other forms of comprehensive education, including health, nutrition, and parent involvement for economically low-income children and their families.

There are many compensatory education programs that cannot be discussed in this brief statement. However, another that was part of President Johnson's War on Poverty is the Elementary and Secondary Education Act (ESEA), which provides compensatory education for the nation's economically poor public school students. This legislation, commonly referred to as Title I, provides compensatory education for public school students and funds for teacher professional development, instructional materials, resources to support educational programs, and parental involvement promotion. The federal government most recently reauthorized ESEA as the No Child Left Behind Act of 2001. This compensatory education program provides financial assistance to local educational agencies (LEAs), which are public school districts. To be eligible for the funds, LEAs must have high numbers of poor children to help ensure that all children meet challenging state academic standards. Federal funds are allocated through four statutory formulas based primarily on census poverty estimates and the cost of education in each state. Basic grants to LEAs are based on the number of children counted, which must be at least 10 and exceed 2% of an LEA's school-age population. Concentration grants are for LEAs where the number of children exceeds 6,500 or 15% of the total school-age population. Targeted grants are based on the same data used for basic and concentration grants except it is weighted so that LEAs with higher numbers or higher percentages of poor children receive more funds. Targeted grants flow to LEAs when the number of schoolchildren (without application of the formula weights) is at least 10 and at least 5% of the LEA's school-age population. Finally, Education Finance Incentive Grants are distributed to states based on the state's effort to provide financial support for education compared to its per-capita income and the degree to which education expenditures among LEAs are equalized in the state. The latter category of ESEA funding is an attempt to encourage states to equalize school funding. Today, there is a great disparity in how public education funds are distributed to public school districts, which use assessed property wealth to determine how much money is provided for students in each school district.

One of the stigmas associated with the early Title I compensatory education programs was the pulling out of certain students from their regular classroom instruction and then providing them with special compensatory education instruction in separate classrooms with trained personnel, who were generally remedial reading or remedial mathematics teachers. The students who were pulled out met certain poverty and low-achievement criteria to be eligible for the services. Unfortunately, while they were out of the regular classroom, they missed out on the basic instruction from their regular classroom teacher that the other students received. This instructional delivery methodology was criticized by educators and prompted development of the schoolwide concept, which meant that all of the students in the school were eligible to receive Title I services regardless of their achievement level. To qualify for the schoolwide model, the school was required to have a percentage of low-income students that was equal to or greater than the school district as a whole. This meant that selected students did not need to be pulled out of their classrooms; rather, compensatory education services could be provided to all of the students in the school at the same time. Because of this schoolwide model, programs such as Success For All were developed and used to provide compensatory education to students who were enrolled in low-income schools. This delivery methodology has continued to be used for Title I services even under the No Child Left Behind Act of 2001 and has eliminated the special assignment to special programs. Another issue for consideration concerns the requirement that students must achieve certain federally prescribed achievement benchmarks over time or schools might lose their funding. These accountability provisions were the cornerstone of President George W. Bush's No Child Left Behind Act that remain in force today but could be modified by the new reauthorization of the law that is currently before President Barack Obama's administration.

In the point essay in this chapter, John A. Oliver and Miguel A. Guajardo (Texas State University–San Marcos), while recognizing that some children require highly specialized and intensive instruction that may not be feasible in an inclusive setting, argue that children should be educated in the least restrictive environment possible. They add, however, that *least restrictive* for children with special needs should be with teachers who have the necessary and sufficient training to help them succeed. In the counterpoint essay, Latish Reed (University of Wisconsin–Milwaukee) advocates for a revised distribution of Title I funds to better serve students in a comprehensive manner. Reed supports an Integrated Comprehensive Services model in which schools draw from and combine a number of funding sources to best meet the individual needs of students. Reed concludes that reallocating funding to support the real-time needs of students is more cost effective than creating fragmented programming that isolates and stigmatizes students.

Richard C. Hunter
University of Illinois at Urbana-Champaign and
Bahrain Teachers College, University of Bahrain,
Kingdom of Bahrain

POINT: John A. Oliver and Miguel A. Guajardo
Texas State University–San Marcos

I n this essay, the authors articulate a position specifically as it relates to ser- vices for exceptional learners or students with special educational needs (SEN) under Title I of No Child Left Behind (NCLB). The debate is framed by acknowledging that the title question cuts across several layers (e.g., access to educational services, instructional curriculum, purpose of public education, collaboration between stakeholders and shareholders, and government fidu- ciary responsibilities at the local, state, and federal levels). The question also deeply probes at least three levels of education, that is, macro level, meso level, and micro level. To adequately address all three of these levels requires deep ethnographic work and is covered elsewhere in this set. Therefore, the question is addressed only at the macro level of educational policy. That is, the question is addressed through a narrative that focuses on excellence, quality, and equity rather than on efficiency, accountability, and choice.

The text that follows includes a brief history of Title I, articulation and sup- port of our position, brief analysis of the current policy along with questions that warrant exploration as we push this debate forward, impact of policy, and some concluding thoughts.

SANKOFA: A BRIEF HISTORY OF TITLE I

Sankofa is a term from the Akan language and a part of the Kwa branch of the Niger-Congo languages of West Africa (Stewart, 1997). The term refers to a West African proverb and accompanying symbol. The proverb states, "Se wo were fi na wosankofa a yenkyi," translated, "It is not wrong to go back for that which you have forgotten." The Sankofa symbol depicts a bird that flies forward while looking backward with an egg in its mouth. The proverb explains that we should reach back and retrieve the best of what we learned from the past in an effort to achieve our full potential as we move forward in the future. This is done all in an effort to better prepare the next generation as symbolized by the egg on the Sankofa bird's back.

This passage is offered to help frame the discussion about the continued importance of compensatory education programs included under Title I of the Elementary and Secondary Schools Act of 1965 (ESEA), now referred to as NCLB. Title I and its compensatory education programs were designed as a federal response to close the achievement gap between economically advantaged and the economically disadvantaged students. Incidentally, most of the economically disadvantaged considered in ESEA were African American. Additionally, many of the students were also generally two grade levels behind non–Title I students. There are many factors that attributed to the previously mentioned disparities. For this essay, the inequities addressed in the *Brown v. Board of Education* (*Brown*) decisions of 1954 and 1955 and later addressed by ESEA are discussed. The *Brown* decisions ushered in a heightened level of concern and interest in the U.S. educational system. In these decisions, the U.S. Supreme Court ruled that segregation of children by race in public schools was unconstitutional. As such, the ruling opened the national debate about the quality of education provided to African American children, and eventually led to broader discussions about the educational needs of all children. More specifically, greater focus was placed on increasing educational opportunities for children from poor families and children with other disadvantages. Unfortunately, *Brown* did not immediately accomplish all that was expected, nor has it to date (see Bell, 2005; Kozol, 2005). Schools were still segregated, and economically disadvantaged students still lacked the equity that many expected *Brown* to deliver. In summary, students lacked equity in instruction, facilities, and resources. This was mostly attributed to the resistance of many Southern states to integrate public schools as the *Brown* decision mandated.

In 1964, Lyndon B. Johnson assumed the office of president after the assassination of President John F. Kennedy. Shortly after taking office, President Johnson signed the Civil Rights Act. The Civil Rights Act signaled that integration had far broader implications than just education. A few of Johnson's most widely known programs and initiatives included a national War on Poverty, the Economic Opportunity Act, Medicare, and the ESEA of 1965. In effect, President Johnson made a connection between addressing issues of poverty and increasing access to educational opportunities.

One of the largest expenditures of Johnson's programs was Title I of ESEA. Title I served as the primary method used by the federal government to address the issues of equality of opportunity. President Johnson was able to pair his commitment to advanced education with a large Democratic majority in Congress to pass social and educational reforms. President Johnson used his political prowess to impress on the House of Representatives to accept and pass his bill with few changes, and then he persuaded the Senate to accept it with no changes. Johnson's crafting and signing of the ESEA into law all happened in less than 3 months. Johnson's determination and strong congressional support led to additional education laws and increased funding to categorical aid that provided extra assistance for children with disadvantages: migrant children,

children for whom English was a second language, delinquent and neglected children, and children with mental and physical handicaps.

Some argue that as a result of Title I, during the 1970s and part of 1980s, states witnessed reductions in the income gaps, improvement in academic achievement of economically disadvantaged students, upgrades in many local school districts, and increases in programs for poor and minority children (Borman & D'Agnostino, 1996; Citizens' Commission on Civil Rights, 1999; Peterson, Rabe, & Wong, 1986). Unfortunately, after the 1980s, the gains receded and the gap steadily widened (Grissmer, Kirby, Berends, & Williamson, 1994).

DISCUSSION OF THE ISSUE

This essay presents arguments that some compensatory education programs and special assignment to special programs under Title I of NCLB are still necessary. Following are reasons why some agree with Title I students leaving regular classrooms to attend special remedial classes with separate teachers.

The issues here involve more than just educational quality, excellence, or efficiency (Cullen & Pratt, 1992). The issues of power and influence are also apparent. Although there are concerns for equity in education, larger social forces play a role in the shaping of educational policies. Therefore, it is necessary to make sense of those forces and learn how they seek to address equity in education. Title I places top priority on assuring that all children, particularly children of poor families, families from culturally different backgrounds, and students with disabilities receive a fair chance at a quality education by providing funding and resources.

One key component of Title I assured that resources would be available to implement innovative strategies to improve educational outcomes for disadvantaged students. In an attempt to assure fairness and equity, Title I provided for the development of special programs specifically for those students most at risk of academic failure through regular instruction. In 1975, the passage of the Education for All Handicapped Children Act, now known as the Individuals with Disabilities Education Act, expanded the Title I definition to include students with disabilities.

It is important to acknowledge that services to students with SEN have experienced moments when services were badly practiced and students suffered abuses. However, the overwhelming practice has operated from a general set of principles that can make and often has made public schooling fairer and more effective than it would otherwise be. Historically, it represents the intention to make sure that students are not neglected, that they learn all they can, and that they are given access to education that they would not have otherwise.

As policy values and direction are concerned, it was during the early 1980s when private conservative think tanks began to push for a shift in the values of education from quality, excellence, and access to efficiency, accountability, and choice. Milton Friedman (1980) published his "personal statement," which quickly became the model for pushing a free enterprise model for changing and providing a direction for public schools. This begins to provide evidence of the shifting landscape of policy and practice. The values informing this direction were not based on sound learning theory or effective educational practices. Instead, it has been based on the values of efficiency, accountability, and choice.

Many support this initiative when they argue that the educational programs being delivered to students with SEN could be and should be improved. Additionally, despite the years of research, it is still not clear which curricula and services are most effective for teaching children with SEN. However, it is clear that educational practices vary widely across states and school districts. Therefore, to improve educational outcomes for students with SEN, the responsibility to do so should not simply be transferred to "regular" education; rather educational stakeholders and shareholders should work and build on the existing theory and effective practices for teacher training, curriculum development, and systems of support for developing and disseminating effective instruction.

It is clear that there are children with SEN who require different services. Therefore, they would also require different settings and instruction that is delivered by a specially trained teacher. Specially trained teachers serve a specific function. They provide a skill set necessary for identifying the appropriate services, accommodations, and instruction that ensures that students with SEN receive an appropriate education. Eliminating all pull-out programs does not eliminate the need that exists for some children. The pull-out programs do not create the need; they simply provide the opportunity and means to respond to some children with SEN.

The proposition to eliminate pull-out programs does not address the structural issue of teacher training programs. Teachers are often trained in segregated curricula (e.g., elementary, secondary, bilingual education, special education). As long as teacher training programs have silos and isolated programs in higher education that teach specialists, they will prepare teachers who are not adequately prepared to teach students with SEN. This is one instance where public policy is only as effective as the appropriateness of its structures; additionally, this too is an example of the lack of readiness for implementations at the local level.

As stated above, this is more than just an issue of quality; it is an issue of power and influence. When students with SEN become merely a minor part of the general education system, they lose their voice in the power circles of the educational system and lose much of their ability to influence policy in the system at the local, state, and federal levels. Robert T. Stout, Marilyn Tallerico, and Kent Paredes Scribner (1995) address several issues about policy decisions and about schools that are considered in those decisions by asking, who is in the room when major policy decisions are made, and who decides? If a director of students with SEN is actively engaged in the hierarchy of the school program, then it is likely that person will be sitting in the room where the policy decisions are made. However, if educators of students with SEN are merely one of many assistants to the general education administration, they likely will not be participants in policy meetings. Unfortunately, their absence removes an important voice for the child with SEN.

IMPACT OF GOOD INTENTIONS

Regular education is in the midst of its own crisis fueled by an eroding tax base, the resegregation of schools, and the pressures associated with unreasonable accountability systems. Calls for efficiency, accountability, and choice have taken precedence over calls for excellence, quality, and equity. Although teachers, administrators, and guidance counselors often are able and willing to make accommodations, these are not always in students' best long-term interest. They give students with SEN a false sense of achievement and competence to avoid the possibilities of stigma and shame. Placing all students, regardless of their abilities, in regular classes has exacerbated the tendency to see disability as something existing only in people's minds. It fosters the view that students are fitting in, when in all actuality they are not able to perform near the normal level. It perpetuates disabilities by not providing the necessary services. Helping students matriculate may be socially necessary or the humane thing to do in some circumstances, but such pretense does not address the more fundamental issue of academic development. In fact, this form of social promotion may create a greater stigma and shame when students with SEN are compared with mainstream students. Empathy, support, accommodation, and acceptance are much more likely to be generated by candid portrayal of a problem, disability, or incompetence.

There are clearly differences in the instruction that students receive in pullout classes compared to the regular education classes. Authentic inclusion of all students is not feasible because some require highly specialized and intensive instruction. Full inclusion of all students is unachievable as a policy for at least two reasons. First, it is illegal. Second, a blanket policy of full inclusion of all students neglects individual differences that are important in academic learning and socialization.

CONCLUSION

The *Brown* decision of 1954 gave hope and progress to many disenfranchised communities, but many think that it also distracted the conversation from the local issues of equity, quality, and access (Bell, 2005). However, the hope and the hype were greater than the progress. Presently, many urban schools find themselves more segregated than ever (Kozol, 2005). A related lesson for the issue at hand is that macro-level policy is important as a statement of our country's values and wishes, but it will only be as effective as the readiness for implementation at the micro level. Until this readiness is established or the necessary investment in local educational systems and consciousness is made, macro policies will continue to be symbolic acts alone. Every child deserves the best education available; however, children should receive that education in the least restrictive environment. Least restrictive for some children with special needs may be in the regular classroom, but for others, it should be with teachers who have the necessary and sufficient training to help them succeed.

This proposition is not presented as an absolute. Children should be assessed on an individual basis. Consistent with this value, mainstreaming students with disabilities without regard for their individual needs is a violation that should not be accepted. There are students with SEN who do well in mainstream classrooms. However, the decision and policy informing placement should never be based on an efficiency model or a zero-sum framework.

RESPONSE TO COUNTERPOINT ESSAY

Title I has been a crucial component for providing access to a better education for students in high-poverty areas. Many urban and poor rural schools have achieved outstanding results with their students as a result of implementing innovative strategies provided by Title I resources. Invariably, high-poverty schools in countries that do not have sources similar to Title I show how central this resource is in creating the potential for major improvements in school practices and student outcomes.

The concerns presented by Latish Reed in the counterpoint essay are not about the necessity of Title I, but rather are centered on the effectiveness of distributing Title I funding and resources. Title I did not create a segregated system in public education, nor has it hindered the capacity of teachers to work with all students. Instead, it has operated as a laudable and noble attempt to consistently address the acknowledged concerns present in public education.

While Title I does not provide a perfect solution, or even a long-term sustainable option, it has provided the necessary impetus to form the foundation for a simply stated, but difficult to achieve, task: to improve educational outcomes for students with SEN. To achieve this goal, the system must be reconstructed with proper mechanisms in place to support the revamp of educational programs and their infrastructures. The challenge with this task is that there is no silver bullet. This issue must be situated within its sociocultural and political conditions of the time, economy, and human resources.

It is difficult not to agree with the idea that schools should be held accountable. However, most recently, the measure of accountability has been academic progress as based on standardized tests. Additionally, it is important to note that academic progress can be measured in a variety of ways. What information, facts, or abilities should we expect students to have at a particular age or grade level? Should all students of a particular age or grade level be expected to know or do the same things? What should they be, and who should set or select them? Should exceptional learners be held to the same standards as other students? The above questions pose interesting intersections. As such, it is also important to point out that measurement of students with SEN can only be understood in the context of measurement in general education and must be grounded in sound learning theory.

We should not confuse the treatment with the cause. The most basic article of faith for students with SEN asserts instruction must be individualized to be truly effective. This is rarely contemplated or observed in most general education classrooms. On the contrary, mainstream teachers must consider the diversity in the group and the extent to which the learning activities they present maintain classroom flow, orderliness, and cooperation. In addition, they generally formulate teaching plans that result in a productive learning environment for the majority of students.

There are clear distinctions in teaching practices of general education and SEN teachers. SEN teachers spend larger amounts of time teaching to assess students. Teaching to assess involves probing to see where weaknesses and strengths lie in student learning. Teaching to assess is also a best practice for general education teachers; however, the frequency and precision of this probing are not the same or necessary for typical learners. SEN teachers also pay particular attention to micro-task analysis. Micro-task analysis involves frequently breaking down lessons into subsegments that most people wouldn't even see as discreet steps. Micro-task analysis is not productive or effective in all settings; for example, in general education, this process would slow the progress of typical students.

Many students with SEN require and do well with highly and carefully structured learning environments, while typical students would find such environments too rigid. To be clear, there are designated differences in the needs of individuals. These designations serve a specific function. They provide a means of identifying the appropriate services, accommodations, and instruction to assure that all students receive an appropriate education. Eliminating special assignment to special programs does not eliminate the necessity or need that exists. The special assignment and special program did not create the need; it simply provided the opportunity and means of servicing the need.

Reed's critique of Title I could have benefited by the use of a critical policy analysis framework. This analysis would focus the target on values, agendas, adoption, implementation, and assessment. This process should then be grounded in context, politics, students, teachers, and advocacy for children.

COUNTERPOINT: Latish Reed
University of Wisconsin–Milwaukee

Throughout the history of the United States, an ongoing debate has been waged about who should have access to a quality public education. Up until the 1950s, segregation based on race was completely acceptable in the United States. When ending segregation, Justice Warren stated in the U.S. Supreme Court's opinion in the 1954 *Brown v. Board of Education* landmark decision, "Separate facilities are inherently unequal." Yet, in an effort to advocate for equity, we have created and endorsed new ways to separate students. Even more than 50 years after the conclusion of legislated segregation, we now legally segregate students based on socioeconomic class via the Title I program. This type of segregation was an unintended consequence of mandating the academic support for economically "disadvantaged" students. Title I funding has created a segregated system in public education based on socioeconomic status. In addition, the program has been inequitably distributed more to primary grades verses secondary students. Finally, Title I programming has not encouraged the building of teacher capacity to work with all students regardless of socioeconomic status. Instead, the program has created another system to deal with "those kids." That said, this argument does not advocate a repeal of Title I funding to some of the neediest public schools in our country, yet advocates for a revised distribution of the funding via the Integrated Comprehensive Services Model (Frattura & Capper, 2007).

INTENT OF TITLE I

The initial intention for Title I was clearly laudable. Its main goal was to provide additional support to schools with higher numbers of disadvantaged students in the areas of reading and math. Funding is distributed based on Title I students enrolled. When a public school's population of students receiving free and reduced lunch is 40% or higher, the school is eligible to receive Title I funds. With the advent of No Child Left Behind, schools have been charged with meeting adequate yearly progress (AYP) on student achievement goals. These goals are established by individual states. If AYP goals are repeatedly not met after a particular period, sanctions are imposed. Sanctions could include withholding or reallocating Title I funding. In essence, if a low-performing school, already operating with fewer resources, fails to make academic gains, further resources will be removed from the school. This is an illogical response and is contradictory to the initial intent of supporting economically disadvantaged students.

CHALLENGES

If the intent of Title I funding is to ensure equity and equality for all students, we are doing so in a context of segregation based on the numerous rules and regulations that accompany the use of Title I funds. Elise Frattura and Colleen A. Capper (2007) posit, "We are promoting a caste system in that we know that the students who meet eligibility for special education, at risk, ESL, and title programs are often typically from low-income families or are racially non-white" (p. 42). These programs, which were intended to strengthen student performance for students from lower socioeconomic statuses, have been used to create a second-class citizenry within public education. Pull-outs, special teachers, and remediated curricula have created new challenges for the very population the funding was supposed to help. Students in special education pull-out programs have an imposed stigma attached to their group or label. Similarly, most Title I services and programs are executed in a pull-out manner based on regulations and restrictions. While students may not be labeled officially, they are still stigmatized by being put in particular groups identified for extra help. Most times, students who need additional academic support are the last to make it known to teachers or classmates. As a matter of fact, many of these students may engage in challenging behaviors that divert the attention of their academic problems. This is not to say that educators should not address the additional academic needs of these students. To the contrary, educators should use innovative and flexible grouping situations that promote a feeling of acceptance by teachers and classmates. Further, Title I programs may not provide the most challenging curriculum and may focus more on remediation than grade-level curriculum. If students continue to miss out on grade-level instruction, it will be difficult for them to ever master grade-level expectations.

A third challenge with Title I funding is its inequitable distribution among grade levels. According to the U.S. Department of Education (n.d.) website,

> In SY 2006–07 Title I served more than 17 million children. Of these students, approximately 60 percent were in kindergarten through fifth grade, 21 percent in grades 6–8, 16 percent in grades 9–12, three percent in preschool, and less than one percent ungraded.

In other words, the Title I funds are not being used to assist older students who may also be disadvantaged. Does data indicate that students in upper grades are not as disadvantaged as those in primary grades? Or does data indicate that the identification of low-income students is not well documented at the upper grades? If that is in fact the case, we are doing a disservice to the older students who are probably more in need of supports as they come closer to the end of their public education career.

Fourth, Title I funding promotes a disjointed service delivery. Given the numerous constraints on how Title I funding can be administered, some staff members are hired with Title I funds only to service Title I students. In many cases, this causes a problem when deciding which students should benefit from Title I–funded instructors or curriculum. Schools begin to split hairs regarding which students can use a Title I–funded computer lab or participate in remediation program based on which students qualify or not. It seems unjust that non–Title I–funded students who could benefit from a teacher's specialty do not have access to those services. In some cases, Title I resources can be eaten up in transportation costs, when in fact students could benefit from teachers who have been trained to deal with some of the challenges presented in their classrooms.

That said, how do these funds promote a message of ensuring that all students are served in an equitable manner? As mandated in the Individuals with Disabilities Education Act, students with special needs are required to be in the least restricted learning environment. Likewise, students from a lower socioeconomic status should be educated. Given the rigorous standards for students receiving Title I–funding supports, the assessments to determine eligibility are sometimes after-the-fact versus preventive. Certainly, teachers have more expertise in assessing student learning than federal legislators. More decision-making authority should be given to teachers and educators who work directly with children daily to determine their needs. School administrators and teachers should determine how to create coherent educational programming for all students.

REALLOCATION

Given the arguments noted here, it would appear that the author does not support schools with higher percentages of disadvantaged students receiving additional funding. Much to the contrary, this funding is important to providing adequate funds in public schools with fewer resources based on lower per-pupil allocations. This author supports a reallocation of Title I funds to serve students in a more comprehensive way. Colleen Capper, Maureen Keyes, and Elise Frattura (2000) propose an integrated use of funding used to support "special" groups of students. Their Integrated Comprehensive Services (ICS) model is against segregating money for specific populations such as Title I–qualified students. Instead, ICS promotes a strategy where schools draw from a number of funding sources to best meet the individual needs of students within a specific context. The four core principles that compose the foundation of ICS are "focusing on equity, establishing equitable structures, providing access to high quality teaching and learning, and implementing change" (Frattura & Capper, 2007, p. xxix). Within the federal legislation for Title I funding, some language has been interpreted to force districts to offer pull-out services specifically for students who qualify for Title I funding. ICS promotes that these funds be used in an integrative way that does not exclude children from the regular classroom setting.

Within the implementation of ICS, practical recommendations to make more effective use of funding set aside for Title I or other special populations emerge. ICS promotes combining different funding sources to support the individual needs of all students. For example, instead of using money to pull students out for services, money should be allocated to create lower class sizes or provide additional support to teachers in classrooms. Another example of a more effective use of support funding is to place a focus on building the capacity of classroom teachers by offering professional development by academic and behavioral specialists to strengthen pedagogy in dealing with classroom challenges. Reallocating funding to support the real-time needs of students is more cost effective than creating fragmented programming that isolates and stigmatizes students.

CONCLUSION

While Title I's intent was to increase equity for students from low socioeconomic backgrounds, an unintended consequence has, in some ways, been an extension of segregation. Also within our current implementation of Title I programs, an inequitable distribution of resources has favored younger students. Finally, the separate delivery of services to students has not fostered capacity building for teachers to address the needs of all students regardless of socioeconomic status. A better use of funding will take an overhaul on the policies and procedures at the federal, state, district, and school levels. We can no longer have policies with good intentions that create additional stigmas for students because they are disadvantaged economically. Providing students with quality educators, competitive and comprehensive curriculum, and learning environments free from segregation is the absolute best we can do for students.

RESPONSE TO POINT ESSAY

In the point essay, John A. Oliver and Miguel A. Guajardo introduced their case for Title I funding by describing the Sankofa symbol, which means, "It is not wrong to go back for that which you have forgotten." While the Sankofa tradition deserves respect, we know that segregation is wrong, and it definitely should not be brought back to help students move forward in a contemporary context. The key argument made in the point essay is that the 1970s and 1980s yielded some reduction in the achievement gaps for disadvantaged students due to additional Title I funds. However, the positive trend began to reverse during the 1990s, and the achievement gap is ever-present today. Oliver and Guajardo noted that this money was allocated so that we could address the challenges of specific populations of students in more innovative ways. Is providing students with separate services considered innovative? Since this funding has not yielded the intended results with these efforts to separate students, is it appropriate to maintain segregated classrooms? Further, if this separate programming is supposed to help students, why is removing the funding a part of NCLB sanctions when schools with disadvantaged students fail to make adequate yearly progress?

While students with special needs are certainly a part of NCLB's intention to provide equitable services to a historically marginalized group, Oliver and Guajardo neglect to fully address the argument surrounding students from lower socioeconomic backgrounds. Title I services are mostly rendered in segregated settings based on income and at-risk factors. Being a poor child in the United States does not necessarily equate to having special needs. Therefore students should not be segregated on income and at-risk basis alone.

Oliver and Guajardo made an excellent point about the ways in which we prepare teachers to address the needs of our diverse student populations. Teachers are prepared in individual silos based on content area, ability, and grade level. This preparation structure has ultimately contributed to the disjointed services rendered to students. Therefore, it does not make sense to replicate segregated settings for our students at the classroom level based on income levels or at-risk factors.

The point essay authors and others have argued that inclusive classrooms can undermine authentic disability diagnoses. They assert that while students may socially fit in, their academic needs are not always addressed, further creating "greater stigma and shame when students with disabilities are compared with mainstream students." I counter that segregated settings perpetuate stigma for students receiving services because they are perceived as different, outside of the mainstream, and ultimately marginalized. Also, when students are educated separately, regular education students do not have the opportunity to interact with students from different ability levels and economic backgrounds. This lack of interaction can reinforce elitist ideology that can replicate classism, racism, and disability discrimination.

My colleagues cloaked the need for segregated services with the statement, "It is illegal." At times, what is legal and what is right may differ. We have seen this throughout our country's history as it pertains to blatant racist laws. These discrepancies can be traced back to our country's constitution where Black people were counted as three fifths of a person and slavery was the law. With the Thirteenth Amendment, the law was changed. Similarly, policies of exclusion may be considered legal, but not necessarily right. For this reason, the policies used to segregate students should be changed to create what *is* right: equitable treatment of students regardless of socioeconomic status.

Finally, I address the notion expressed in the point essay that "a blanket policy of full inclusion of all students neglects individual differences that are important in academic learning and socialization." In this essay, I do not argue that *no* pull-outs or special remediation should occur for students in need of special services. To the contrary, teachers and administrators who have the expertise to address gaps in students' education and services should have the right and responsibility to make appropriate decisions regarding how resources are best used to serve students—hence the need to revise our current distribution of Title I funding.

FURTHER READINGS AND RESOURCES

Bell, D. (2005). *Silent covenants:* Brown v. Board of Education *and the unfulfilled hopes for racial reform.* New York: Oxford University Press.

Borman, G. D., & D'Agnostino, J. V. (1996). Title I and student achievement: A meta-analysis of federal evaluation results. *Education and Policy Analysis, 18,* 309–326.

Capper, C. A., Keyes, M. W., & Frattura, E. (2000). *Meeting the needs of students of ALL abilities: How leaders go beyond inclusion.* Thousand Oaks, CA: Sage.

Citizens' Commission on Civil Rights. (1999). *Title I in midstream: The fight to improve schools for poor kids.* Washington, DC: Author.

Cullen, B., & Pratt, T. (1992). Measuring and reporting student progress. In S. Stainback & W. Stainback (Eds.), *Curriculum considerations in inclusive classrooms: Facilitating learning for all students* (pp. 175–196). Baltimore: Paul H. Brookes.

Frattura, E., & Capper, C. A. (2007). *Leading for social justice: Transforming schools for all learners.* Thousand Oaks, CA: Corwin.

Friedman, M. (1980). *Free to choose: A personal statement.* New York: Harcourt Brace Jovanovich.

Grissmer, D. W., Kirby, S. N., Berends, M., & Williamson, S. (1994). *Student achievement and the changing American family.* Santa Monica, CA: RAND.

Kozol, J. (2005). *The shame of the nation: Restoration of apartheid.* New York: Crown.

Peterson, P. E., Rabe, B. G., & Wong, K. W. (1986). *When federalism works.* Washington, DC: Brookings Institution Press.

Stewart, J. (1997). *African proverbs and wisdom.* New York: Kesington.

Stout, R. T., Tallerico, M., & Paredes Scribner, K. (1995). Values: The "what?" of the politics of education. In J. D. Scribner & D. H. Layton (Eds.), *The study of educational politics: The 1994 commemorative yearbook of the Politics of Education Association (1969–1994)* (pp. 5–20). London: Falmer.

U.S. Department of Education. (n.d.). *Improving basic programs operated by local education agencies (Title I, Part A).* Retrieved from http://www2.ed.gov/programs/titleiparta/index.html

COURT CASES AND STATUTES

Brown v. Board of Education, 347 U.S. 483 (1954).

Brown v. Board of Education, 349 U.S. 294 (1955).

Elementary and Secondary Education Act of 1965, 20 U.S.C. § 6301 *et seq.* (1965).

Individuals with Disabilities Education Act, 20 U.S.C. §§ 1400–1482 (2006).

No Child Left Behind Act, 20 U.S.C. §§ 6301–7941 (2006).

Should gender-based student loan forgiveness be used to increase the percentage of male teachers and administrators in public schools?

POINT: Paul Green, *University of California, Riverside*
COUNTERPOINT: Mona Bryant-Shanklin,
Norfolk State University

OVERVIEW

In spite of efforts to make public education staff more representative of the groups who live in U.S. society, certain groups continue to hold a proportionally high number of these positions. According the U.S. Bureau of Labor Statistics (BLS, 2011), women hold 73.8% of all educational positions including librarians and teaching assistants at the elementary, secondary, and postsecondary levels. Examining the various levels of schooling, women account for 97% of preschool, pre-K, and kindergarten teachers, 81% of those working in elementary and middle school instruction, 57% of high school educators, and 45.9% of college-level instructors. Additionally, just over 85% of all teachers employed in special education and 63% of school administrators are also women. Clearly, women have come to dominate education as a profession.

Over the course of the 20th century, the social perception of teaching as an extension of motherhood created the conditions that now allow women to occupy a greater proportion of these professional positions. Yet, the question remains, why are so few men now pursuing teaching careers? One reason that it may be difficult to get men to pursue teaching as a profession is due to the low pay. In 2010, men working in all industries had an average annual income of just under $43,000. That same year, employees from both sexes who ended their educations with the completion of a bachelor's degree earned an average of a little less than $54,000. However, the average beginning teacher holding just a bachelor's degree earns less than $35,000 (BLS, 2011). Given the high costs of completing a college degree in today's economy, such low salaries may certainly be a deterrent to those looking for careers that will allow them to support themselves. These salaries may be especially unappealing to those who will want or need to serve as the primary wage earner within their family units.

Another reason why schools find it difficult to attract male teachers is the fact that colleges and universities simply do not produce very many of them. Whether due to the low salaries or for other reasons, men are not enrolling in teacher education programs at the postsecondary level. As such, even men who hold college degrees lack the certification and pedagogical training needed to qualify to teach in elementary and secondary schools. Indeed, the highly qualified provisions attached to classroom teachers under No Child Left Behind (NCLB) further inhibit the ability of schools to attract male teachers since this legislation closed many alternative qualification methods that do not require teacher education courses, certificates, or degrees. Essentially, the lack of males studying to enter teaching as a profession limits the number of candidates available to work in either public or private schools.

Additionally, elementary, secondary, and postsecondary schools have a hard time drawing both men and women into either teacher preparation programs or teaching as a profession due to the social perception accorded to this field of practice. Compared to other countries in the world, teachers in the United States receive little respect. Daily, media outlets report stories of teachers suffering disrespect, threats, and even violence stemming from interactions with students, parents, administrators, community members, and even other educators. Although NCLB, state laws, and school district policies generally require most teachers to complete a college education, this does little to help the way that U.S. society perceives and treats teachers. Consequently, the poor status accorded to teachers and those who work in public schools may also help to deter many interested and intellectually qualified male candidates from pursuing these roles even if they are willing to accept the low salaries that accompany these positions.

Related to the low status of the teaching profession is the increasingly feminized view of careers in this area. Regarded as a nurturing career, teaching provided an easy way for educated women in the 19th and early 20th centuries to justify professional employment outside of the home. Functioning in the limiting, yet predominant social, perception of the time, early female teachers used the presumption that women are best caretakers of children to compel their way into the profession. While this presumption is no longer as dominant as it once was, the strong presence of women within the teaching profession helps to communicate the idea that teaching is a female profession. As a result, similar to nursing, schools have to work harder to attract and retain qualified male applicants.

Recognizing the low number of males now pursuing and working as teachers in the United States, states, colleges, universities, and schools have resorted to various methods to attract male candidates. Both public and private entities use partial and full scholarships to recruit men into the profession. For example, Men for Excellence in Elementary Teaching in Missouri, Call Me Mister in Florida and South Carolina, and Men Equipped to Nurture in Maryland all provide financial support to male college students who agree to complete a certain number of years of service in schools in those states. Targeting this issue nationally, the Pearson Teacher Fellowship and the New Teacher Project assist both schools and those interested in teaching in finding each other, learning to acclimate to the profession, and identifying and obtaining professional development that effectively promotes retention especially in high-need schools and school districts.

Concentrating on individuals who already possess the education and credentials needed to serve as classroom teachers, loan forgiveness programs also offer financial incentives to help keep people in the profession. Generally speaking, loan forgiveness programs pay off a portion of an individual's educational debt in exchange for working in a certain profession or high-need area. More established loan forgiveness programs focus on bringing more teachers into high-need areas such as math, science, and special education, or into schools identified as low performing or financially impoverished. Expanding on this concept, the two essays in this chapter consider the impact of loan forgiveness reserved for male teachers as a tool for increasing their presence in the profession.

The essays in this chapter focus on the need for more males in education and whether loan forgiveness programs are a viable, and fair, way to recruit more males into the profession. In the point essay, Paul Green (University of California, Riverside) argues in the affirmative, stating that poor compensation is one reason for the lack of diversity in the teaching corps. He concludes that loan forgiveness programs are an essential ingredient for attracting more men, particularly African American men, to the education field. Mona Bryant-Shanklin (Norfolk State University) takes the view in the counterpoint essay that loan forgiveness programs that target males only are inherently discriminatory. Further, she argues that such programs do not provide a real answer to the problem since they may temporarily address the shortage of males in education but are unlikely to provide a long-term solution.

Saran Donahoo
Southern Illinois University Carbondale

POINT: Paul Green
University of California, Riverside

The "perfect storm" is how Gene A Budig, a member of the College Board's Center for Innovative Thought, describes the current state of teacher recruitment and retention. According to Budig (2006), "The nation's citizens, business leaders, and politicians have been warned repeatedly about an impending disaster, a 'perfect storm' that is brewing, and yet their responses have been temperate and at times, even dismissive" (p. 114). The recruitment and retention of male teachers and administrators in city public schools is even worse. While the dearth of male teachers and administrators in public schools is due to several factors, rectifying the problem of poor compensation and providing loan forgiveness have been identified as keys to increasing the percentage of male teachers and administrators.

The paucity of diversity in the teaching and administrative workforce has become a serious educational issue. While the faces of students educated by our schools have changed, the faces of administrators and teachers preparing these students have not kept pace. According to the National Center for Education Statistics (NCES), 90% of public school teachers were White, 6% Black, and fewer than 5% other races. Nationally, 40% of public schools had no teachers of color within the teaching or administrative staff. Three quarters of all teachers are women, and over 91% of women teach at the elementary level.

A closer examination of the NCES 2006 data reveals emerging trends. Today, 40% of all public school students are members of minority ethnic groups. In many cities, minority ethnic pupils compose the majority of enrollment, with Hispanic students now constituting the largest minority group in the United States. Yet, teaching remains dominated by European Americans, primarily women (NCES, 2006; NEA, 2010).

Statistical projections reveal that while the diversity of students in public schools is expected to rise, the diversity among teaching staffs is expected to remain unchanged or even decline. These trends also impact the school administrator workforce. As a rule, educational administrators have traditionally been selected from the teacher workforce. The decline in the diversity of the pool of teachers leaves even fewer opportunities for the development of school administrators who reflect the diversity of their student populations.

The NCES (2006) data reveal a widening gap in the gender, racial, and ethnic makeup of the teaching workforce as compared to the expanding diversity of students in public schools across the United States. Thus, one challenge is to increase the proportion of African American, Hispanic, Native American, and Asian-Pacific Islander teachers. Another challenge is the matter of gender and teaching. Because the teaching force comprises primarily women, the need to recruit and retain more men into the profession is self-evident (NCES, 2006; NEA, 2010).

TEACHER DIVERSITY GAP

The College Board has called for the immediate close of the teacher "diversity gap" in its report, *Teachers and the Uncertain Future* (NEA, 2006). The report recommends abandoning the expectation that diversity of the teaching workforce will resolve itself. It advises that institutions of higher learning must devise targeted recruitment programs to attract minority ethnic students. One of the key components of these programs must be generous financial aid and eventual loan forgiveness tied to years of service (NCES, 2006; NEA, 2010).

Schools serving inner-city students face the challenge of preparing children from disadvantaged neighborhoods to be productive citizens. Teachers and administrators perform a critical role in public schools, particularly in inner-city school districts where children often have less support in their homes and neighborhoods. But inner-city districts often have difficulty attracting and retaining qualified teachers and administrators, let alone qualified male minority teachers and administrators. According to federal statistics in the Schools and Staffing Survey, 34.7% of central city schools had difficulty hiring a math teacher compared with only 25.1% of suburban schools (NCES, 2006; NEA, 2006).

Inner-city communities and rural areas with the highest percentages of poor and students of color are experiencing the greatest challenges in recruiting high quality teachers, particularly male teachers. According to the National Education Association (2010), U.S. public schools reflect diversity primarily in their student populations but not in their teaching and administrative ranks. While efforts have been made by urban school districts to increase the numbers of minority ethnic teachers, such as African American males, many districts fail to hire these teachers proportional to the increasing number of minority ethnic pupils in schools. Each year the minority male teacher and administrator shortage becomes more acute.

The NEA (2006, 2010) predicts that a critical shortage of male teachers and administrators as role models could contribute to the growing urban educational achievement gap between African American, Hispanic, and White students. The minority teacher shortage presents a dilemma for education associations that seek to close the "diversity teaching gap" (Budig, 2006, p. 116). At a time when the demand for minority teachers is rising, the supply is falling. In school districts across the United States, the number of minority ethnic teachers and administrators continues to decline (NEA, 2010).

CLOSING THE TEACHER DIVERSITY GAP

The week after President Barak Obama urged more Americans to become teachers, Education Secretary Arne Duncan issued a call for more men to become teachers. Duncan stressed that a specific need exists for more African American men to teach in elementary and middle schools (U.S. Department of Education, 2011). For more than 30 years, educational research has explored the decline of male teachers in public schools. Data suggest that male teachers and minority male teachers have disappeared from the teaching profession (NEA, 2006).

The recent decline in the numbers of African American males who now enter the teaching force provides one example of why the number of minority teachers had declined. The role of teacher was held in high esteem throughout the African American community prior to desegregation. For decades, African American communities and their teachers were responsible for providing education to more than 2 million African American public school students. African American male teachers performed not only as teachers but also as counselors, role models, and spiritual leaders in the school and the community. While segregation denied African Americans access to careers outside of their community, it provided African American students the benefit of being educated by well-educated teachers in the African American community (Brown, 2005; Tillman, 2004).

More than a decade after the U.S. Supreme Court's landmark desegregation decision in *Brown v. Board of Education* (1954), over 40,000 African American teachers and administrators in 17 southern and border states were removed from their positions as administrators and teachers (Brown, 2005). The loss of African American teachers and administrators who served as dedicated educators and role models was accompanied by the closure of many historically African American schools. Linda Tillman (2004) asserts that the loss of African American teachers and their schools negatively affected the academic achievement of African American students.

Since the mid-1970s, state policymakers, leaders of education associations, researchers, and school leaders have called for more diversity among teachers and administrators. Today, inadequate schooling often leaves some minority students ill prepared and unmotivated for higher education. Many minority students face numerous educational obstacles that prevent them from pursuing a career in teaching. For 3 decades, educational reforms have led to the adoption of standardized tests for teachers, like the National Teachers Exam (NTE), or the Praxis I and II. Many states now require these tests for teacher certification. A review by Joann Jacullo-Noto (1991) of students who fail these examinations showed that a disproportionate number are African American students and male. In response to this failure, several states (e.g., Louisiana, Colorado, Texas, Georgia, Mississippi, Alabama, Florida) require universities with teacher preparation programs to produce a certain percentage of students who successfully complete the NTE as requirement for maintaining their teacher education programs.

Many teacher education programs at historically Black colleges and universities faced similar problems with their teacher education programs because students holding education majors are not passing the state-required standardized tests for entrance into the teaching profession. One example is Southern University in Baton Rouge, whose campus was threatened with closure because its students were not passing the standardized test at the 80% passage rate. By adding test-taking seminars and classes focused on test-taking strategies, Southern University's teacher education program was able to increase its test passage rate and maintain its teacher education program.

Social and cultural competencies are additional areas that June Gordon (2000) mentions as trouble spots that African American, Native American, Asian American, and Latino students, especially males, face in the process of becoming accomplished teachers. The social and cultural competencies discussed here refer primarily to poor academic preparation in secondary schools and with the difficulties of social and cultural adjustment to life. These competencies require constant adjustment by students throughout their journey to become accomplished teachers (Lee, 2005).

In adjusting to the social and academic culture of higher education, students often attempt to gather and process information using learning strategies that have been rewarded previously in similar situations (Lee, 2005). If students perceive that their own culturally learned behaviors for processing information are incompatible with the required cognitive style of the task, dysfunction (e.g., cognitive and emotional conflict, poor academic performance, low self-esteem) often results. The instructional methods typically used in lower schooling and higher education are often incompatible with the cognitive styles and experiences of culturally and linguistically different students.

In most schools, the normative style of cognition is consistent with that of the European American cultural group. Students from African American and Hispanic backgrounds are often taught information in a European-American context and presentational style that may be opposed to their preferred manner of learning; thus, some African American and Hispanic pupils perform more poorly in comparison to their majority culture learners (Anderson, 1988). Most teacher education programs at historically White colleges and universities replicate the normative style of cognition with few courses or research that affirms the value of cognitive cultural diversity. The loss of social and cultural competencies and skills prevent some minority students, particularly males, from building important cognitive and social skills critical for academic success.

Research also shows that ethnic minority males are not pursuing the teaching profession because they have other career opportunities open to them. Gordon (2000), in her book *The Color of Teaching*, interviewed teachers, counselors, and other educational professionals from four ethnic minority groups to understand why more teachers of color are not pursuing education as a profession. Gordon found that many students of color did not find the profession of teaching a lucrative career choice. Research shows that many of the best and brightest college graduates continue to choose more financially lucrative careers such as engineering and computer animation, where recent graduates can earn starting salaries greater than the salary teachers in large metropolitan areas earn only after 10 years in education (Crosby, 2001).

States with the highest salaries tend to have the highest proportion of male teachers, the NEA says. Michigan has the highest percentage of male teachers (37%) and also has the highest teacher salaries. Mississippi, with the lowest percentage of male teachers, is ranked 49th in teacher pay. Salaries are low for teachers compared to salaries for other professionals, which lowers prestige and social value of a career in teaching for many potential minority teachers.

Gordon (2000) also discovered that ethnic minority students were dissuaded to teach by poor compensation benefits (health and child care, pension) offered by school districts. Less than 1% of African American students indicated any interest in the profession of teaching. According the NEA (2010), the declining numbers of Black and Hispanic students majoring in education is steeper than the overall decline in education majors. Gordon makes clear that fewer ethnic minority males in particular will select teaching as a career if salaries and compensation packages remain lower than in other professions.

RECRUITMENT AND RETENTION

States and urban school districts continue to face daunting challenges to recruit and retain men and men of color as members of the teaching profession. These challenges persist because of the NTE or Praxis, social and cultural obstacles, and low compensation offered to teachers. As mentioned above, Southern University in Baton Rouge provides a clear example of how states and teacher education programs can remedy poor NTE performance through test-taking seminars and classes focused on test-taking strategies to improve passage rates. Chance W. Lewis (2006) believes that "teacher education programs need to make their cultures on campus and within classes more 'welcoming' for African American teacher candidates to increase their chances of becoming certified or licensed teachers" (p 229).

Salary and compensation have a deleterious effect on the number of men and men of color who chose teaching as a profession. According to the *Teachers and the Uncertain American Future* report, "Our schools will never get the teachers they need with the salaries now offered" (NEA, 2006, p. 19). The report recommends (a) that states and school districts increase salary expenditures by an average of 15% to 20% now and by 50% within the foreseeable future; (b) that general salary schedules reward experience, a demonstrated ability to improve student achievement, and the attainment of new knowledge, experience, and skills that can be used to advance learning; (c) that schools pay teachers more in mathematics, science, bilingual, and special education; and (d) that generous loan forgiveness—up to 20% per year—be provided to encourage all students to teach in the most challenging urban and rural schools.

The Teacher Recruitment and Retention Act is intended to triple the amount of loan forgiveness for teacher education graduates who choose to work in poor school districts. The bill is intended to increase the amount of loan forgiveness from $5,000 to $17,500. The initiative targets teachers with specialties in math, science, and special education. The bill has been proposed in several sessions of Congress and has yet to be passed.

The "perfect storm" appropriately depicts the dilemma of the teacher diversity gap. Budig (2006) states, "Despite the impressive progress the nation has made in advancing the civil rights agenda, equal [educational] opportunity remains only a promise to many" (p. 116). The research is clear: If states and school districts seek to increase the numbers of men and men of color, financial incentives like loan forgiveness are essential to closing the teacher diversity gap.

COUNTERPOINT: Mona Bryant-Shanklin
Norfolk State University

The federal government has the option to cancel either all or part of an educational loan. This option is called *loan forgiveness*. Low supply and high demand factors fuel the continuance of various loan forgiveness programs. The Higher Education Act, Title IV authorizes many of these programs in the public sector for the purposes of recruiting and retaining qualified professionals in specific fields. There are also state-run programs, which urge residents to participate in loan forgiveness, particularly in health and education, where critical shortages of personnel exist. Although there are also private programs that fund recruiting and retention efforts, these programs generally do not venture into loan forgiveness. Traditionally, loan forgiveness programs attract students and others to work with populations or in places where there is great need. The field of education has traditionally had the need for qualified educators who are willing to work in high-need (poverty) areas or with populations of children who are at risk of academic failure. Loan forgiveness programs provide for partial or complete loan forgiveness and have specific guidelines that might vary by program. The eligibility criteria for many programs include (a) the year the original loan was dispersed, (b) the type of loan, (c) years of teaching service, and (d) teacher qualifications.

Typically, loan forgiveness programs require recipients to do or have in their backgrounds one or more of the following: (a) the obligation to perform volunteer work, (b) a military service background or promissory obligation, (c) an understanding that they will work in areas of high need or with at-risk communities, and (d) other criteria which might be a part of the specific loan forgiveness program.

The first federal student loan forgiveness program began with the National Defense Student Loan Program of 1958, which was aimed at public school teachers. Today, students in the field of education secure student loans and join the numbers of students who are eligible for loan forgiveness. The goal of loan forgiveness is to ensure that highly qualified teachers are available to help educational systems move toward influencing the imbalance between the supply and demand of these teachers. Loan forgiveness programs serve as an incentive for teachers to remain in the field, return to the field, or enter the field from other professions.

Loan forgiveness programs for teachers generally forgive either a portion or the entire amount of a loan. For example, the National Defense Education Act provides for a graduating percentage of loan forgiveness, which increases each year. Forgiveness requires teachers to teach full-time in designated schools and with specific populations. A growing number of programs have need for teachers proficient in foreign languages and science, technology, engineering, and mathematics subject areas. Traditionally, high-need areas targeted for teacher loan forgiveness have included (a) low-income families, (b) children with disabilities, and (c) early intervention programs.

Many loan forgiveness programs focus on the population with whom teachers work. Fewer loan forgiveness programs consider the circumstances of the actual borrower. Some programs do however consider personal factors by looking at the borrower's income or his or her years working as a public servant. Generally, persons recruited into loan forgiveness programs are considered based on one's teaching status, the location of the educational facility, the amount of time the teacher works with a certain population, one's years of service, and one's willingness to teach in a shortage area.

LOAN FORGIVENESS BASED ON GENDER

The use of loan forgiveness programs based solely on gender (e.g., targeting males) is debatable. Not at issue is the obvious and apparent shortage of male teachers and administrators in education, particularly in the lower grades. What is at issue is the legitimacy of awarding males loan forgiveness based solely on their gender. Such an action is not justified historically and should not be now allowed. To do so is inherently discriminatory. Other reasons for disallowing loan forgiveness based on gender might include the following:

1. The establishment of a precedent that is economically unsustainable

2. The blatant abolishment of national and institutional standards that state that teachers should be hired based on being highly qualified and not because of their gender, racial, ethnic, or linguistic backgrounds

3. The question of personal and professional values and ethics

4. A subscription to a practice that has not clearly proven to be advantageous to children, male or female

5. The lack of evidence that males will be retained in the field of education at rates higher than females.

These reasons are discussed as follows.

Precedent

Establishing a gender-based student loan forgiveness program establishes a bad and financially unsustainable precedent. There has to be a level of accountability (e.g., prior repayment history, accrued assets) established first for any financial loan program to work. Persons being permitted to take advantage of a loan forgiveness program based solely on their gender would be untenable, unless there is evidence that the person is responsible and accountable. Additionally, depending on when a male makes the decision to become a teacher, motivated mainly by the temptation of not having to repay student loans, it may be difficult to establish accountability if the major debt is forgiven or nullified prior to the establishment of a payment history. Without a viable payment history, one cannot know if the money used to fund such a program would literally become a responsible entity in creating any one or several of the following:

There may be a more deserving recipient of loan forgiveness. There will be those who argue that if any group should be forgiven student loan repayments, it should be women. The American Association of University Women reports that loan repayment is a greater burden for women, who earn 77 cents to every dollar that men earn, equating to a less substantial lifetime earning potential.

There may be recipients more or less likely to default on their loan. There are data to suggest that gender is a predictor of default behavior in the repayment of student loans. For example, males appear to be more likely to default on their student loans at a higher rate than females, although there is some disagreement with this belief.

The sincerity and dedication of professionals should be considered. If the profession of teaching is targeted for loan forgiveness based on the gender of the borrower, which profession will then become the next target of gender-based loan forgiveness? It is conceivable that males could begin to enter a field of study or a profession simply to obtain a free or nearly free education, thus creating a state of induced "male privilege." While male privilege as it exists in this country has been the target of civil rights legislation for years, we do not want to create yet another layer of this beast only to have to deal with the consequences later. Though desirous, those seeking greater gender equity in the classroom "by any means necessary" would be wise to take care in honoring the integrity of the profession built by past generations of teachers who sincerely sought to teach for intangible reasons. This generally is still the case. The fallout created by recruiting less-than-sincere persons into the field who only wish to avoid a debt would surely become evident sooner or later. Allowing for loan forgiveness based on gender is not a movement that could sustain itself over time. We cannot afford for our children to become the sacrificial lambs of such intentions.

Teacher Quality

A loan forgiveness program based on one's gender rather than teacher quality is an imprudent idea. There would have to be some assurance that a person receiving loan forgiveness is capable of first performing as a teacher. Gender alone is no criteria for assuring qualifications. Male teachers tempted to take advantage of a loan forgiveness program based solely on gender may or may not be highly qualified or possess the characteristics necessary to be a good teacher.

Providing loan forgiveness where gender is the determinant of the award avoids, and perhaps even dismisses, the issue of basic skills that are necessary for any individual who decides to teach. Basing the decision to teach on being forgiven thousands of dollars of debt, most especially when the decision is made prior to adequate pedagogical training or background, might open the floodgate to fill our classrooms with teachers who may or may not meet the standard of being highly qualified. While doubtful that a loan forgiveness program based on gender would create a "rush to teach" by all male loan recipients, there certainly would be those whose actual qualifications to teach would be in question. We know that while academic prowess and specific measurable skill sets are necessary qualities contributing to being considered a highly qualified teacher, there are also other qualities that many educators would consider equally important. One must be cognizant of personal characteristics or abilities that are a part of the fabric that many teachers possess, which include the following:

- A personal and professional conviction to teach, absent monetary gain

- The ability to make personal and professional sacrifices (e.g., salary, time, prestige)

- The ability to persevere what many would consider to be deterrents to teaching (e.g., the overreliance of educational entities to use tests alone to determine both teacher qualifications and student abilities, sometimes disallowing students the full advantage of a free and appropriate education; the necessity to work with difficult and sometimes unsupportive parents, faculty, and administrators; increased accountability measures that, though well intentioned, may interfere with valuable teaching and learning time in the classroom)

- The acumen and desire to teach. Many teachers include a love of children as one of their key reasons for joining the profession. This among other qualities may contribute to creating a passion for teaching, which in turn likely contributes to separating mediocre teachers from effective teachers. Without passion, it is difficult to even imagine that being male will magically create the type of teachers many institutions seek.

One must take care to look closely at teacher characteristics, backgrounds, and motivations to teach. This type of attention to detail would help to assure that teachers have the "right stuff" to perform effectively as a classroom teacher.

Ethical Question

Then there is the ethical question. Traditionally, teachers have been held to a higher standard than the general population, serving as role models in the community and life mentors for the children they teach. The motivation to teach is intricately tied to the values that teachers possess. Although a difficult argument to make, the motivation to teach spurred only by nonpayment of student loans puts into question one's values and ethical practices. The lure of loan forgiveness and the opportunity to dodge a debt may be viewed as somehow morally flawed. Unlike some other professions, a teacher's moral character is still important in many communities in this nation. Teachers have been and continue to be dismissed for questionable moral character. The morality of having loan forgiveness as one's sole motivation to teach is one that is debatable. However, it is an issue to be considered.

Teacher Gender and Child Advantage

Then there is the issue of gender effects in the classroom. This line of research can be viewed from at least two perspectives: (1) the impact of gender on the teacher and (2) the impact gender on the student. The results of the research are mixed and spotty. For example, some research reports that among female preservice mathematics teachers, significant statistical effects of gender on performance in mathematics self-efficacy exist. Other research examining student achievement scores and student autonomy in classrooms taught by female teachers support the notion that the performance of students increases as task autonomy increases. In male-taught classrooms, the measure of student autonomy appears to remain constant.

With regard to achievement, some research reports that teacher gender differences do make a difference in the achievement of children in the classroom. Again, the evidence is mixed. There is very little firm and consistent evidence that teacher gender matters with regard to achievement. Rather than teacher gender, it appears that teacher ability and quality are factors that really matter. Male and female teachers bring different qualities to the classroom, which is not to be considered qualitatively better or worse, just different. For example, males and females differ in the way that they manage the classroom and how they determine the learning abilities of their students. In looking at possible gender effects on disciplinary procedures, social interactions, and test score performance, the results indicate that there are few if any differences based on teacher gender. Other research has demonstrated a language advantage among children in classrooms of female teachers. In these same classrooms, there appears to be no effect on mathematics learning. Even in college environments, research supports the notion that gender is not important in determining college student achievement. Generally, teacher gender may have little or no impact on student learning. These are just a few examples of gender influence in the classroom; but they indicate the ongoing need for further investigation regarding gender effects, most especially if the discussion of using gender as a determinate of loan forgiveness is to be considered seriously. Ability, knowledge, and commitment should be at the crux of creating a viable teaching force, rather than gender. In our haste to populate classrooms with underrepresented groups, we must remember to honor quality first.

Male Teachers and Retention

Data on loan forgiveness or any other recruitment and retention methodologies do not fully support the notion that males have higher career retention rates than do females given similar opportunities. Past research has shown that traditionally males may leave the professional earlier due to the increased responsibility that comes with acquiring a family; however, with changing demographics and the growing number of single female headed households, the same could be said of females. Based on the examination of the Chicago Teacher Advancement Program (a program providing financial incentives for teachers while increasing teacher retention rates and student academic achievement), there appears to be no difference with regard to retention between teachers who did or did not receive incentives. The appearance that men leave teaching at a greater rate may simply be reflective of the relatively low number of men in the profession. Regardless of numbers, recent retention research supports the belief that men and women leave the teaching field for many of the same reasons.

Additionally, it is important for researchers to examine the specific characteristics of teachers who stay with their jobs. These individuals seem to have a perseverance that is necessary for any dedicated professional in any field. While loan forgiveness based on gender could result in a temporary solution to gender inequity in teaching, it is unlikely to provide a long-term solution.

CONCLUSION

Using gender as a method of attracting males into the teaching field is an idea that makes little sense both from a research point of view and simply based on common sense. While it is clear that the profession lacks adequate representation of male teachers, offering loan forgiveness as a way of increasing those numbers lacks justification. Perhaps the only justification for male teachers being awarded loan forgiveness or other financial advantage would be if male teachers were asked to teach "differently" than females (e.g., increased preparation, rigor, job tasks). This might make this notion more palatable. One of the most obvious reasons for not establishing loan forgiveness programs for males is that gender-based student loan forgiveness programs are discriminatory. Unlike programs seeking to right the wrongs for females in certain fields due to past discrimination, male inequity in the classroom has more to do with choices made by males than discrimination. Thus, in the absence of past discrimination, reversing a trend by offering male advantage is not in question. There is no way to disguise the inherent discrimination of gender-based loan forgiveness.

As a last point, although there is a need to recruit and retain high quality males (and females) into the teaching profession, using a gender-based loan forgiveness approach is shortsighted. Other methods of recruitment and retention should be thoroughly investigated prior to a fully vested effort of any type. For example, raising teacher salaries for both female and male teachers would perhaps be a more attractive option for all involved and serve as a clear and equitable recruitment strategy for males as well as females. Low wages for the majority of teachers regardless of gender remains a central point of discussion among politicians, educators and the public year after year. Recruiting males with loan forgiveness, in the face of losing more teachers due to low salaries and the lack of other incentives, not to mention the current budget crises faced by the government, is a foolish notion. As parents, citizens, and lawmakers, we need to put our money where our mouths are. Higher salaries for well-deserving, underpaid professionals would do much to recruit highly qualified and highly motivated teachers regardless of gender.

FURTHER READINGS AND RESOURCES

American Association of University Women. (2011). *Breaking through barriers for women and girls: AAUW federal policy agenda for 2011–2012*. Retrieved from http://www.aauw.org/act/issue_advocacy/upload/federalPolicyAgenda.pdf

Anderson, J. A. (1988). Cognitive styles and multicultural populations. *Journal of Teacher Education, 24*(1), 2–9.

Brown, K. (2005). *Race, law and education in the post-desegregation era: Four perspectives on desegregation and resegregation*. Durham, NC: Carolina Academic Press

Budig, G. A. (2006, October). A perfect storm. *Phi Delta Kappan, 88*(2), 114–116.

Cantrell, P., & Sudweeks, R. (2009). Technology task autonomy and gender effects on student performance in rural middle school science classrooms. *Journal of Computers in Mathematics and Science Teaching, 28*, 359–379.

Chudgar, A., & Sankar, V. (2008). The relationship between teacher gender and student achievement: Evidence from five Indian states. *Compare: A Journal of Comparative Education, 38*, 627–642.

Crosby, B. F. (2001). *The $100,000 teacher: A teacher's solution to America's declining public school system*. Herndon, VA: Capital Books.

Gordon, J. (2000). *The color of teaching*. New York: Routledge.

Harrast, S. (2004). Undergraduate borrowing: A study of debtor students and their ability to retire undergraduate loans. *NASFAA Journal of Student Financial Aid, 34*, 22–37.

Jacullo-Noto, J. (1991). Minority recruitment in teacher education. *Urban Education, 26*, 214–231.

Lee, C. (2005). The state of knowledge about the education of African Americans. In J. E. King (Ed.), *Black education: A transformative research and action agenda for the new century* (pp. 45–72). New York: Routledge.

Lewis, C. W. (2006). African American male teachers in public schools: An examination of three urban school districts. *Teacher College Record, 108*(2), 224–245.

National Center for Education Statistics (NCES). (2006). *Characteristics of schools, districts and staffing survey* (Report 2006-313). Washington, DC: U.S. Department of Education.

National Collaborative on Diversity in the Teaching Force. (2004, October). *Assessment of diversity in America's teaching force: A call to action*. Washington, DC: National Education Association.

National Education Association (NEA). (2006). *Teachers and the uncertain future*. Washington, DC: Author.

National Education Association (NEA). (2010). *NEA and teacher recruitment: An overview.* Washington, DC: Author.

Orum, J. (2006). *Institutional strategies to improve government student loan repayment.* Ministry of Advanced Education, British Columbia. Retrieved from http://www .aved.gov.bc.ca/studentaidbc/schoolofficials/documents/institutional-strategies.pdf

Tillman, L. (2004). African American principals and the legacy of *Brown. Review of Research in Education, 28,* 101–146.

U.S. Bureau of Labor Statistics (BLS). (2011). *Labor force statistics from the current population survey.* Washington, DC: Author. Retrieved from http://www.bls.gov/cps/ home.htm#charemp

U.S. Department of Education. (2011). *Secretary calls Black men to the blackboard.* Retrieved from http://www.ed.gov/blog/2011/02/secretary-calls-black-men-to-the- blackboard/

U.S. Department of Education Federal Student Aid. (2011, February). *Stafford loan forgiveness program for teachers.* Retrieved from http://studentaid.ed.gov/PORTALSWeb App/students/english/cancelstaff.jsp

COURT CASES AND STATUTES

Higher Education Act, 20 U.S.C. § 1001 *et seq.* (2006).

National Defense Education Act of 1958, 20 U.S.C. § 401 *et seq.*

INDEX

English Language Learners (ELL)
heritage language maintenance,
3:187–188, 3:190, 3:192,
3:193–194
individual differences, 3:199, 3:201
instructional approaches, 3:160,
3:186–205
See also Achievement gaps; Bilingual
education; "English-only"
curriculum; Immigrants
"English-only" curriculum
advantages, 2:109, 3:188, 3:193,
3:194–195
cost-effectiveness, 3:188
criticism of, 2:111–116, 2:118, 3:188,
3:197–201
implementation, 2:111
instructional approaches, 2:120–122
legal mandates, 2:119, 2:122, 3:191,
3:192, 3:193, 3:200
models, 2:119–120, 3:191, 3:203–204
political issues, 2:111–112, 2:118, 3:190,
3:191–194, 3:200, 3:202
pull-out programs, 2:119, 2:120, 3:191,
3:195
research on, 2:112–114, 3:195
supporters, 2:109, 2:110, 2:117–122,
3:190, 3:193–194
Entwisle, Doris R., 1:243–244
Epperson v. Arkansas, 4:xxv, 4:22, 4:185,
4:196
Epstein, Joyce L., 7:88–89, 7:90
Equal Access Act (EAA)
application, 4:220–224
effectiveness, 4:216–231
enactment, 4:216, 4:219, 4:233
gaps, 4:225–230
goals, 4:225
impact, 4:74
legal cases, 4:xxvi, 4:217, 4:219–220,
4:225, 4:226–227, 4:228,
4:229–230, 4:234
limitations, 4:xxvi, 4:50, 4:220–224,
4:227–231
order and discipline exception,
4:229–230
provisions, 2:201, 4:216–217, 4:219,
4:225, 4:229, 4:233–234
Equal Pay Act, 3:207
Equality
in curriculum and instruction, 2:xix–xx
distinction from equity, 6:179

of educational opportunity, 6:15–16,
6:148, 6:152, 6:264–265
state constitutional requirements,
6:xviii–xix, 6:1–2, 6:22, 6:148,
6:152
tension with local control, 6:xxv,
6:2–3, 6:110–111
See also Fourteenth Amendment
Equity
charter schools and, 1:16, 6:282–283,
7:144
choice programs and, 1:106–107
digital divide, 10:xvi–xvii, 10:20,
10:38–39, 10:65, 10:198,
10:210–211, 10:215
distinction from equality, 6:179
gender, 1:190, 7:xxviii
in gifted education, 6:116–117
horizontal, 3:173, 6:66, 6:116, 6:152,
6:179, 6:188
increasing, 3:xix, 7:248, 7:250–251,
7:261, 9:xxvii–xxix, 9:227–228
of inputs or outcomes, 9:196–197
in special education, 6:95, 6:98–99
in tax systems, 6:66–67
vertical, 3:173, 6:6, 6:66, 6:116, 6:152,
6:180, 6:188
See also Discrimination; Financing
equity; Inequities
Equity audits, 7:108
Equity suits
arguments, 3:15–16, 6:xx, 6:144–145,
6:183
in federal courts, 3:xxvi, 6:xxi, 6:14,
6:193, 9:191
goals, 7:253
outcomes, 3:xxvi, 3:169–170, 3:174,
6:153, 6:200
property tax issues, 3:173, 6:63–64, 6:72,
6:168–169
in state courts, 3:xxvi, 3:170, 3:180–182,
6:xxi, 6:14, 6:25, 6:152, 6:194,
9:191
*See also San Antonio Independent School
District v. Rodriguez*
Erastians, 4:95
e-readers. *See* e-books
Ericsson, K. Anders, 9:146
ESEA. *See* Elementary and Secondary
Education Act
ESL. *See* English as a Second Language
ESP. *See* Education Support Professionals

Religious music
arguments against allowing, **4:**114–118
arguments for allowing, **4:**106–112
educational value, **4:**106, **4:**107–110,
4:111–112
Establishment clause violations, **4:**104,
4:114–116
at graduation ceremonies, **4:**47–48,
4:116–117
at holidays, **4:**109–110, **4:**114–115, **4:**118
legal cases, **4:**104, **4:**107–110, **4:**111,
4:116–117
Lemon test and, **4:**104, **4:**107–110, **4:**113,
4:114–115
opting out of performing, **4:**110–111,
4:116, **4:**118
policy arguments against using,
4:117–118
in public schools, **4:**xxii, **4:**47–48,
4:103–118
Religious schools
academic performance, **4:**14
admissions, **1:**149–150
advantages, **4:**4, **4:**5, **4:**13–14
affordability, **1:**148
church-state separation issue,
1:40–41, **1:**46, **1:**93, **4:**xviii, **4:**1–2,
6:267–268, **6:**272–273
curricula, **1:**54
federal government and, **1:**39–40
funding, **1:**29–30, **1:**39, **2:**199, **6:**246,
6:283
history, **1:**xxiii–xxiv, **1:**72–73
Islamic, **1:**54, **1:**55, **1:**66, **6:**255–256
Jewish, **1:**xxv, **1:**125–143
nonsectarian approach, **1:**149
parents' rights to choose, **1:**39, **1:**46,
1:73, **4:**25
Protestant, **1:**22
Quaker, **2:**246
racial discrimination by, **4:**32
Roman Catholic, **1:**xxiii–xxiv, **1:**22,
1:39–40, **1:**44, **1:**98–99, **2:**199,
4:294–295, **8:**38
scholarships, **1:**95, **1:**98–100, **1:**104,
6:262
science curricula, **1:**116, **4:**31
tuition levels, **6:**262
See also Faith-based charter schools
Religious schools, government aid to
arguments against, **4:**9–14, **4:**19, **4:**26–32
arguments for, **4:**7–9, **4:**19, **4:**21–26

bans on state aid, **1:**95, **1:**96, **2:**199
child benefit test, **4:**xix, **4:**6, **4:**11, **4:**18
ethnocentric charter schools, **1:**29–30
for field trips, **4:**xx, **4:**2, **4:**6
indirect, **4:**11–12, **4:**26, **4:**27, **4:**28, **4:**29,
4:30
for instructional materials, **4:**7, **4:**27,
4:28
legal cases, **4:**xviii, **4:**1–2, **4:**4–7, **4:**18,
4:27–29
Lemon test for, **4:**xviii, **4:**xxv, **4:**6, **4:**18,
4:22–24, **4:**27
prohibitions, **4:**2, **4:**11–12
for special education, **4:**7, **4:**19, **4:**28
state aid types, **4:**4, **4:**11–12, **4:**18
state bans, **1:**95, **1:**96, **2:**199, **4:**4
for students with disabilities, **4:**18, **4:**24
tax credits for tuition, **1:**92, **1:**150,
6:267–268, **6:**272–273
for textbooks, **4:**xx, **4:**5, **4:**17–32
for transportation, **4:**xix–xx, **4:**1–14
See also Vouchers
Religious symbols
arguments against allowing, **4:**129–135
arguments for allowing, **4:**123–129
contexts of displays, **4:**127–128
educational value, **4:**124–125,
4:128–129, **4:**134
endorsement test and, **4:**xviii–xix, **4:**120,
4:121, **4:**123, **4:**126–127, **4:**128,
4:132
Equal Access Act and, **4:**229
free speech rights and, **4:**128–129
gang use of, **4:**268, **4:**272–273, **4:**280
Jewish, **4:**272
legal cases, **1:**26, **4:**120–122, **4:**124–127,
4:131–133
Lemon test and, **4:**123, **4:**124–127, **4:**131
Nativity scenes, **4:**121, **4:**126–127, **4:**128,
4:132
in public schools, **1:**26, **4:**xxii–xxiii,
4:120–135
secular purposes of displays, **4:**123–126,
4:128–129, **4:**132–133, **4:**134
Ten Commandments, **4:**xxii–xxiii, **4:**113,
4:120–121, **4:**124, **4:**126,
4:131–132, **4:**133
wearing, **4:**93, **4:**272, **4:**296
See also Religious garb
Religious texts
cultural importance, **4:**171–172
as literature, **4:**xxiv–xxv, **4:**168–182

teacher training programs, **9:**88–89
See also Milwaukee
Wisconsin Center for Educational Reform,
2:63
Wisconsin v. Yoder, **1:**xx–xxi, **1:**112–113,
1:114, **1:**123, **4:**74, **4:**273–274
Woessmann, Ludger, **7:**137
Woida, Chloe, **2:**207–208
Wolf, Patrick, **6:**248
Wolman v. Walter, **4:**xx, **4:**2, **4:**6, **4:**18, **4:**27
Wolstencroft, Helen, **2:**215
Women
administrators, **3:**219, **7:**94–95,
7:100–101, **7:**104, **7:**105–106
career paths, **7:**105
Catholic nuns, **4:**276, **4:**287
earnings, **3:**120–121
elected officials, **7:**103
higher education graduates,
3:114–115
Muslim garb, **4:**268, **4:**275, **4:**276,
4:280–281, **4:**288, **4:**296
principals, **7:**100, **7:**101, **7:**103, **7:**104
school board members, **7:**103, **7:**118,
9:15
superintendents, **7:**104
teachers, **3:**255–257, **3:**259, **3:**269–270,
7:94, **7:**97, **7:**101, **7:**104
violence against, **3:**206–207
voting rights, **3:**207–208
See also Gender
Wong, Kenneth K., **7:**5, **7:**7, **7:**17, **7:**258
Wood, R. Craig, **6:**206–207
World Health Organization, **2:**169
Wright, Wayne E., **2:**119
WSF. *See* Weighted student funding
Wyke v. Polk County School Board, **5:**81
Wyner, Joshua S., **3:**86
Wyoming, charter schools, **7:**132

Yahoo Groups, **10:**199
Year-round schools
alternative reforms, **1:**251–252
benefits of, **1:**xxvii–xxviii, **1:**236,
1:239–246
charter schools, **1:**5
cost savings, **1:**245, **1:**252
as distraction from reform efforts,
1:246–253
intersession activities, **1:**239–240,
1:241–242, **1:**244, **1:**246
models, **1:**239, **1:**242

number of, **1:**236–237, **1:**239, **1:**245
planning, **1:**243, **1:**244
research on, **1:**239, **1:**240–244, **1:**245,
1:246
schedules, **1:**236, **1:**237, **1:**239,
1:241–242
student outcomes, **1:**236–253
See also School years
Yemeni Americans, **2:**129–130
Yeung, Ryan, **3:**177, **8:**53
Young, K. Richard, **5:**243
Youth culture. *See* Popular culture
Youth Risk Behavior Survey, **5:**29
YouTube, **2:**217, **8:**183, **10:**169, **10:**182
Yuan, Kun, **2:**58

Zamecnik v. Indian Prairie School District,
4:263–264
Zeichner, Kenneth, **3:**41
Zelman, Susan Tave, **1:**221
Zelman v. Simmons-Harris
arguments, **6:**244
conditions for voucher constitutionality,
1:30–31
criticism of public schools, **6:**245–246
dissents, **6:**255
impact, **6:**242, **6:**250, **6:**283
majority opinion, **1:**93, **1:**95, **1:**96–97,
4:7, **4:**23–24, **6:**xxiii
vouchers seen to benefit families,
1:40–41
Zero tolerance policies
alternatives to, **5:**45
case-by-case reviews, **5:**25–26, **5:**30
criticism of, **5:**xx–xxi, **5:**27–34
for cyberbullying, **10:**155, **10:**161
definition, **5:**xx, **5:**22
for drugs and alcohol, **5:**19–22,
5:26–27, **5:**29, **5:**31, **5:**204
due process and, **5:**xx, **5:**20, **5:**49, **5:**50
effectiveness, **5:**25, **5:**43
enforcement, **5:**25–26, **5:**30–33, **5:**43,
5:44, **5:**51
historical background, **5:**22–23,
5:24–25, **5:**39–40
impact, **5:**23–27, **5:**28–34, **5:**43–45
introduction of, **5:**xviii, **5:**xix–xx, **5:**22,
5:23
legal challenges, **5:**xx, **5:**19–20, **5:**49–50
objectives, **5:**22, **5:**25
other offenses included, **5:**32, **5:**33, **5:**40,
5:204